THE BEST

PLACES TO KISS

IN HAWAII

A Romantic Travel Guide

COMPLETELY REVISED **3rd EDITION** AND UPDATED

by
Linnea Lundgren

BEGINNING PRESS

Other Books in the

BEST PLACES TO KISS™
Series:

The Best Places to Kiss in the Northwest, 7th Edition $16.95

The Best Places to Kiss in Northern California, 5th Edition $16.95

The Best Places to Kiss in Southern California, 4th Edition $13.95

Any of these books can be ordered directly from the publisher.

Please send a check or money order for the total amount of the books, plus $5 for shipping and handling per book ordered, to:

Beginning Press
13075 Gateway Drive, Suite 160
Seattle, WA 98168

All prices are listed in U.S. funds.
For information about ordering from Canada or
to place a credit card order, call (206) 444-1616.

Visit our Web site to order on-line:
www.bestplacestokiss.com

Art Direction and Production: Studio Pacific, Deb McCarroll
Cover Design: Studio Pacific, Deb McCarroll
Managing Editor: Laura Kraemer
Editor: Kris Fulsaas
Printing: Publishers Press
Contributors: Paula Begoun and Elizabeth Janda

BEST PLACES TO KISS™

is a registered trademark of Beginning Press
ISBN 1-877988-25-1

This book is distributed to the U.S. book trade by:
Publisher's Group West
1700 Fourth Street
Berkeley, CA 94710
(800) 788-3123

This book is distributed to the Canadian book trade by:
Raincoast Books
8680 Cambie Street
Vancouver, B.C. V6P 6M9
(800) 663-5714

"As usual with most lovers

in the city, they were

troubled by the lack

of that essential need

of love—a meeting place."

Thomas Wolfe

Publisher's Note

Travel books have many different criteria for the places they include. We would like the reader to know that this book is not an advertising vehicle. As is true for all *The Best Places to Kiss* books, the businesses included were not charged fees, nor did they pay us for their review. This book is a sincere, unbiased effort to highlight those special parts of the region that are filled with romance and splendor. Sometimes those places, such as restaurants, inns, lodges, hotels, and bed and breakfasts, were created by people. Sometimes those places are untouched by people and simply created by God for us to enjoy. Wherever you go, be gentle with each other and with the earth.

"What of soul was left,

I wonder, when the

kissing had to stop?"

Robert Browning

Contents

The Fine Art of Kissing

Why It's Still Best to Kiss in Hawaii

Hawaii is an exceptionally desirable place to kiss. In fact, it is probably one of *the* premier places to kiss in the world. For those of you who have never been to Hawaii, we'll begin by saying that much of it, without question, is a true tropical paradise. When you first see these jewel-like islands, it takes very little effort to imagine how they looked to the first non-native visitors over two centuries ago: unspoiled jade green hills and silver-capped blue waves meeting one another in all their majestic, primeval glory. Today, Western and Eastern cultures have done much to change the flawless appearance of these islands, but the quintessential splendor and legendary scenery are still there in great abundance.

Paradise doesn't often mix well with modernization, and Hawaii has suffered large-scale development by both Japanese and American corporations over the past 20 years, with the greatest influx in just the last decade. Through the 1950s, when the most prized hotel rooms rented for about $10 a night and "The Beach at Waikiki" was a popular song, the islands were relatively unmarred. Much of that had to do with accessibility. To put it mildly, the Hawaiian Islands are out in the middle of nowhere: 2,400 miles from the nearest coast (equidistant between Japan and the west coast of the United States). Back in the 1950s, visiting these Polynesian playgrounds meant a long, arduous journey.

Needless to say, times have changed. Easy access from nearly every corner of the globe makes Hawaii one of the most-visited locales in the world, with the preponderance of tourists coming from the U.S. mainland and Japan. About 7 million vacationers a year come here searching for a taste of tropical heaven. Frequent-flyer award programs and enticing, reasonably priced vacation packages make Hawaii an affordable destination. A week's stay at a hotel or condominium, including car and round-trip airfare from the West Coast to the island of Oahu, can cost as little as $395 per person. With deals like this, the islands' exotic personality at times seems little more than a memory.

It takes some effort to find the truly enchanted, idyllic side of these tropical islands, but it can be done. In those special places, the kissing will be as amorous as you ever dreamed possible.

The Islands

There are six major islands in the Hawaiian archipelago that are prime destinations for remarkably romantic sojourns. Of these, the big four, from south to north, are the Big Island of Hawaii, renowned for the volcanic activity of Kilauea; Maui, home to the overdeveloped but exquisite Kaanapali Coast as well as the underdeveloped, old Hawaiian town of Hana; the bustling island of Oahu, where the heavily visited city of Honolulu and perhaps the best-known beach in the world—Waikiki—can be found; and Kauai, a late bloomer as a worthy destination, with some additional catching up to do after the disastrous repercussions of Hurricane Iniki in 1992. Less known and vastly less developed, the islands of Molokai and Lanai, nestled in a rain shadow between Oahu and Maui, provide the ultimate in authentic tropical seclusion; their gentle spirit is evident from the moment you arrive.

Three other small islands complete the lineup. Niihau, just southwest of Kauai, is privately owned and restricted. Helicopter flights to isolated parts of the island are offered, but interaction with the natives is strictly prohibited, and the lack of amenities, expense of the flight, and minimal local cooperation make it a pricey, joyless getaway. There is little real reason to go, apart from fascination with its quarantined status.

The tiny island of Kahoolawe lies slightly southwest of Maui. For decades, the U.S. Army and Navy used it as a target for testing and training their bombers and pilots, rendering the land desolate and virtually uninhabitable. Efforts are now being made to restore and develop the island, but how, when, and by whom are unknown at present.

At the very end of the Hawaiian island chain, some 1,100 miles northwest of Oahu, awaits the Midway Atoll. Formerly owned by the U.S. Navy, this two-mile-long sandy island is now a wildlife refuge catering to tourists searching for pristine beauty and a chance to be close to nature. Each fall, thousands of albatross descend upon Midway to nest and raise their young, making it a bird-lover's paradise. If bird-watching is not your calling, however, the abundance of these large birds can be overwhelming; you may be better off visiting Midway at other times of the year, when you can entertain yourselves with snorkeling, scuba diving, or deep-sea fishing. Accommodations here consist of renovated Navy officers quarters and aren't anywhere near as fancy as what you'll find on Oahu or Maui, but Midway offers something much more special: a remote wildlife destination that most people never see.

How do you choose which island to visit? Each island has its own personality, amenities, and landscapes. Depending on your tropical preferences, you can find an island that fits your romantic inclinations. The chapters that follow will help you make a choice. You can settle on just one destination, selecting a particularly secluded place to stay, and embrace for your entire visit, or you can just as easily island hop and experience many different aspects of the Aloha State.

If you haven't been to Hawaii before, your first thought may be to start on the island of Oahu. Although Oahu has limited romantic possibilities (it's just too crowded), you may still be curious to see this tourist mecca for yourselves. If you do choose to visit Oahu, we recommend that you go there first. Because it is the most popular island and the most densely populated, it can be a jarring place to end your vacation after spending time on the comparatively tranquil islands of Maui, Kauai, the Big Island of Hawaii, Lanai, and Molokai. Peace and quiet are not the order of the day (or night) for Honolulu or Waikiki. However, if upscale designer boutiques, abundant nightlife, the excitement of city life, and beaches overflowing with sun worshippers are on your list of romantic wants, whenever you schedule a visit to Oahu will be just fine. If the two of you are searching for a more relaxed, peaceful vacation, away from beachgoing masses, head to any of the islands *except* Oahu.

Getting Around

The easiest way to travel between the islands is via airplane and, for some of the islands located only a few miles apart, via passenger-only ferryboats. Three airlines provide all interisland air service: **HAWAIIAN AIRLINES** (800-367-5320 mainland, 800-882-8811 interisland; www.hawaiianair.com), **ALOHA AIRLINES** (800-367-5250; www.alohaair.com), and **ALOHA ISLAND AIR** (800-323-3345; www.alohaair.com). Passenger-only ferry service is available from Maui to Lanai via **EXPEDITIONS** (808-661-3756, 800-695-2624 interisland; daily; reservations required), and from Maui to Molokai via the **MAUI PRINCESS** (808-667-6165, 800-275-6969; www.maui.net/~ismarine; Tuesday and Thursday only; reservations recommended).

Hawaii's main tourist office, the **HAWAII VISITORS AND CONVENTION BUREAU** (2270 Kalakaua Avenue, Suite 801, Honolulu, HI, 96815; 808-923-1811, 800-481-9898; www.gohawaii.com) provides information for all the islands. Phone numbers and web sites for the visitors bureaus on the other islands are as follows:

Maui Visitors Bureau:
(808) 244-3530, (800) 525-MAUI; www.visitmaui.com

Kauai Visitors Bureau:
(808) 245-3971, (800) 262-1400; www.kauaivisitorsbureau.org

Big Island Visitors Bureau:
(808) 961-5797, (800) 648-2441; www.bigisland.org

Destination Lanai:
(808) 565-7600, (800) 947-4774

Molokai Visitors Association:
(808) 553-3876, (800) 800-6367 mainland, (800) 553-0404 interisland; www.molokai-hawaii.com

Midway Phoenix Corporation:
(888) MIDWAY-1; www.midwayphoenix.com

Rental cars are as much a part of the scenery on Hawaii as palm trees, although infinitely less attractive. Without a car, it is all but impossible to experience the awesome beauty hidden along winding stretches of roads and highways. Once you arrive, you are likely to understand why a rental car is a necessity for sightseeing activities that don't involve tours. It is less important to have a car if you plan to stay in Honolulu or near Waikiki, where excellent bus service and taxis are readily available, but even then you may want to consider a one- or two-day rental to take in Oahu's less-developed beaches and less-traveled interior.

There are some great car rental deals to be found, particularly through some of the 100 local rental companies, as opposed to the big national chains such as Hertz, Budget, Alamo Rent-A-Car, National Rent-A-Car, Thrifty, and Avis. While booking through a local firm can indeed be a bargain, do not wait until you get here to rent a car, particularly during high season when there won't be any available. If you want to compare prices, call a travel agent who can handle it for you.

Romantic Suggestion: Be sure to check whether the property you are staying at offers a package that includes a car. Many of them do.

The Most Romantic Time to Travel

As impossible as it may seem, Hawaii's beautiful weather doesn't really have an off-season, although we wouldn't encourage anyone to visit during the near-90-degree humid heat of July and August. These months are almost as popular as the Christmas–New Year holiday season (December 20–January 4), because families seem to flock to the islands anytime school isn't in session. Not surprisingly, those sought-after winter dates are not only the most crowded and most expensive period, they also fall in the midst of the islands' rainy season. But even during this span, you are likely to encounter occasional 68-degree evenings, 75-degree afternoons, and as many sunny days as rainy ones. In terms of perfection, the most idyllic weather conditions are to be found during fall and spring, when the weather is almost always a dry 80 degrees.

Weather conditions on each island can vary. Some sections of the islands are known for their drier conditions and may be preferable during winter. For example, on Maui, Kapalua and Hana are wetter areas in comparison to Wailea, which is more arid; Poipu Beach on Kauai is drier than Napali Coast; and the east side of Oahu has more rain than the Diamond Head side. Staying in one of the drier areas doesn't mean you won't see rain during the winter, but it does improve the odds that you'll have the tropical vacation of your dreams instead of a soaking-wet nightmare. Or simply learn to enjoy the rain. Hawaiian winters may not be sunny but they are usually warm, and the sound and smell of a tropical downpour is delightful to the senses—not to mention the sight of a delicate, ephemeral rainbow brought on by the rains.

Romantic Note: High season here runs from mid-December through the end of March. Low season runs from April to mid-December with the exception of some summer months. The difference in hotel prices usually varies from $10 to $30 per night.

Can't We Kiss Anywhere?

You may be skeptical about the idea that one location is more romantic than another, whether it's in Hawaii or your own neighborhood. You might think, "Well, it isn't the setting, it's who you're with that makes a place special." And you'd be right. But aside from the chemistry that exists between the two of you without any help from us, some locations can facilitate and enhance romance, and others can discourage and frustrate the magic of the moment. More so than any other place we've written about, this can be true for Hawaii. Hawaii's burgeoning high-rise development can literally be the other side of Eden. Perhaps the romantic expectations most couples bring to this South Pacific paradise make it all the more disappointing when a tender embrace is marred by screaming kids, slamming car doors, or a noisy exhaust fan under your private balcony. Location isn't everything, but when all the right details are shared by a loving couple, chances are undeniably better for achieving unhindered and rapturous romance.

With that in mind, here is a list of the things we do not consider even remotely romantic: places with garden or mountain views punctuated by the blare of traffic noise; hotels with impressive lobby and pool areas but mediocre rooms (particularly ones with outrageous price tags); crowded beaches; anything overly plastic or overly veneered; noisy restaurants, even if they are very elegant; most tourist spots (particularly those with facilities for tour buses); the latest to-be-seen-in night spots (romance is looking at each other, not at the people sitting across from you); and row after row of overcrowded condominium developments.

Romantic Note: In Hawaii, sightseeing possibilities are even more abundant than condos and luaus (and that's saying a lot). We have highlighted the best excursions for each island. When it comes to outdoor tours involving the water or gloriously scenic sights, it is difficult to make a mistake. The only negative may be the crowds; the water and the vistas will be just as you envisioned—ecstatically breathtaking. Cultural centers and museums offer a colorful, insightful perspective on life in Hawaii throughout the generations. Take advantage of these whenever you can. Although they can often feel like tourist traps, the information they offer is intriguing and thought provoking.

You Call This Research?

This book was undertaken primarily as a journalistic effort and is the product of ongoing interviews, travel, thorough investigation, and critical observation. Although it would have been nice, even preferable, kissing was not the major research method used to select the locations listed in this book. If smooching had been the determining factor, several inescapable problems would have developed. First, we would still be researching, and this book would be just a good idea, some breathless moments, random notes, and nothing more. Second, depending on the mood of the moment, many kisses might have occurred in places that do not meet the requirements of this travel guide. Therefore, for both practical and physical reasons, more objective criteria had to be established.

You may be wondering how, if we did not kiss at every location during our research, we could be certain that a particular place was good for such an activity? The answer is that we employed our reporters' instincts to evaluate the heartfelt, magnetic pull of each place we visited. If, upon examining a place, we felt a longing to share what we had discovered with our special someone, we considered this to be as reliable as a kissing analysis. In the final evaluation, we can guarantee that when you visit any of the places listed, you will be assured of some degree of privacy, a beautiful setting, heart-stirring ambience, and romantic accommodations. What you do when you get there is up to you and your partner.

Romantic Warnings

Candid, genuine reviews are the hallmark of *The Best Places to Kiss* series. We understand how disappointment can affect your ability to pucker up. Even the best places can have drawbacks or failings that you need to know about. That is why we have incorporated

"Romantic Warnings" into our reviews. Sometimes an exquisite bed and breakfast fronts a busy intersection, or an outstanding restaurant may be cursed with a belligerent waitstaff. Whatever it is that might affect your interlude together, we want you to be prepared in advance. Our reviews don't always please the proprietors of the places we include, but we are dedicated to our readers first and foremost.

On that note, we cannot emphasize the following point enough: **Many of the brochures and ads for the various hotels, resorts, and restaurants in Hawaii make them look infinitely better than they are in reality.** After reading scintillating descriptions and seeing enticing pictures, we were often shocked (as many unsuspecting tourists have been) when we found establishments that did not begin to live up to the promises touted in their advertising materials.

Another problem we ran into repeatedly is the fact that on the islands, smoking and nonsmoking sections seem to run into one another. Because most restaurants are open-air and the trade winds are almost constant, it is hard to contain the smoke in one area. Even in hotel rooms this can be a problem, because if you leave the doors to your lanai open to enjoy the sounds of the ocean, you might end up with smoky smells that are definitely not coming from the sea. In hotels, one way to avoid this problem is to request a smoke-free room and ask whether that whole section of the hotel is smoke-free.

Rating Romance

The three major factors that determine whether or not we include a place are:

- **Privacy**
- **Location/view/setting**
- **Ambience**

Of these determining factors, "privacy" and "location" are fairly self-explanatory, but "ambience" can probably use some clarification. Wonderful, loving environments are not just four-poster beds covered with down quilts and lace pillows, or tables decorated with white tablecloths and nicely folded linen napkins. Instead, there must be other engaging features that encourage intimacy and allow for uninterrupted affectionate discourse. For the most part, ambience is rated according to degree of comfort and number of gracious appointments, as opposed to image and frills.

If a place has all three factors going for it, inclusion is automatic. But if one or two of the criteria are weak or nonexistent, the other feature(s) have to be superior before the location will be included. For example, if a breathtakingly beautiful panoramic vista is in a spot that's inundated with tourists and children on field trips, the place is not included. If a fabulous bed and breakfast is set in a less-than-desirable location, it is included if, and only if, its interior is so wonderfully inviting and cozy that the outside world no longer matters. Extras like complimentary champagne, handmade truffles, or extraordinary service earn brownie points and frequently determine the difference between three-and-a-half- and four-lip ratings.

Romantic Note: Hawaii is inherently romantic, but it is also a unique tourist destination. Often we found majestic scenery and sensual beaches surrounded by condominium developments and overrun by substantial crowds. Other times we stayed at stupendous resort hotels with 500 rooms—not exactly intimate or private by anyone's standards. Our basic guideline for selecting a specific place has always been to search out smaller, more intimate, and out-of-the-mainstream spots, particularly when it comes to accommodations. Hawaii caused us to rethink our usual modi operandi. We were in a predicament: Should we ignore a magnificent setting because of its current popularity or a luxurious hotel because of its size, or should we adapt our standards to the unique attributes of the Hawaiian Islands? We decided on the latter, and consequently you will read many reviews that sound something like "There are too many people for this to be truly romantic, but . . ." or "This is too large to be genuinely intimate, but. . . ."

Kiss Ratings

The lip rating preceding each entry is our way of indicating just how romantic we think a place is and how contented we were during our visit. The following is a brief explanation of the lip ratings awarded each location.

No lips	=	Reputed to be a romantic destination, but we strongly disagree
:bust_in_silhouette:	=	Romantic possibilities with potential drawbacks
:bust_in_silhouette::bust_in_silhouette:	=	Can provide a satisfying experience
:bust_in_silhouette::bust_in_silhouette::bust_in_silhouette:	=	Very desirable
:bust_in_silhouette::bust_in_silhouette::bust_in_silhouette::bust_in_silhouette:	=	Simply sublime
Unrated	=	Not open at the time this edition went to print, but looks promising

Romantic Note: If you're planning to celebrate a special occasion, such as an anniversary or birthday, we highly recommend telling the proprietors about it when making your reservation. Many bed and breakfasts and hotels offer "special-occasion packages," which may include a complimentary bottle of wine, breakfast in bed, fresh flowers, and special touches during turndown service, such as dimmed lights and your beloved's favorite CD playing in the background to set the right romantic mood. Restaurants are also sometimes willing to accommodate special occasions by offering free desserts or helping to coordinate a surprise proposal.

Cost Ratings

We have included additional ratings to help you determine whether your lips can afford to kiss in a particular restaurant, hotel, or bed and breakfast. (Almost all of the outdoor places are free; some charge a small fee.) The price for overnight accommodations is always based on double occupancy; otherwise there wouldn't be anyone to kiss. Unless otherwise indicated, eating establishment prices are based on a full dinner for two (which includes an appetizer, entrée, and dessert for each person), excluding the cost of liquor. Because prices and business hours change, it is always advisable to call each place you plan to visit, so your lips will not end up disappointed.

Most of the accommodations listed in this book have an extensive and diverse price list for their rooms, based mostly on the view and the time of year (high season is from mid-December through the end of March; low season is from April to mid-December). Our cost ratings include both the lowest and the highest prices available regardless of the season, and are based on a property's published rates. They do not take into account special promotion packages or available upgrades. If you are traveling at anytime other than high season, you may want to consider booking the least expensive room and asking for an upgrade when you arrive. Most hotels and some condominium rental properties will be pleased to do that for you. (Although it never hurts to ask, upgrading between December 20 and January 15 is virtually impossible.)

Romantic Suggestion: It takes an assertive tourist to locate special packages or upgrades, but it definitely beats paying the overpriced published (or "rack") rate.

Lodgings

Inexpensive	**Less than $130**
Moderate	**$130 to $180**
Expensive	**$180 to $230**
Very Expensive	**$230 to $350**
Unbelievably Expensive	**More than $350**

Restaurants

Inexpensive	**Less than $30**
Moderate	**$30 to $50**
Expensive	**$50 to $80**
Very Expensive	**$80 to $110**
Unbelievably Expensive	**More than $110**

Romantic Warning: Our cost ratings do not include the price that some hotels charge to park your rental car for you. If free self-parking is not available, you may get stuck paying up to $15 per day for your car to be valet parked. When booking your reservation, ask if parking is included in the daily rate for your room and if a parking lot is provided where guests can park for themselves. This way you won't be surprised by an accumulation of daily charges.

Romance in a Condominium

The number of condominiums available for rent in Hawaii is nothing less than staggering. Reviewing these properties was literally an overwhelming, albeit necessary, task. There are great advantages to staying in a condominium complex: They are generally much less expensive than the larger resort hotels; there are no extra costs such as service people to tip, phone surcharges, or pricey mini-bar treats; and they often have hotel-style front desk check-in and service. Condominiums also offer more space, fully equipped kitchens where meals can be cooked (saving the cost of repeatedly eating out), and separate dining and living room areas.

What are the negatives? Other than the lack of porters and concierges, there are very few. Of course, not all condominium complexes are created equal. Some pile people on top of each other like a stack of pancakes, while others have no air-conditioning—a definite drawback on hot, breezeless nights. It's often explained that the trade winds cool things off, but we can assure you this isn't always true. Another drawback is that, for the sake of saving money, families tend to stay in condominiums, which means that the grounds and pool area may not be all that serene because of playing children. Also, because the condominiums in rental pools are privately owned, the furnishings in the individual units can vary drastically, from luxurious to absolutely tacky.

The best prices for a condominium stay are to be found on Kauai ($100 and up a night), while Maui condo rentals can start at $120 for just average properties. We've done most of the research for you, but if you purchased a travel package and the property you have been given is not listed in this book, be sure to stipulate categorically the type of unit you want or don't want, and *get it in writing*. Do not risk a spoiled vacation by finding yourselves with unsatisfactory accommodations.

Ask the following questions before renting a condominium:

- Is it near a main road, and if so, can traffic noise be heard?
- How far is it from the airport?
- How far *exactly* is the nearest beach, and is it safe for swimming and snorkeling?
- If the unit has a view, what type of view is it?

- Does anything obstruct the view, and if so, what?
- What size beds are provided?
- How far is the property from any activity or amenity you are personally interested in, such as golf, nightlife, restaurants, an accessible jogging path, or grocery stores?
- Is maid service provided?
- Is air-conditioning and/or a phone provided?
- Is a rental car part of the package?

Romantic Note: Speaking of condominiums, at some point during your visit in Hawaii you are very likely to receive a sales pitch from a time-share salesperson. In exchange for sitting through a presentation, you will be offered a free rental car for one day, a dinner sail, a visit to a wax museum, or some other attraction (many of which are not very romantic or even very interesting). There is a great deal of consumer information about time-shares you should know before you deal with a provocative sales performance (and these people are pros). Do your homework before you inadvertently get involved with something you may be better off resisting.

Romance in a Bed and Breakfast

Professionally run bed and breakfasts are hard to find in Hawaii. It's not that they don't exist, it's just that the vast majority of them are represented exclusively by bed-and-breakfast agencies, and these companies don't make it easy for travel writers. (They are very protective, and dislike giving out names and numbers without a booking.) Licensing is very complicated and politicized, so a vast number of bed and breakfasts are run illegally. Also, most bed and breakfasts don't advertise, and only a handful are listed in the phone book. That means we often couldn't scope out a property before booking. But booking and then assessing is a highly inefficient way to weed through literally hundreds of bed and breakfasts. Usually we seek out potential candidates, eliminate all but the best, and then book before we do a final review for inclusion. Given the number of establishments, with descriptions that often sound infinitely better than they actually are, it can take an amazing amount of time to distinguish between the merely ordinary and the truly superb when staying overnight is the only research option.

Bed and breakfast Hawaii-style is more informal (and vastly less expensive) than what you may be used to in, say, Northern California or New England. Many of the hosts work at other jobs, have families, or are retired, and it can feel more like a home stay with a relative than anything else. However, a wide variety of accommodations are available—everything from separate cottages to apartments located on your own floor of an oceanfront home. We did our best to uncover as many of the more professionally run, comfortable, and plush places as we could. Given the limited number we've included, if you prefer bed-and-breakfast accommodations (something we wholeheartedly endorse), using a local agency is the best way to go. Be specific about your requirements, expectations, and needs, and *get everything in writing*. Your lips (and pocketbooks) will be eternally thankful if you do.

Romantic Note: The only bed-and-breakfast agency we found with consistently high standards for the properties it chooses to represent is **HAWAII'S BEST BED AND BREAKFASTS** (808-885-0550, 800-262-9912 mainland; www.bestbnb.com). Its office is located on the Big Island, but it handles properties all over the state.

A Room with a View

Incredibly sensual views abound in Hawaii, and the very thought of its rocky cliffs, sun-drenched beaches, and opalescent blue ocean can be enough to fill your heads and hearts with anticipation even before you start packing. Most people go to Hawaii with the expectation of seeing as much of these spectacles as possible. It isn't surprising to discover that the better the view and proximity to the water, the steeper the price tag for your room. Most hotels add sizable price increments as the view improves from a peekaboo glimpse of the Pacific to the most coveted prize, an unobstructed, full frontal vista of the rolling surf. Be aware that sometimes an expensive ocean view is visible only through thick foliage, way off in the distance, or over a massive rooftop, or may be glimpsed from a window or lanai above a noisy pool. When you ask for a specific room or certain features, make your request and get an answer *in writing*. Do not settle for the words "ocean view" on your confirmation. There is a lot of leeway in that description, and that could set you up for a burn that isn't from the sun.

Is a room with a view necessary? That depends primarily on your budget. Many lovely properties that have minimal water views or magnificent mountain views (sans cars) and a beach nearby are wonderful places to stay. But it would be misleading to say that waking to the sound of the waves surging against the shore and a view of the endless ocean isn't more romantic and breathtaking, because it is. Balancing the quality of various accommodations against view and beach accessibility was a major factor in all our lodging reviews.

Romantic Warning: Expensive doesn't always mean most desirable. Even hotel properties with well-known names can have their drawbacks, such as a mountain or garden view highlighted by a well-trafficked street or parking lot, or rooms in need of renovation. Read our recommendations carefully; sometimes reputations die hard, which can make for some lackluster kissing places.

Love Among the Golf Courses

Almost as big a draw as the beaches and exquisite scenery are the assortment of world-class golf courses in Hawaii. Set on hillsides, bordering the ocean, wrapped around premier resort properties, these links make the islands a golfer's utopia. Golf tournaments abound, golf carts circle about in the distance, and you are just as likely to overhear conversations discussing the beautiful layout of a course as you are to hear praise for the beautiful beaches. This book is not about golfing, but we would be remiss not to mention this attraction for affectionate couples who may want to go for one or more under par. All of the islands have several excellent courses to choose from, and the more popular ones are listed for each individual island or town area. Even if you are not fond of golf, these courses are so magnificent that you may find yourselves drawn to this sport that has so many island visitors so firmly under its spell.

To Luau or Not to Luau?

More luaus take place on the Hawaiian Islands today than ever took place in all of the islands' combined pre-statehood history. Every major hotel and even some minor ones as well as large and small restaurants host luaus on a nightly basis. There are even special restaurants with incredible outside settings dedicated only to luaus. No matter which one(s) you choose to attend (and we mention a couple of possibilities), you will behold a totally contrived, artificial reenactment of a once time-honored Hawaiian ritual. The rampant commercialization of this tradition has dashed whatever authenticity might have existed. Although we recommend avoiding luaus, the lure to attend at least one will be hard to resist. So if you're in the mood, go anyway, although one should be plenty. You will find the dancing colorful enough, and the music can be quite entertaining (performance quality varies greatly). The traditional *kalua* pig (a whole pig cooked in an *imu*, or underground pit) is often very good, but you don't get very much of it because there usually isn't enough to go around. The dinner is served buffet-style, which means a large crowd lining up at the same time for usually mediocre food (including coleslaw, potato salad, overly sweet punch, and standard white cake with coconut frosting). It isn't very Hawaiian, but it isn't all that easy to find the *real* Hawaii anymore.

The Lei of the Land

Many package deals include a lei greeting at the airport or hotel. Although it is a wonderful welcome, a lei is most appreciated when given by one loved one to another. The custom of presenting a sweetly scented garland of tropical flowers is one of Hawaii's most endearing expressions of *aloha* (love). The tradition is said to have begun in the days when kings and queens ruled the islands. Royalty were greeted with many gifts, including flowing necklaces of flowers.

Although those days are long past, lei greetings have evolved into a traditional way of saying *aloha* to everyone, royalty or not. Lei making has also become quite an art form on the islands. Leis can be made from simple plumeria blossoms, beautifully woven jasmine flowers, trailing vines, sweet-smelling *pikake*, or rare (and very expensive) *niihau* shells. Except for the intricate, multistrand *niihau* shell leis that can cost thousands of dollars, leis are available almost everywhere, on all the islands (we even saw them at convenience stores), at prices ranging from $4 to $30. Downtown Honolulu's Chinatown has the greatest profusion of lei shops, some of which have been family owned for many generations.

Surf's Up

Please read this section carefully together. Water safety can never be emphasized too much. Just ask any hospital emergency room staffer in Hawaii about respect for the power of the ocean. The water beckons with a siren's call that cannot be ignored, and the desire to rush hand-in-hand into the surf will be intense, absolute, and easy to do with nary a wince or shrug: After all, the water temperature is an optimal 75 to 80 degrees year-round. But the brilliant blue of the water can mask the turbulence and force of the surf and tides. Although the ocean may appear calm or flat when you enter, moments later you are likely to confront a crashing set of waves that can tumble you out of control back onto the beach. The following are specific guidelines to consider whenever you are tempted to re-create that beach scene in *From Here to Eternity*:

- Waves come in sets, and even though all you presently see are small waves, bigger ones may be on the way.

- Never turn your back on the ocean. Watch for what is coming your way.

- If you do encounter a breaking wave, do not try to outswim it or ride it ashore. Your best option is to duck or dive under it. The waves pass over you rather quickly, but be ready: The next one is on its way.

- Remember that tidal undertow and rip tides can pull you farther out than you want to go.

- Never swim alone (besides, alone isn't romantic).

- If you can't swim, do not play in high, rolling waves. At first the water may seem only knee-deep, but it can become 15 feet deep in the blink of an eye.

- Distances over water can be deceiving. Judge your endurance conservatively.

- Do not step barefoot on coral reefs (coral cuts are painful and can become infected) or on rocky ground where sea urchins and eels are prevalent.

- It is best to watch surfers from high ground. Avoid being in the water at the same time with a group of surfers if you are not savvy to surfer etiquette. You can easily get hit by a surfer or a runaway surfboard.

- There are sharks in these waters, but they prefer fish to humans. Shark attacks are infrequent and rarely result in a fatality. If you do see a shark, do not panic; swim quietly away, get out of the water, and tell a lifeguard of your sighting.

Romantic Note: When you are snorkeling, the temptation to remove some of the sea's alluring natural gifts can be hard to resist, but be strong and refrain. The ocean is not a gift shop, and what you remove is not easily replaced. Be respectful of nature's wonders and leave them there for the next couple to enjoy.

Romantic Note: The beaches in Hawaii are some of the most spectacular in the world. They are often somewhat difficult to reach around the massive hotel properties and private homes here, but they are accessible. Remember, *all beaches in Hawaii are public.* No beach can be privately owned; they are all available for use by everyone. Signs may not be visible or might not exist at all, but that doesn't mean you can't use the beach.

Whale Watching

If you have always secretly longed to witness firsthand the passage of whales on their yearly migration to warmer waters (where the humpback whales give birth to their young), the Hawaiian Islands are a great place to live out your fantasy. December to April is the best time to witness this odyssey, particularly when the weather conditions are clear and sunny. Be sure to start your search early, about the time when the sun is radiantly warming the cooler morning air. As you stand at the edge of the shore, scanning the Pacific realm, you will have a tremendous view of the open waters. Find a comfortable sandy spot or grassy knoll, snuggle close together, and be patient. This performance is intermittent at best and requires careful observation and diligence. But be prepared for an amazing encounter.

Imagine the scene. You are slowly studying the calm, azure waters. Suddenly, in the distance, breaking the still of a silent, sun-drenched Hawaiian winter morning, a spout of bursting water explodes from the surface. A giant, arched black profile stands out boldly against the blue sea, followed by an abrupt tail slap and then stillness once more. It's hard to explain the romance of that moment, but romantic it is. Perhaps it's the excitement of seeing such an immense creature gliding effortlessly through the water with playful agility and ease. Or perhaps it's the chance to celebrate a part of nature's mysterious aquatic underworld together. Whatever it is, discover it for yourselves if you have the chance.

Romantic Note: There are good whale-watching spots on many of the islands, but the southern shores of Maui are particularly prime. Boat excursions can take you out for more intimate viewing. On Maui, the most enlightening whale-watching cruises are sponsored by the **PACIFIC WHALE FOUNDATION** (808-879-8811, 800-WHALE-11; www.pacificwhale.org), with daily departures from Maalaea Harbor and Lahaina Harbor. The guides are authorities from the foundation, and they fill the two-hour expedition with everything you ever wanted to know about whales and more. Prices start at $31 per person, but be sure to inquire about special rates too.

What to Pack

As many times as we've been to Hawaii, we still engage in a never-ending discussion about what we should and shouldn't pack. It seems self-evident, yet it is of great concern given the variety of experiences and attractions available and the inevitable heat. Obviously a lot depends on your itinerary, but we offer some basic suggestions to help lighten your luggage.

Be assured that shorts and a short-sleeved shirt of any kind are acceptable at 99 percent of the places you will visit. Even tank tops for both women and men are fine in most casual restaurants and shops. We were often surprised at what is considered acceptable. These islands have an amazingly nonchalant, laid-back temperament. However, the dress code does change when you go out for a posh evening of dining and dancing. Many of the finer restaurants require women to wear nice resort wear and men to wear jackets. But don't worry about bringing a jacket along—almost all of the fancier restaurants have jackets you can borrow while you dine, and some are much less strict than their policy implies. If you choose to attend a luau or other evening entertainment, the dress depends on the type of place. The fancier the venue, the more clothes you have to wear.

During the winter months, nights can get a bit on the cool side. For Hawaii that means in the low 70s or high 60s. A lightweight cotton sweater or jacket is all you should need to ward off the slight evening chill. Cotton slacks are also a good idea on those occasions. As far as footwear goes, given the varied number of hiking trails available and your own level of endurance, good hiking boots can be an asset, particularly on the island of Kauai.

Romantic Note: We always pack our own snorkels, fins, and beach towels so we can indulge our urge for underwater viewing at a moment's notice without worrying about rentals. But don't be concerned if you don't have your own; there are plenty of rental places all over the islands (prices range from $5 to $12 per day).

Sunscreen: Don't Leave Home without It

Nothing can destroy a romantic holiday or your ability to kiss faster than a sunburn, and the Hawaiian sun can burn fast and furiously. If you pack nothing else, you must pack a sunscreen with an SPF (sun protection factor) of at least 15 or greater. It doesn't have to be expensive as long as it has a high SPF rating. Because of FDA regulations, all sunscreens protect from sunburn (UVB rays) equally, based on the SPF number. But when it comes to UVA rays, which cause silent, long-term damage, there is no rating listed on sunscreens. In order to ensure that you are getting equal protection from both UVA and UVB rays, make sure the active ingredients on the label include one of the following ingredients: titanium dioxide, zinc oxide, or avobenzone. For sunscreens with the least risk of irritation, consider one that only uses pure titanium dioxide as the active ingredient; look for the words "chemical free" or "nonchemical" on the label if you are interested in this type of protection. Try to purchase a sunscreen before your departure: The hotels and stores in Hawaii charge a hefty fee in comparison to what you would pay at a drugstore on the mainland.

Be sure to apply sunscreen at least 20 minutes before you go out in the sun. You can get burned just in the time it takes to walk from your car to the beach and spread out your blanket. Apply sunscreen evenly and generously, covering every inch of exposed skin. Don't forget the tops of your feet, thin hair spots, the hairline, where your hair parts, ears, and eyelids. It is also essential to reapply sunscreen after you swim or exercise.

Getting Married in Hawaii

One of the most auspicious times to kiss is the moment after you've exchanged wedding vows. In Hawaii, locations for your wedding can vary from a lush garden perched at the ocean's edge to a specially built chapel at an elegant beachfront hotel to a private suite in an exclusive condominium. As an added service to those of you in the midst of prenuptial arrangements, we have indicated which properties have impressive wedding facilities. For more specific information about the facilities and services offered, please call the establishments directly. They should be able to provide you with menus, prices, and all the details needed to make your wedding day as spectacular as you have ever imagined.

Many of the more notable island hotels increasingly specialize in weddings and renewals of vows, and some of them handle more than 60 weddings a month. These noteworthy packages are gaining popularity because the hotels make it so easy for you, and they can be surprisingly affordable. Some resorts have romance directors or wedding organizers whose sole job is attending to the details of your nuptials, no matter how simple or complex the event. If you do decide to utilize the exotic surroundings of Hawaii for one of the most romantic interludes of your life, there are plenty of options available. Simply choose a hotel based on the reviews provided in the following chapters, ask for the wedding or romance planner, and tell him or her your budget. They'll take it from there; you just need to bring the wedding dress, the tux, and the rings. It really is that simple.

Romantic Suggestion: For a free wedding brochure with information about getting married in Hawaii, write to the **HAWAII VISITORS AND CONVENTION BUREAU** (2270 Kalakaua Avenue, Suite 801, Honolulu, HI, 96815; 808-923-1811, 800-481-9898; www.gohawaii.com).

A Brief History

Beginning about A.D. 1200, when the first Polynesian settlers (believed to be Tahitian) arrived on these islands, and culminating in the multibillion-dollar tourist industry of today, Hawaii's history is a fascinating and spellbinding saga. Because of Hawaii's geographic location and exotic, tumultuous past, its identity and culture are distinctly different from the mainland's; however, Hawaii was associated with the United States long before it became the 50th state in 1959.

Although the islands are often characterized as a peaceful, untroubled corner of the world before missionaries and colonists came bringing sickness, Western religion, and capitalism, this is not a totally accurate or complete depiction. Before the European discovery of these islands by Captain Cook in 1788, the tribes here were continually at war, vying for position and dominance; human sacrifice was a customary religious practice; and there was a caste system (*kapu*) in place that made life miserable for some and luxurious for others.

It wasn't until the arrival of Western civilization that human sacrifice was stopped and the *kapu* system was eliminated. However, Western civilization also changed the unspoiled glory of the land forever, bringing new diseases, non-native animals and plants, intense foreign commerce through whaling in the 1840s, agriculture in the form of sugar and pineapple plantations in the 1850s and 1860s, and the elaborate and virtually overflowing tourist industry of the present.

Perhaps the most notorious and controversial interaction between the United States and Hawaii occurred in 1893, when Queen Liliuokalani, after trying to reinstate her rightful control over the islands, was overthrown by American Republican forces in Honolulu and placed under house arrest. Seven years later Hawaii became a territory of the United States, and the monarchy was officially defunct.

Over the past 20 years, the plantation fields of pineapple and sugarcane have slowly lost their financial productivity and been superseded by high-rise hotels and condominiums. Almost all of the local population to one degree or another, directly or indirectly, works for the massive tourist industry.

From ancient Polynesians crossing the oceans more than 800 years ago to the jam-packed streets of Waikiki today, there is much to discover regarding the history of Hawaii. We encourage you to take the time to delve into this remarkable chronicle. It would be a shame to come all this way and not find the real Hawaii, because it does exist—not at tourist attractions or on the beaches, but in the sacred sites (*heiaus*) still found on the islands, in the wild beauty of uninhabited regions, and in the endeavors of Native Hawaiians to reclaim their culture amid the melting pot of peoples that have made Hawaii their home.

"The sound of a kiss is not so loud

as that of a cannon, but its echo

lasts a great deal longer."

Oliver Wendell Holmes

Oahu

Kahuku

Kailua

Honolulu   Hawaii Kai

Kapolei

Waikiki   Kahala

Diamond Head

Oahu

Oahu—known as the gathering place—is home to 80 percent of Hawaii's inhabitants; most of the population is concentrated in Honolulu around Waikiki Beach. With its white, sandy beaches, busy streets, and immense high-rise hotels; its numerous shopping centers dotted with designer boutiques; and its myriad restaurants and clubs, Waikiki is certainly the hub of the action. However, visitors who concentrate their time and energy in only this area are missing out. Decidedly an island of contrasts, Oahu offers as much tropical beauty as the less populous islands—and much, much more.

You can escape the crowds to some degree by heading east to **DIAMOND HEAD** and **KAHALA**, where the hotels thin out and elite residential areas are the norm. The sandy beaches here are gorgeous (one is even called Sandy Beach), but they are popular with local surfers, so kiss-worthy privacy can be a problem. Nevertheless, these beaches are definitely less crowded than Waikiki, which is a considerable kissing advantage.

Sunsets on Oahu's northwest shore are extraordinarily majestic. You can park your car and walk along any number of astonishingly beautiful beaches. **SUNSET BEACH** and **WAIMEA BEACH** are particularly stupendous. These areas are also celebrated surfing spots, with awesome, thundering waves and no crowds. Farther south, near **KAENA POINT STATE PARK**, glorious scenery abounds, and a formidable surf crashes against rocks interspersed with patches of sand. Although this part of Oahu is primarily residential and undeveloped (sans hotels and condominiums), much of it is run-down, with communes of makeshift houses scattered along the coast.

From Honolulu, head northwest through the center of the island for a beautiful drive between the **WAINAE AND KOOLAU MOUNTAIN RANGES**, which rise imperially on either side of the road. An expansive series of residential neighborhoods line the north shore, which means the beach is obscured by homes. But remember, *all* of the beaches on all of the islands are public (even if they look private), so keep your eyes open for access paths. You are more likely to find an empty stretch of beach in

---

Brochures that promise ocean views from the rooms may be misleading. Be sure to get specifics about what kind of view you can really expect, and get it in writing.

this area than anywhere else on Oahu. Even if you don't, you are guaranteed to find fewer crowds than you would in Waikiki.

Popular locations, such as 1,800-acre **WAIMEA VALLEY ADVENTURE PARK** (808-638-8511; open daily; $24 per person) and the **POLYNESIAN CULTURAL CENTER** (808-293-3333, 800-367-7060; www.polynesia.com; open Monday–Saturday; $27–$95 per person depending on package), make interesting day trips and provide entertaining insights into the history of the Polynesian people. Just be ready for busloads of people and a theme-park atmosphere; crowds of tourists flock to these places, so while they may be fun and educational, they are of little to no romantic interest.

Although we don't often recommend tourist attractions, we do urge you to take the time to see the **USS *ARIZONA* MEMORIAL** at Pearl Harbor (808-422-0561; www.nps.gov/usar; open daily; free admission). Poignant and moving, this memorial is dedicated to the U.S. military lives that were lost during World War II's Pearl Harbor attack.

West Oahu

While much of Oahu has been heavily developed, the west coast has barely been touched and retains much of its pristine beauty. Regardless of where you stay on the island, the beaches and sights of West Oahu are worth a day trip, not only to see the island's varying landscape of volcanic shores and arid hillsides, but to escape the city life of Waikiki. If you're really lucky, you may even spot a pod of spinner dolphins offshore as you drive along Farrington Highway (Highway 930).

Kapolei

Hotel/Bed and Breakfast Kissing

❧❧❧❧ **IHILANI RESORT AND SPA, Kapolei** The Ihilani Resort and Spa's location might be too far from the city lights of Waikiki for some, but if privacy and calm are part of your romantic agenda, this exclusive getaway is just for you. As the first of three intended hotels on the 642-acre Ko Olina Resort, Ihilani stands alone, with a tranquil lagoon on one side and the crashing Pacific on the other.

No expense has been spared in the 387 sophisticated rooms, and the effect is stunning. From the generous flower-trimmed lanais to the high-tech electronic comfort-control systems to the spacious marble bathrooms, you won't be disappointed. Plush bedspreads, Berber carpeting, teak and wicker furnishings, and soft taupe or pale green complement each room. The majority of the rooms are oceanfront (facing the crystal-clear lagoon and the lovely swimming pool) or ocean-view (facing the open ocean). Views from both sides are remarkable, but if you're hoping to savor as many amazing Hawaiian sunsets as possible, request an ocean-view room. For those who can afford to splurge (and we mean *really* splurge), the luxury suites are the way to go—each is wonderfully opulent, and several have indoor whirlpool tubs and outdoor Jacuzzi tubs.

Gifts from the **IHILANI SPA**, such as soothing foot gel, are left on your pillow each night with turndown service. The 35,000-square-foot spa has six tennis courts, a fitness center outfitted with the latest equipment, a lap pool, and enough therapeutic treatments and services to make you feel completely pampered. Finally, we must mention the one-and-a-half-mile-long beach walk that begins just beyond the hotel's pool. If you time your stroll properly, you can begin walking early in the evening and catch the sun sinking into the sea as you head back to your sweet oasis. **Ko Olina Resort, 92-1001 Olani Street; (808) 679-0079, (800) 626-4446; www.ihilani.com; very expensive to unbelievably expensive and beyond; recommended wedding site.**

Romantic Note: The hotel's somewhat casual, poolside **NAUPAKA TERRACE** (expensive; breakfast, lunch, and dinner daily) is great for breakfast or lunch, but save room for a special dinner at the more formal **AZUL** (see Restaurant Kissing). You are in for one of the best fine-dining experiences on Oahu.

Restaurant Kissing

❤❤❤❤ **AZUL, Kapolei** We considered ordering a whole grilled Maine lobster the night we dined at Azul, but this is not the kind of place where you'd feel comfortable using your fingers or making a mess of your napkin. Genteel and elegant, Azul has mastered the art of refined dining. Soft-hued murals depicting Mediterranean seascapes enrich the dimly lit, handsome dining room, accented with dark wood and choice white linens. Exceedingly proper, attentive waiters address you by name and cater to your every need over the course of the long, savory, multicourse meal. All entrées include appealing Mediterranean starters, such as roasted scallops wrapped in pancetta with black truffle butter. The innovative menu varies nightly, with tantalizing items like pepper-crusted ahi topped with seared foie gras, and rack of lamb with a focaccia crust. Take the time to linger over dessert and coffee; like everything else here, they are superb. **Ko Olina Resort, 92-1001 Olani Street, at the Ihilani Resort and Spa; (808) 679-0079, (800) 626-4446; www.ihilani.com; very expensive; dinner Monday, Wednesday, Friday, and Saturday; call for seasonal closures.**

South Oahu

Honolulu/Waikiki

In the south-shore area of Waikiki, they really did "pave paradise and put up a parking lot." All this development services millions of tourists a year who want some semblance of tropical bliss without forgoing convenience and the excitement of a big city. Nearly perfect year-round temperatures and the famous beach at Waikiki, with its vast, aqua-blue, shallow waters and silky, golden sand, are what draw the masses. But Waikiki is so densely populated with tourists (about 80,000 daily) that it isn't really most people's idea of paradise anymore. Actually, kissing on the beach at Waikiki can be problematic—if you close your eyes for a moment and move ever so slightly, you may end up kissing someone you don't know. On a warm day, the shoulder-to-shoulder lineup of oiled bodies is staggering. However, at night, when the crowds are across the street shopping at the endless promenade of stores and markets or sampling the varied nightlife offerings, this warm and exquisite beach is almost yours for the taking.

The **INTERNATIONAL MARKETPLACE** is one of the most popular places to shop along the Waikiki strip. You are likely to get good deals on just about anything, but you'll also be cornered by determined salespeople. A more relaxed shopping area (if such a thing exists) is the **ALOHA TOWER MARKETPLACE**, just a couple of miles west of Waikiki. This open-air shopping center features designer boutiques, art galleries, casual eateries, and a more leisurely pace. Parking can be tricky and expensive, but a trolley runs back and forth from the central part of Waikiki for only $1 each way.

Hotel/Bed and Breakfast Kissing

❀❀ ALI'I TOWER AT THE HILTON HAWAIIAN VILLAGE, Waikiki

One of the largest resorts in the state, the Hilton Hawaiian Village can be, to say the least, overwhelming. Situated on 20 acres of prime but crowded beachfront property, the Hilton boasts fantastic ocean views from its unbelievable 2,545 guest rooms comprising four sky-rise towers. In addition to multitudes of boutiques and cafés, the village provides two outdoor swimming pools and more than 20 restaurants and lounges.

The secret to surviving these conditions is to stay in the Ali'i Tower. Here you can sample all the Hilton offers, and then retreat to the sanctuary of your room or swim in the private pool. Drawing on the concept of a "hotel within a hotel," the Ali'i Tower consists of only 348 rooms (small in comparison to the enormous size of the Hilton Hawaiian Village). Guests in the tower enjoy extra touches of privacy, including a separate check-in desk, their own concierge staff, and a building that's off-limits to regular Hilton guests (a white-gloved doorman makes sure of that).

Although guest rooms have all the necessary amenities, the decor and furnishings are fairly nondescript and standard (like the rest of the Hilton's rooms). However, this is easily forgotten once you see the second-floor pool and hot tub overlooking Waikiki Beach. Adjacent to the pool area are a fitness center, massage room, and cocktail bar, which serves complimentary appetizers between 5 and 7 P.M. Again, only Ali'i guests can use these amenities, making it a very pleasant place to kiss in the midst of hotel madness. **2005 Kalia Road; (808) 949-4321, (800) 221-2424; www. hawaiianvillage.hilton.com; very expensive to unbelievably expensive and beyond; recommended wedding site.**

Romantic Suggestion: When you decide to leave your secluded surroundings, enjoy dinner at either of the Hilton's well-known restaurants, **BALI BY THE SEA** or **GOLDEN DRAGON** (see Restaurant Kissing for reviews of both).

❤❤❤ **ASTON WAIKIKI BEACHSIDE HOTEL, Waikiki** In many ways this is one of the most unusual hotel properties on Oahu, and it is a welcome change of pace. As you leave busy Kalakaua Avenue and venture into the elegant marble lobby filled with carefully chosen antiques, you seem to enter an entirely different world. Only 79 rooms (most on the small side) fill this boutique hotel. Intimate and cozy, each room features Chinoiserie decor (a blending of Eastern and Western styles), pastel peach fabrics and walls, hand-painted Asian screens, plush furnishings, an attractive marble bathroom, and twice-daily maid service. Oceanfront rooms are soundproofed, a much appreciated touch considering the busy location. A complimentary continental breakfast is served in the hotel's small but charming parlor area, and special touches like candles and champagne waiting in the room at check-in can be arranged in advance.

Overall, the ambience is refined, and the service is friendly and eager to please. Once you step inside this oasis, you won't miss the overbearing, impersonal atmosphere found in the countless other hotels that line the Waikiki strip. **2452 Kalakaua Avenue; (808) 931-2100, (800) 922-7866 mainland; www.aston-hotels.com; moderate to very expensive.**

Romantic Note: Since the hotel is set directly across the street from the beach, ocean-view or partial ocean-view rooms are preferred. Other rooms tend to be quieter, but that is because they face a cement wall or have no windows at all.

❤❤❤❤ **HALEKULANI, Waikiki** Without a doubt, this the most desirable place to stay in all of Waikiki. Halekulani means "house befitting heaven" and this aptly named luxury hotel stands alone as a tranquil, serene oasis in the heart of hectic Waikiki. Quiet splendor and the fragrant scent of jasmine enfold you as you step from the busy street into an open-air lobby replete with glimpses of the ocean, small waterfall-fed pools, imported marble pillars framing gracious corridors, and lovely garden landscaping. A beautifully tiled oceanside swimming pool beckons, flaunting a brilliant, painted white orchid underneath the shimmering blue water. Upon arrival, you are greeted in gracious *aloha* style and ushered to the privacy of your own room to register. Waiting for you is a complimentary basket of tropical fruits and chocolates (and sometimes champagne if it happens to be a special occasion).

All 456 guest rooms face the hotel's secluded oceanside courtyard, and each one surrounds you in several shades of white, from the plush carpet and crisp bed linens to the sparkling bathroom tiles. Such simplicity ensures that nothing in the room competes with the outstanding view. Throw back the shutters and step out onto your spacious lanai, where you can survey the courtyard below and the ocean beyond. Some rooms allow you to soak in the ocean views from the vantage point of a glass-enclosed shower, provided you slide open the partitioned doors or shutters. Other romantic touches include fresh flowers, Halekulani's own line of bath amenities (including sunscreen), plush bathrobes, showers automatically set at the ideal temperature, and deep soaking tubs. If you do venture from this oasis, the hotel provides complimentary tickets to the Honolulu Symphony, the Honolulu Academy of Arts, and The Contemporary Museum as part of their "For you, everything" package.

Although Halekulani's prices might sound steep, they are surprisingly comparable to those of Oahu's less luxurious properties. In fact, Halekulani's rates feel much more reasonable in light of the hotel's extraordinary accommodations and service. **2199 Kalia Road; (808) 923-2311, (800) 367-2343; www.halekulani.com; very expensive to unbelievably expensive and beyond; recommended wedding site.**

Romantic Note: Halekulani's two restaurants, the exorbitant and sophisticated **LA MER** and the more casual **ORCHIDS** (see Restaurant Kissing for reviews of both), offer attentive service, unpretentious settings, and a refreshing amount of open-air seating.

❀❥ **HAWAII PRINCE HOTEL, Waikiki** This twin-towered hotel, sheathed in rose-colored glass, makes no excuses for catering to the business crowd. Corporate clientele is the hotel's bread and butter, but we decided to include it anyway, because in Hawaii, you should always mix business with pleasure.

Despite the suit 'n' tie customers, the hotel has many redeeming features for romance. All 521 rooms have floor-to-ceiling windows opening to oceanfront views; the sunsets here are the talk of the town; the large pool and whirlpool are spectacular; and the rooms, while modestly decorated, are quite pleasing. The hotel stands apart from the Waikiki crowds, but that also means the beach is farther away too. Luckily, it's only a five-minute walk or a complimentary shuttle away. The Prince fronts the Ala Wai Yacht Harbor, which can be quite a sight during December when thousands of holiday lights adorn the sailboats' masts.

The hotel offers several restaurants, including the view-filled **PRINCE COURT** (808-956-1111; moderate to expensive; breakfast, lunch, and dinner daily). For those of you who come to putt in paradise, the Hawaii Prince is the only Waikiki hotel with its own 27-hole course, which is a short shuttle ride away. **100 Holomoana Street; (808) 956-1111, (800) 321-OAHU; www.westin.com; very expensive to unbelievably expensive and beyond; recommended wedding site.**

❀❥ **HYATT REGENCY, Waikiki** Directly across the street from Waikiki Beach stands this massive twin-towered hotel complex, which rises 40 stories above the water. Centered around a large atrium lobby with a cascading waterfall, the hotel's first two floors are a maze of boutiques and jewelry stores.

Those who have more than shopping in mind will appreciate the Hyatt's spacious guest rooms, located upstairs above the mall. Each of the 1,230 rooms is appointed with attractive wood furnishings; stylish, brightly colored linens; and a private, narrow lanai. Our only hesitation about recommending the Hyatt is the lack of soundproofing. While listening to the sensuous surf is romantic, hearing your neighbors above you and the noisy traffic below is not. Guests who are willing to pay extra have exclusive use of sundecks and Jacuzzi tubs perched at the top of both towers. Otherwise, you can catch the rays on the third floor, which boasts a lovely sunning deck and a pint-sized pool. **2424 Kalakaua Avenue; (808) 923-1234, (800) 233-1234; www.hyattwaikiki.com; expensive to unbelievably expensive and beyond.**

Romantic Suggestion: We recommend only one of the Hyatt's five restaurants for affectionate dining. CIAO MEIN (808-923-CIAO; moderate to expensive; reservations recommended; dinner daily) boasts several semicasual dining rooms. Although the black-and-white Italian motif looks slightly out of place beside Chinese sculptures and hand-painted vases filled with exotic flowers, the unusual blend of Chinese and Italian cuisine is a big success. The unique menu items are all artistically presented and well executed, from the sesame asparagus and black mushrooms with oyster sauce appetizer to the mouthwatering meringue Napoleon appropriately called Double Happiness. If you'd rather enjoy a private meal on your lanai, opt for the in-room romantic dinner. This four-course meal (unbelievably expensive) includes champagne and a complimentary photograph to commemorate the occasion.

❧ **MANOA VALLEY INN, Honolulu** Professionally run bed and breakfasts are rare commodities in Hawaii. The Manoa Valley Inn is the only historical inn of its kind on Oahu, which is the primary reason we recommend it. Those who like the personal touches of a bed and breakfast will appreciate this 1915 country inn, set in a relatively quiet residential neighborhood near the University of Hawaii. It once reveled in ocean views, but now Waikiki's high-rise skyline looms in the distance—not so alluring in the daytime, but lovely at night when the city lights twinkle.

Eight rooms are available: seven in the main house and one separate cottage. The three rooms on the top floor share a bath, which is rather *un*romantic, but the others have private baths and offer some amorous potential. All feature weathered black-and-white photographs, massive antique carved-wood or iron beds, and period wallpaper. Private baths, with antique fixtures still operable, are dismal with an unbecoming institutional look. The inn's sparse selection of Victorian furniture is in need of renovation, but such pieces add a touch of authenticity.

Continental breakfast is served on the expansive covered backyard lanai, definitely the coziest spot for two at any time of day. Although the other common rooms house interesting and authentic antiques, they are timeworn and somewhat dreary. Still, this is a unique, historical alternative to luxury living in Waikiki. **2001 Vancouver Drive; (808) 947-6019, (800) 634-5115; inexpensive to expensive.**

❧ **OUTRIGGER HOTELS HAWAII, Oahu** We can't mention "Hotel Kissing" in Hawaii without at least commenting on the Outrigger Hotels. This well-known island chain has 30 hotels scattered across the four main islands, 20 of them on Oahu. Yet once you've seen one, you've virtually seen them all. Outriggers offer welcome budgetary relief from Waikiki's otherwise painful prices, while providing standard hotel accommodations, good service, and even the occasional ocean view for relatively reasonable prices. Generally well kept and conveniently located, these hotels are ideal for tourists who want to enjoy Waikiki but don't want to spend a lot of money for luxury (or a lot of time in their rooms). **Various locations; (800) 462-6262; www.outrigger.com; inexpensive to expensive.**

❧❧❧ **THE ROYAL HAWAIIAN, Waikiki** For obvious reasons, this hotel is commonly referred to as the "Pink Palace of the Pacific." Yet for all its color, you just might miss this soft-pink building on your way through Waikiki because of its location behind a shopping center. From its construction in 1927, the formidable, colorful hotel has withstood the decades with continued glamour and panache. You can virtually feel the history as you walk through the luxurious lobby and meander down the tropical, tree-lined pathways.

When booking a stay here, do not be misled into thinking that the newer oceanfront tower has the better accommodations. Although these are the only units with lanais, most of these rooms are rather small, with standard bathrooms and furnishings. If you must stay in the tower, opt for the corner rooms with wraparound lanais. For romance, book a room in the original, historic wing instead, where you'll never want for space, luxury, or style. Intricately hand-carved wooden doors open into rooms with high ceilings, lush fabrics, Italian-tiled baths, and interesting antiques. No two rooms are decorated the same, a refreshing change of pace in Waikiki. Some rooms have canopy beds, four-poster beds, low beds, or high beds, so be specific about what you want. Of course, no matter where you stay, pink accents abound, from the bath towels to the floor mats. To compensate for the lack of a lanai, open your windows, and let the fresh ocean air drift through your room. Sweeten things up even more by digging into the banana bread that awaits in your room. It's a complimentary treat for newly arrived guests.

Not many restaurants or bars sit directly on the beach at Waikiki, but The Royal Hawaiian boasts two: the **SURF ROOM** (moderate to expensive; breakfast Monday–Saturday, lunch and dinner daily, brunch Sunday) and the **MAI TAI BAR** (inexpensive; afternoon and evening cocktails and appetizers daily). Although the Surf Room can get crowded and the food is rather standard, the expanse of beach is beautiful and Sunday brunch here is lively and pleasant. And with a delightful view of the gardens, the Mai Tai Bar is a wonderful, casual setting for sipping cocktails as the day ebbs into night. **2259 Kalakaua Avenue; (808) 923-7311, (800) 782-9488; www.royal-hawaiian.com; unbelievably expensive and beyond; recommended wedding site.**

Romantic Note: The pool area is unusually small for a hotel with more than 500 rooms, and it can get extremely crowded at the height of the afternoon. Although the pool area opens to the beach, the sardine factor on the sand is equally as high.

❦❦ **SHERATON MOANA SURFRIDER, Waikiki** Built in 1901, the Moana Surfrider was Waikiki's first hotel property; today the place still awes visitors with its turn-of-the-century splendor. Sparkling crystal chandeliers hang from the ceiling in the grand lobby, thick columns and winding staircases add that plantation-style touch, while extravagant tropical bouquets bring a brilliance to the already gleaming white interior. Sadly, the Sheraton's 791 air-conditioned guest rooms have not retained much, if any, of the lobby's old-world charm and intimacy. In spite of ongoing renovations, even the hotel's historic wing is surprisingly disappointing, with drab color schemes and standard hotel furniture. On the bright side, new reproduction Hawaiian quilts enhance the beds, and the wood accents in the historical section add an elegant touch. The Moana's nostalgic past, impressive lobby, and prime beachfront location are the real reasons these rooms are worth your affectionate consideration.

Outside, afternoon tea is served on a lovely wraparound porch called **THE BANYAN VERANDA** (see Restaurant Kissing), where a magnificent, towering banyan tree shades the oceanfront courtyard. We also recommend a romantic dinner for two at the Moana's reputable **SHIP'S TAVERN** (see Restaurant Kissing). It's the perfect place to savor delectable continental cuisine and spectacular ocean views. **2365 Kalakaua Avenue; (808) 922-3111, (800) 782-9488; www.moana-surfrider.com; expensive to unbelievably expensive; recommended wedding site.**

❦❦ **WAIKIKI JOY HOTEL, Waikiki** Moderately priced (and reasonably romantic) accommodations are as rare as a rainy day in Waikiki. But in

High season is from mid-December through the end of March. Low season runs from April to mid-December. Not only do rates go down in low season, but business hours may be more limited too.

our search for economical luxury, the 94-room Waikiki Joy Hotel stood out as an affordable find. Furthermore, the boutique-style hotel caters to couples and the corporate crowd—a definite advantage if you're seeking an escape from the little ones (yours or anyone else's).

The modest, attractive open-air lobby is enhanced by Italian marble, stately white pillars, and a small waterfall pond. A postcard-size pool located off the lobby offers little to no privacy, but you won't mind once you've seen the upstairs rooms, which all feature large Jacuzzi soaking tubs. The rooms and suites themselves are not extravagant, but they are nicely appointed with wicker furnishings and pastel tones of pink, lilac, and gray. Some suites include a full kitchen and wet bar. All rooms and suites are soundproof and have a slightly outdated but admirable stereo system. Views aren't a selling point here, and the hotel staff is refreshingly honest about that point. A continental breakfast, served on the first-floor veranda area, is included with your stay.

The beach may be a few blocks away, but considering the price (and the lack of competition in this price range), the Waikiki Joy is an affectionate surprise that lives up to its name. **320 Lewers Street; (808) 923-2300, (800) 922-7866 mainland; www.aston-hotels.com; moderate to very expensive.**

❀❀❀ **WAIKIKI PARC HOTEL, Waikiki** A sister property of the elegant HALEKULANI (see review above), the Waikiki Parc Hotel lacks its sibling's oceanfront drama and opulence, but don't let that deter you from booking a room here. You can't find rooms, ocean views, and service of this caliber anywhere else in Waikiki at such reasonable rates. (Ask about the hotel's special packages, too.) Situated above a modest but comfortable lobby, each of the 298 rooms is simply decorated with a soft white and Pacific blue color scheme, bamboo furnishings, ceramic-tile floors, inlaid rugs, and white shutters that open onto a cozy lanai. Rooms above the 19th floor are considered deluxe, thanks to their "over the rooftop views." Other view choices include partial ocean views (you'll see other hotels), city and mountain vistas, and direct views of other hotels. On the eighth floor, sunbathers and swimmers can dally away at the pool, which is often all yours for the taking. **2233 Helumoa Road; (808) 921-7272, (800) 422-0450; www.waikikiparc.com; moderate to very expensive.**

Romantic Note: Connected to the Waikiki Parc Hotel, and a magnet for sushi lovers, is **KACHO** (inexpensive; breakfast, lunch, and dinner daily). This petite restaurant, elegantly though sparsely appointed, serves fresh udon and even fresher sushi. Although not romantic by any stretch of the imagination, the **PARC CAFE** (inexpensive; breakfast, lunch, and dinner daily) is considered a buffet-lover's paradise. The Hawaiian-style buffet lunch is a local favorite that's served twice a week.

Restaurant Kissing

❤❤❤ **ALAN WONG'S RESTAURANT, Honolulu** If you drive along South King Street too quickly, you might miss this excellent restaurant, hidden away in a nondescript neighborhood. So cruise by carefully, valet park, journey upstairs to the third floor of an office building, and prepare your palate for Pacific Rim dishes that are perfectly spiced and seasoned. Sliced Chinese-style duck with refried taro and Asian guacamole makes an excellent appetizer or, for a more steamy show, try "da bag": steamed clams, *kalua* pig, shiitake mushrooms, and spinach, all cooked and sealed in a foil bag. Choosing an entrée is difficult, since everything on the menu is wonderful. The signature ginger-crusted *onaga* with miso-sesame vinaigrette is delectable, and the braised Kahua Ranch lamb with potato gnocchi is equally satisfying. Specials change nightly and are worth a try. When the dessert menu arrives, crème brûlée lovers can indulge their taste buds with five flavors of custard individually presented in Chinese-style soup spoons.

Alan Wong's intriguing cuisine is served in an upbeat atmosphere with delicate halogen lights, island-print table coverings, and wicker-and-iron chairs—not exactly romantic, but the main reason to come here is the magnificent food. Because this restaurant is geared primarily toward groups, the room can become increasingly noisy with voices and laughter as the evening progresses. Service is professional, and each dish is explained in great detail when brought to your table. **1857 South King Street, third floor; (808) 949-2526; moderate to expensive; reservations recommended; dinner daily.**

Romantic Note: A seven-course chef's tasting menu is available for $85 per person. Yes, that does fall into our unbelievably expensive category, but if you're celebrating a special occasion and you're true connoisseurs of Hawaiian cuisine, this is the perfect place to indulge.

❤❤❤ **BALI BY THE SEA, Waikiki** Alluring ocean views are guaranteed no matter where you sit at this sophisticated open-air restaurant. Set above Waikiki's waterfront, Bali by the Sea offers unforgettable sunsets to start your evening off right. Warm tropical breezes waft through the plush, sage-colored dining room, where you will want to linger by candlelight long after your dessert plate is cleared. The varied menu includes Hawaiian-inspired and continental favorites such as sautéed prawns with vanilla red curry sauce, roasted salmon with lentil and pancetta casserole, and Hawaiian ahi steak served broiled or blackened. Throughout the year, the chef offers special four-course dinners designed to complement the season and showcase what's fresh from sea and land. As for desserts, they change nightly and never disappoint. **2005 Kalia Road, at the Hilton Hawaiian Village; (808) 941-2254; expensive; dinner Monday–Saturday.**

❧❧❧ **THE BANYAN VERANDA, Waikiki** A white banister encloses this idyllic wraparound terrace dining room, which fronts the sapphire blue Pacific. From any angle it is one of the most enticing spots on the island for breakfast, Sunday brunch, or afternoon high tea. High-backed wicker chairs, teak floors, and open-air seating create an authentic island setting, and a harpist enhances the breezy mood as light winds blow through the venerable banyan tree in the courtyard. White-glove service from a polite staff can be gracious but a little on the haughty side. If you don't mind the formality, you will relish the romance that overflows from this picturesque setting. **2365 Kalakaua Avenue, at the Sheraton Moana Surfrider Hotel; (808) 922-3111; www.moana-surfrider.com; expensive; breakfast Monday–Saturday, high tea and dinner daily, brunch Sunday.**

❧❧ **THE CONTEMPORARY CAFE, Honolulu** You wouldn't guess it, but this is one of the more interesting places to kiss in Hawaii. It's close to Waikiki, yet it feels miles away. A winding drive up through the exclusive Makiki Heights neighborhood brings you to The Contemporary Museum, a spectacular 1920s estate that now houses modern art exhibitions and a lovely café. Although it is just a casual café, the unique location away from hordes of tourists, the stylishly sparse decor, and the light and healthy menu make it worth mentioning. You'll find such delights as cold soba salad with baked tofu, pita pizza of the day, vegetarian sandwiches, or specials such as Malaysian shrimp salad of succulent tiger prawns, green papaya, and leafy lettuce in a tasty peanut dressing. End your meal on a rich note with a scoop of gelato or a slice of banana-cranberry bread. When you've finished, enjoy strolling through the three and a half acres of beautifully landscaped gardens. The property is dotted with massive, unusual sculptures and magnificent trees framing peekaboo views of Waikiki and the great blue beyond. **2411 Makiki Heights Drive, at The Contemporary Museum; (808) 523-3362; inexpensive; $5 per person museum admission fee; lunch Tuesday–Sunday.**

Romantic Suggestion: Take the time to walk through the museum's exhibits. The $5 admission fee applies even if you only come for the café, but most likely you'll be glad to have paid once you see the noteworthy exhibits.

❀❀❀ **GOLDEN DRAGON RESTAURANT, Waikiki** Harbored on an oceanfront marina, this series of luxurious, open-air dining rooms resembles the interior of a mansion, brimming with exquisite Oriental antiques, shoji screens, and Chinese statues. Candles flicker at well-spaced tables draped in white linens, complemented by mahogany floors and pillars. Despite the enticing, potentially pretentious surroundings, service is decidedly friendly. The sizable menu includes standard Cantonese favorites such as wonton soup and potstickers, in addition to more unusual dishes like jellyfish with sesame shoyu and ocean scallops seared with lychees (a must if you've never tried this interesting tropical fruit). Our only complaint is that the scallops are slightly undercooked, but that won't dissuade us from recommending the Golden Dragon again and again for its enchanting ambience. **2005 Kalia Road, at the Hilton Hawaiian Village; (808) 949-4321; inexpensive to expensive; dinner Tuesday–Sunday.**

❀❀ **HANOHANO ROOM, Waikiki** The view is the attraction at the Hanohano Room, and the major, if not only, reason to mention this established restaurant. Ensconced on the 30th floor of the Sheraton Waikiki, you can dine amid vast, majestic views of the ocean, mountains, and endless sky. Prices are fairly astronomical in light of the kitchen's failings, and there is nothing distinctive about the interior. Yet there is that view. Sunset can be quite an experience from up here, as long as you stick to cocktails and snacks served in the small bar area, which has fine access to the view and a pianist who plays gently into the night. **2255 Kalakaua Avenue, at the Sheraton Waikiki; (808) 922-4422; very expensive; reservations recommended; dinner daily.**

❀❀❀ **INDIGO, Honolulu** Nestled in the heart of Waikiki's historic Chinatown, Indigo is coloring the local dining scene with fabulous flavors. Provocative modern art and authentic Chinese antiques contribute to an intriguing atmosphere in the first of several dining rooms, but we recommend holding out for a table in the open-air brick courtyard, where the real romance awaits. Here, you will feel as if you've been transported across the globe to another time and place. Tiki torches illuminate two-person tables tucked next to a genuine Chinese pond teeming with goldfish and floating water lilies. A second handful of larger tables overlook a neighborhood park complete with a small, melodic rock waterfall. (Views of the park are most pleasant at nightfall, when gatherings have thinned out.)

Service can be inattentive, but thankfully every dish prepared by Indigo's chef is done to perfection. Bao buns with Okinawan potatoes and sun-dried cherries are a sweet, unique beginning, and almost as delicious as the lobster potstickers with soy-ginger sauce. Norwegian salmon cakes with smoked chipotle mayonnaise and stir-fried asparagus with black bean–butter sauce are sublime and artistically presented on lovely platters with pickled vegetables, chutney and salsa, and chive pillow noodle cakes. Leave room for the appropriately named "Explosions to Heaven"—fried bananas with coconut gelato; it's guaranteed to end your evening on a heavenly note. **1121 Nuuanu Avenue; (808) 521-2900; www.places.com/indigo; moderate; dinner Tuesday–Saturday.**

❦❦ **KEO'S IN WAIKIKI, Waikiki** Every celebrity imaginable, and then some, has eaten at Keo's. The proof is on the wall. Peruse the gallery of pictures as you enter and see how many stars you recognize. This is definitely Waikiki's to-be-seen-in hot spot. Even if you don't care about who's who, come anyway to experience the intriguing surroundings and incredible Thai cuisine.

The dining room overflows with exotic floral arrangements, palm trees, wooden screens, and golden statues. Unfortunately, the restaurant resides next to a busy bus stop, and when the windows are open (which is often), conversations come to a halt whenever a bus goes by. Top all this off with an exposed ventilation system accompanied by lines of halogen lights, and sensory overload can take hold. Luckily, the delicious entrées don't overtax the taste buds. Delight the palate with creatively prepared, evenly spiced Thai entrées, such as lime-kissed papaya salad, roll-your-own spring rolls, rich Panang curry, or the famous Evil Jungle Prince, a medley of vegetables, fresh basil, and red chiles in a coconut sauce. The Evil Princess drink (jackfruit, pineapple juice, orange juice, and coconut) makes a refreshing accompaniment. A scoop of coconut ice cream or sorbet should cool off your hot lips (at least for the time being). Reservations are recommended and a must on Friday and Saturday nights. Don't overlook this place for a romantic lunch either; beat the noonday heat by hiding yourselves in the back of the restaurant where it's dark and cool. **2028 Kuhio Avenue, at the Ambassador Hotel; (808) 943-1444; inexpensive to moderate; reservations recommended; breakfast, lunch, and dinner daily.**

❦❦❦ **LA MER, Waikiki** Housed on the second floor of what was originally a private beachfront estate at the Halekulani, this dining room is characterized by subdued etched paneling and delicious ocean views. Fresh ocean air (and the sound of next-door evening entertainment) spills into the elegant dining room. Guests are greeted with glasses of champagne, then escorted to spacious, secluded tables topped with flickering candles. Although the menu offers delectable, award-winning Pacific Rim selections, prices can be extremely expensive. Yet when you see the time that was put into the presentations, you might understand why. The filet of *kumu,* wrapped in a rosemary salt crust shaped like a fish, is certainly showstopping, as is the pistachio and coconut ice cream covered by a shell of spun sugar. To get the most for your money, choose one of the three available prix fixe dinners. This is a slightly more affordable (yet still unbelievably expensive) way to taste a little bit of everything. **2199 Kalia Road, at the Halekulani; (808) 923-2311; www.halekulani.com; very expensive to unbelievably expensive; reservations recommended; jackets required; dinner daily; recommended wedding site.**

❤️❤️ **NICHOLAS NICKOLAS, Waikiki** Looking for a sexy nightspot where you can observe Waikiki's twinkling city lights from 36 floors up? Then look no further than Nicholas Nickolas. Tables for two, adorned with white linens and single red roses, hug the supper club's window-lined perimeter, but cozy leather booths are also available. The predominately American-style cuisine is just average—a major disappointment, considering the prices. Service is attentive to the point of being ludicrous, unless you are comfortable with a parade of tuxedoed men waiting on you. Still, Nicholas Nickolas is one of the few intimate late-night options in Waikiki, and it is a prime place to kiss. Just come for drinks, dancing, and maybe dessert (bananas Foster is a deliciously sweet option). **410 Atkinson Drive, 36th floor, at the Ala Moana Hotel; (808) 955-4466; expensive; dinner daily; recommended wedding site.**

❤️❤️ **NICK'S FISHMARKET, Waikiki** Nick's Fishmarket has been serving great fresh fish for more than 30 years, and it continues to hold its own against competition from the highly touted chefs flocking to Waikiki. On the downside, it has also held on to its original decor. The dimly lit dining rooms are dated and a tad too cave-like for some tastes, but the high leather booths and adequately spaced tables with high-backed chairs offer a surplus of cozy spots for two. Service is friendly yet professional, and the kitchen takes time and care with every item on its extensive menu. Large portions of Hawaiian fish are presented in a variety of remarkably tasty sauces, most notably the best-seller: *opakapaka* served with oven-roasted-tomato–butter sauce. What really caught our curiosity was the "vanbana pie," recently named the "Fantasy Dessert of the Year." Try this banana pudding–vanilla ice cream–Ritz Cracker creation and see if your tropical dream comes true. **2070 Kalakaua Avenue, at the Waikiki Gateway Hotel; (808) 955-6333; expensive; dinner daily.**

Romantic Warning: Half of Nick's Fishmarket serves as a nightclub in the late evening, with an open bar, a dance floor, and live entertainment. Sounds from the bar definitely carry into the restaurant and can be a romantic deterrent if you're not in the mood for the evening's musical selections.

❤❤❤ **ORCHIDS, Waikiki** Halekulani does everything to perfection, and the Orchids restaurant is no exception. Provocative floral arrangements and white-linen tables fill the terraced, open-air dining room, which is graced by eucalyptus hardwood floors. Scintillating views counterpoint a gala of flavors and tastes, from the appetizers all the way through to dessert. Orchids focuses primarily on seafood from around the world, including a fine selection of shellfish. Stuffed calamari seasoned with a tomato-tarragon sauce and a paella perfect for two are entrées worth ordering. End your evening by sharing a slice of coconut cake, Orchids' signature creation that deserves a "Best Dessert Award" in our book. **2199 Kalia Road, at the Halekulani; (808) 923-2311; www.halekulani. com; moderate to expensive; breakfast, lunch, and dinner daily; recommended wedding site.**

Romantic Alternative: If you'd like to admire views of Halekulani's grounds and the ocean in a more casual atmosphere, gaze and graze at the hotel's **HOUSE WITHOUT A KEY** (808-923-2311; inexpensive to moderate; breakfast, lunch, and light dinner daily). This poolside terrace dining room serves a small but eclectic assortment of ethnic cuisine. Simple combinations or a delicious chicken fajita salad are relatively reasonable, and the service is sheer perfection.

❤❤❤ **SHIP'S TAVERN, Waikiki** "Tavern" is a misnomer for this elegant dining room. Named after the old-fashioned luxury liners that brought the wealthy and adventurous to Waikiki, Ship's Tavern is the Sheraton Moana Surfrider's "flagship" restaurant. You don't have to be adventurous to eat here, since the dishes are straightforward, but being wealthy might help. Linen-cloaked tables arranged with romantic privacy in mind line an expanse of windows that overlook the beach below and sultry ocean sunsets beyond. Colorful bouquets of exotic flowers lend the ultraformal setting a tropical flair.

Continental dishes appear on the menu, from classical seafood bouillabaisse and Chateaubriand of beef tenderloin to Pacific mahi mahi à la Oscar. Finish the evening off with a dish of Kona coffee chocolate crème brûlée, guaranteed to make your dreams even sweeter. **2365 Kalakaua**

Avenue, at the Sheraton Moana Surfrider; (808) 922-3111; www. moana-surfrider.com; very expensive; dinner daily; recommended wedding site.

Outdoor Kissing

❀❀❀ **HONOLULU MAUKA TRAIL SYSTEM, Honolulu** If you are one of the many who believe that Oahu's natural beauty has been diminished by overbuilding and overpopulation, you need to venture into the Honolulu Mauka trail system. An afternoon in the Tantalus area will restore your faith in the power of nature. Fertile stands of lush bamboo and fragrant eucalyptus line the **PUU OHIA TRAIL,** which rambles through groves of wild fruit trees and other tropical treasures. Sections of this three-quarter-mile hike are steep but not too difficult if you have proper shoes (*proper* is the operative word here). If you still long for more natural wonders once you reach the highest point of this trail, you can take the **MANOA CLIFF TRAIL,** then continue on the **AIHUALAMA TRAIL,** and make the gorgeous descent into **MANOA VALLEY. Oahu Division of Forestry: (808) 587-0166.** *Call the Division of Forestry for maps and descriptions of all the hikes in the Honolulu Mauka trail system. They are free and can be picked up at 1151 Punchbowl Street, Room 131, Honolulu. To reach the various trailheads for most of the hikes, follow Round Top Drive up to its highest point, where it becomes Tantalus Drive; parking lots along the road indicate where to stop.*

Romantic Suggestion: With so many intersections and varying trails, you really need to obtain a map and specific descriptions before setting out. Getting lost in paradise may be fine for a fantasy, but in reality it's not too fun.

❀❀❀ **LYON ARBORETUM, Honolulu** If you've been curious about the names of the exotic flora that seem to envelop the Hawaiian Islands (and you're looking for slightly cooler air), Lyon Arboretum is the place to go. Every imaginable kind of tropical flower, plant, and tree is exhibited in this enchanting public garden set deep in the lush folds of the Manoa Valley. Bring walking shoes and stroll hand in hand up a stone road through dense forests, where you'll hear only the wind, birds, and whispers of love. With its 193 acres and several gardens to explore, the two of you may have this paradise all to yourselves. It's the closest thing to jungle love we've found on Oahu. **3860 Manoa Road; (808) 988-7378; free admission, donation of $1 per person suggested; open Monday–Saturday.** *Drive north on University Avenue, which turns into Oahu Avenue after you pass the*

*University of Hawaii campus. Pass East Manoa Road, then turn right
onto Manoa Road. Signs will first direct you to Paradise Park, then to
Lyon Arboretum.*

Diamond Head

Go ahead, close your eyes. The chances of accidentally kissing a stranger
on the beach here are much slimmer than on the beach at Waikiki. Diamond Head summons you away from the crowds and mayhem of urban
Waikiki. You won't be totally alone, but you'll have a lot more room to
enjoy the surf, sand, and sunshine.

There isn't a better place to witness spectacular views of Waikiki's shoreline and cityscape (or to kiss) than the top of **DIAMOND HEAD CRATER**.
Early morning is really the only time when the heat isn't too unbearable for
the steep hike, but once you reach the top, you'll be glad you made the less-
than-an-hour-long trek. A bottle of water, strong legs, and shoes with good
traction are advised. A map and a flashlight for the long, dark tunnels are
also helpful.

Hotel/Bed and Breakfast Kissing

❤❤❤❀ **COLONY SURF HOTEL, Diamond Head** "A Bit of Bali on
Hawaii" best describes this luxurious, boutique hotel separated from the
hustle and bustle of downtown by a quiet expanse of parks and beaches.
Although outward appearances prove uninteresting, you'll be pleasantly
surprised once you step inside the elegant, marbled lobby, warmed by Balinese art and furnishings and cooled by the wind that breezes through
open windows. The 50 rooms, which reside five to a floor, share the same
decor and size; only the views differ. Light, spacious, and private, each
room is accented by cool white and beige fabrics, textured wallpaper, a
low-profile king-size bed, Balinese art, and contemporary teak furniture.
Private lanais face the blue water, Diamond Head crater, or a combination
of both. Romantic extras include thick robes, Aveda bath amenities, CD
players, in-room refrigerators, and evening turndown service.

Although there's no pool at the hotel, you are only a few steps from a
small, uncrowded beach; plus you have access (for a nominal fee) to a
private fitness center next door. A bountiful continental breakfast is served

---

*Disposable underwater cameras take surprisingly good photographs. We recom-
mend purchasing one to take along on snorkeling adventures and boat rides so you
won't have to worry about getting your nondisposable camera wet.*

downstairs, and trays are provided if you want to savor the morning goodies on your private patio. Come evening, don't miss a dinner at DAVID PAUL'S DIAMOND HEAD GRILL (see Restaurant Kissing), an innovative and contemporary restaurant that fits beautifully into this elegant hotel. **2885 Kalakaua Avenue; (808) 924-3111, (888) 924-SURF; www. colonysurf.com; expensive to unbelievably expensive.**

Romantic Note: Colony Surf also operates private, long-term rental condominiums, which we don't recommend for several reasons: They lack air-conditioning, room service, and other amenities, and the decor is dated. Besides, few places can compare to hotel rooms at the Colony Surf.

❤❤❤ THE NEW OTANI KAIMANA BEACH HOTEL, Diamond Head

As travel writers, we have learned never to judge a book by its cover, and the New Otani is a case in point. Pulling into the hotel's narrow driveway and crowded parking lot, you may initially doubt that romantic possibilities can be found here, but put your worries aside. Although the hotel's exterior, hallways, and carpeting are a little worse for wear, each of the suites and guest rooms (except the standard ones that face the neighboring condo complex) has the makings for a satisfying getaway. Private balconies, expansive floor-to-ceiling windows, and pastel fabrics and wall coverings create an inviting atmosphere. Many of the 124 units have impressive up-close and personal views of the churning blue ocean, while others face neighboring Kapiolani Park. Of special amorous interest are the five spacious, beautifully designed suites situated on the hotel's top floor. Sensually appointed with Jacuzzi tubs and boutique furniture, they leave little doubt that the extra expense will provide an experience you and yours will appreciate. Either way, downtown Waikiki sparkles in the distance—far away enough for you to enjoy peaceful nights and quiet mornings. **2863 Kalakaua Avenue; (808) 923-1555, (800) 356-8264; inexpensive to unbelievably expensive and beyond.**

Restaurant Kissing

❤❤❤ DAVID PAUL'S DIAMOND HEAD GRILL, Diamond Head A

fiery sunset reflecting off nearby Diamond Head Crater isn't the only sight turning heads in Waikiki. In the shadow of this famous landmark resides the outstanding and elegantly appointed David Paul's, a restaurant that almost equals the beauty outside. Colorful works by a local artist bring

---

Be sure to pack comfortable walking shoes. Sandals may not provide enough traction for the various hikes on each island.

energy into the stunning dining room, while marble, blond woods, brushed metals, and glass accents add a contemporary touch. For optimum kissing opportunities, the handful of window tables or the curved booths fronting one side of the restaurant are ideal. When the sunset fades, the lights dim and candles illuminate each table. If that's not enough for your romantic wants, a piano and vocal duo complement with melodies of love.

The "New American" cuisine David Paul's features is equally as engaging as the surroundings. Drawing on Hawaiian, Southwest, and Asian flavors, the dishes dazzle and delight. Taste the imagination of the chef with such signature dishes as Kona coffee rack of lamb, *kalua* duck, or the bursting-with-flavor tequila shrimp with firecracker rice. Linger a while over dessert; as the night goes on, the crowds disperse, leaving the two of you to enjoy the love songs in peace. **2885 Kalakaua Avenue, at the Colony Surf Hotel; (808) 922-3734; www.davidpauls.com; expensive to very expensive; lunch Monday–Friday, dinner daily.**

💋💋💋 **HAU TREE LANAI, Diamond Head** Share a sunset beneath the sprawling *hau* tree at this lovely beachside terrace restaurant. Ocean breezes drift past cozy tables covered with white tablecloths and shaded by pink umbrellas. After night falls, tiki torches glow, the glorious tree is lit with twinkling white bulbs, and soft classical guitar music accompanies your meal. Choose from menu selections such as grilled steak, lobster, and various fresh seafood dishes—pretty standard fare, but the main reason to come here is the setting, not culinary wizardry. The atmosphere is best described as informal; breakfast and lunch are the most casual as swimmers and sunbathers pass by. **2863 Kalakaua Avenue, at The New Otani Kaimana Beach Hotel; (808) 921-7066; moderate; breakfast, lunch, and dinner daily.**

💋💋 **MICHEL'S, Diamond Head** The ambience here is unquestionably sensual. In fact, it would be hard to find more amorous surroundings. The plush open-air dining room is nestled directly on the beach and offers panoramic views of the ocean surf, Waikiki's skyline, and unobstructed sunsets. The dining rooms exude elegance at every turn. Cozy, candlelit tables for two are draped in white linens, adorned with classical place settings, and set beneath dimly lit crystal chandeliers and gilded mirrors.

Unfortunately, the kitchen's talents are not as impressive as those of the interior decorator or Mother Nature. Continental cuisine may be a welcome change for those who have tired of the Pacific Rim rage, but the entrées and desserts aren't as innovative or tasty as we had hoped they would be (especially at these prices). The salads, however, are excellent. As for the service, it tends to fluctuate between underattentive and overattentive throughout your three-hour meal. **2895 Kalakaua Avenue; (808) 923-6552; expensive to very expensive; reservations recommended; dinner daily; recommended wedding site.**

Kahala

Just east of Diamond Head is Kahala, with its well-tended neighborhoods, gated luxury homes, and handful of lovely beaches. There's one beachfront hotel here and two fabulous restaurants that we found worthy of your romantic consideration.

Hotel/Bed and Breakfast Kissing

❤❤❤❤ **KAHALA MANDARIN ORIENTAL HOTEL, Kahala** When we last set foot inside this 371-room hotel, it was in the midst of an $82-million renovation. With such extensive efforts now complete, we are delighted to report that the Kahala Mandarin is definitely worth the ten-minute drive from the bikini-clad crowds of Waikiki into the upscale and quiet Kahala neighborhood. Situated between the Waialae Country Club Golf Course and the beach, the hotel caters to those seeking to sun and smooch in relative solitude. The hotel's most stunning feature is the lagoon surrounding the inner part of the hotel. Three Atlantic bottlenose dolphins, two sea turtles, and plenty of colorful fish make their home in these crystal-clear waters. Near the swimming pool (popular with the kiddies) is a wonderful stretch of beach where you can hide beneath a private cabana (for a fee) and heat up those lips.

With the exception of the individually decorated and ultra-expensive suites, all rooms are elegantly appointed with teak wood furniture and floors, wooden blinds, Hawaiian artwork, CD player, and large TV. The spacious, tiled bathrooms truly are couple-friendly with double sinks, two closets, robes and slippers, a glass-enclosed shower, and a deep soaking tub. Book a room with a king-size bed and you'll fall in love underneath the elegant canopy. Rooms in one of the two towers provide the best views, although be forewarned that, for privacy reasons, not all have balconies. For more seclusion and romantic charm, we recommend the Lagoon Rooms, especially those facing the beachfront or inner lagoon.

After a day spent sunbathing, watching the dolphin program, or taking a complimentary scuba lesson in the pool, enjoy dinner at the casual, open-air **PLUMERIA BEACH CAFE** (moderate to expensive; breakfast, lunch, and dinner daily) or upstairs at **HOKU'S** (see Restaurant Kissing).

No matter where you turn in the Kahala Mandarin, beauty and art are everywhere. The hotel's efforts in bringing authentic Hawaiian art to almost every corner of the property, from the private rooms to the public rest rooms, are noteworthy and impressive. The museum-like collection is one more aspect that sets this hotel apart from the rest. **5000 Kahala Avenue; (808) 739-8888, (800) 367-2525; www.mandarin-oriental.com; very expensive to unbelievably expensive and beyond; recommended wedding site.**

Restaurant Kissing

☙☙☙ **HOKU'S, Kahala** The stars that twinkle in the Hawaiian sky aren't the only ones shining. Far from Waikiki's bright lights, Hoku's—translated as "star" in Hawaiian—brightens up the nighttime dining scene with innovative entrées, an energized feel (untypical of so many hotel restaurants), and one of the best beachfront dining locales on Oahu.

Cherry-wood furniture and paneling, vaulted ceilings, an open kitchen (which can be noisy if you sit nearby), and a sprinkling of exquisite glass and metal sculptures make the two-tiered, indoor restaurant feel open and inviting. Ocean views, sans sunbathers, surfers, and so forth, are the trademark of each table.

If you can handle the steep price, try the chef's choice: a scrumptious five-course feast that caters to your preferences. With a wok, tandoori oven, and *kiawe* grill at the kitchen's disposal, choices range from stuffed naan to grilled lobster. You can't go wrong with the wok-seared Hawaiian prawns, deliciously salty and garlicky, or, for some comfort food à la the tropics, taste the herbed *onaga* (red snapper) served on creamed spinach. Rack of lamb, courtesy of a Colorado ranch, hits the high mark for tenderness. Although desserts could be more interesting, we won't complain about the coffee crème brûlée tower topped with a scoop of coffee ice cream. How heavenly can you get? **5000 Kahala Avenue, at the Kahala Mandarin Oriental Hotel; (808) 739-8779; expensive to very expensive; lunch and dinner daily.**

☙☙☙ **KAHALA MOON CAFE, Kahala** The upscale Kahala neighborhood, ten minutes east of Waikiki, is home to one of Oahu's best restaurants. Kahala Moon Cafe—more restaurant than café—is nicely appointed with modern Hawaiian art, pale mint walls, a spectacular *koa*-wood bar, and breathtaking floral arrangements created by the multitalented chef. Candlelit tables draped in white linens are arranged throughout two adjacent dining rooms, and there are a handful of two-person tables lining a cushioned bench that runs the length of one wall. Unfortunately, some of these seats can feel too close for kissing comfort. Service is extremely gracious, with an attention to detail that is unsurpassed.

The contemporary American cuisine draws on influences from the Pacific Rim, but unlike many restaurants that only serve surf 'n' turf, Kahala Moon's menu is well rounded. You'll find plenty of filling comfort foods, including robust portobello mushrooms in a balsamic–roasted garlic jus or lamb shank so tender it falls off the bone into the accompanying rosemary cabernet jus and wild mushroom risotto. And when it comes to dessert, there are few things in life as succulent and sweet as a ripe mango, but we discovered something equally tantalizing here: the warm mango bread pudding, one of the most luscious desserts on the island. **4614 Kilauea Avenue; (808) 732-7777; moderate to expensive; dinner Tuesday–Sunday.**

Hawaii Kai

Restaurant Kissing

❤❤ **ROY'S RESTAURANT, Hawaii Kai** Restaurants tucked into business parks aren't our idea of a romantic dining option, especially in Hawaii, but luckily at Roy's you'll fall in love with the food rather than the location. Plus, the drive out to Hawaii Kai is a good excuse to escape wacky Waikiki.

An open kitchen is the centerpiece of this second-floor dining room, while vivid modern art graces the walls. Window seats look out to palm trees and the ocean beyond, but unfortunately the view also takes in the busy highway. Brightly adorned tables are packed in rather tightly, and since this restaurant is almost always booked, don't expect any privacy or quiet conversation time. What you can expect is professional service and well-executed dishes. One of Roy's signature dishes is the must-try crab cakes accented by an outstanding spicy sesame sauce. Continue pleasing the palate with other flavor-filled dishes such as the miso-marinated butterfish or seared *shutome* with macadamia nut–coconut sauce. Roy's signature dessert, a chocolate soufflé, demonstrates that simplicity is often sublime. **6600 Kalanianaole Highway; (808) 396-7697; www.roys restaurant.com; moderate to expensive; reservations recommended; dinner daily.**

Romantic Note: Reservations are recommended, but if you call too late and the dining room is already full, the first-come, first-served lower level is devoted to those who didn't plan ahead. The same menu is offered in the casual bar and outdoor patio area, in addition to live Hawaiian-style entertainment consisting of steel guitars and soft melodies.

Outdoor Kissing

❀❀❀❀ **KOKO HEAD DISTRICT PARK, Hawaii Kai** Due east of Diamond Head is the rugged terrain and breathtaking shoreline of Koko Head District Park. **HANAUMA BAY NATURE PRESERVE**, a volcanic crater open to the sea on one side, is the big attraction on this side of the island. The crater features prime snorkeling among some of the most abundant, amazing, and colorful sea creatures you will encounter anywhere (see Romantic Note below). Even if you decide to skip snorkeling, be sure to drive through this park for the views and the chance to experience as much of Oahu as possible. Every turn of the road brings new panoramas of deep blue waves turning to white mist as they crash against the volcanic-rock shoreline. You won't be all alone on this drive, but the crush of tourists does seem to thin out over here. There are plenty of lookout points where you can stop, linger over the view, take pictures, and, most importantly, share a kiss or two. **(808) 395-3407.** *On Oahu's southeast shore.*

Romantic Note: Despite efforts to limit the number of people at **HANAUMA BAY NATURE PRESERVE** (808-396-4229; $3-per-nonresident admission fee, $1 parking fee per vehicle; open Wednesday–Monday), the area can still seem crowded. However, this is still the best spot to snorkel on Oahu. While you must deal with the crowds when you first arrive, once submerged you enter a totally different, much more peaceful world of bright fish and shapely coral. Access to the bay is limited, based on parking spots available. Come in the morning as early as 6 A.M. when the sun is not too blistering and most of the tourists are still in bed.

East Oahu

Kailua

Located about 40 minutes northeast of Waikiki is the town of Kailua, which goes about its business at a drastically different, far less hectic pace. You won't see a single high-rise here. The drive through the Koolau Mountain Range via the Pali Highway is reason enough to at least check out this charming residential area and its excellent beaches. Year after year **KAILUA BEACH PARK** has been rated by various travel magazines as one of the best beaches in the country. With its soft, white, sandy beaches and aqua waters, it'll rate high with you, too, for kissing.

Hotel/Bed and Breakfast Kissing

❤❤ **MANU MELE BED AND BREAKFAST, Kailua** Travel to Oahu's windward side for an attractive alternative to the Waikiki scene. Manu Mele (meaning "bird song") is a residential bed and breakfast with two simply but attractively appointed guest rooms. Both rooms open to a pool area and well-tended garden courtyard, and each is completely self-sufficient, with air-conditioning, a TV, microwave, and coffeemaker. A complimentary welcoming breakfast of fresh fruit and muffins awaits in your room's refrigerator and will keep you going on the first day of your stay. A nearby path leads to a sweeping, fairly empty stretch of sun-kissed sand at Kailua Bay. The only drawback to this kissing bargain is the adjacent thoroughfare. Cars whiz by and the sound is less than idyllic, but the price, the proximity to the beach, and the owners' professionalism and attention to detail more than compensate. **153 Kailuana Place; (808) 262-0016; www.pixi.com/~manumele; inexpensive; minimum-stay requirement.**

Outdoor Kissing

❤❤❤ **LANIKAI BEACH, Kailua** Soft, warm waves lap against the sandy, white shore of Lanikai Beach, and the water is crystal clear. Dotting the horizon are two small islands, both seabird sanctuaries. The scene resembles an impossibly perfect picture from one of those brochures advertising a tropical paradise, but this is no illusion. Located at the edge of an affluent neighborhood, Lanikai Beach is a wonderful place to enjoy the serenity and peacefulness of the pale aqua ocean, not to see or be seen as in Waikiki. *This beach is just south of Kailua, along Mokulua Drive. Watch for walkways and signs stating* "PUBLIC RIGHT-OF-WAY TO BEACH."

    Romantic Suggestion: If you can muster the energy for an extremely early morning, try to experience at least one sunrise here. It is an event not soon forgotten.

All beaches in Hawaii are public. As long as you can find public access, you are welcome to enjoy the beaches everywhere.

North Shore

Kahuku

Hotel/Bed and Breakfast Kissing

❤❤❤ **HALE O'HONU, Kahuku** If you've got your hearts set on a dream-vacation rental home, look no further. Sheltered on Oahu's spectacular North Shore, this self-sufficient beachfront house is as pretty as a postcard. Set overlooking a white-sand beach and crystal blue Kawela Bay (one of the few remaining feeding grounds for endangered Hawaiian green sea turtles), the contemporary two-story home feels relatively secluded, with neighbors on only one side.

Ample windows allow for cool breezes and lovely water views on the home's lower floor, where you'll find two bedrooms, a fully equipped kitchen (provisions are up to you), and a cheerful, airy living room appointed with blond hardwood floors and comfortable wicker furnishings. Unfortunately, during summer's peak, the upstairs master bedroom is suffocatingly hot, even when the windows are open and the ceiling fan is running at high speed. If it's just the two of you, consider sleeping in one of the downstairs bedrooms, although you'll want to take advantage of the large, glass-enclosed soaking tub upstairs in the master bathroom. When the sun has gone down completely, watch the stars emerge in the night sky from the steamy privacy of the outdoor hot tub in the backyard. **(808) 247-6821; www.w-ink.com/honu; very expensive; minimum-stay requirement.**

"You may conquer with the sword,

but you are conquered by a kiss."

Daniel Heinsius

Maui

Kapalua *
* Napili
Kahana *
Kaanapali *
Wailuku
Huelo
* Paia *
* Haiku
Lahaina *
* Haliimaile
* Makawao
Kihei *
* Kula
Wailea *
* Hana

Maui

Of all the nicknames that define the Hawaiian Islands, Maui's seems truest to form. "The Magic Isle" certainly casts a spell on all who sink their toes into the sandy beaches, breathe the crisp morning air atop mighty Haleakala, or journey into the heart of the jungle near Hana. Surely the garden of Eden looked something like Maui—well, at least the Maui of 30 years ago. Maui's magic is no longer a secret, and the island's increasing popularity and growth have left their mark, especially in the sprawling condominium complexes that crowd the sunniest, sandiest beaches. Even so, the scenery is still graced with plenty of tropical forests, green fields of sugarcane, azure waters, and pristine beaches. Yes, the handful of mostly single-lane main roads that outline the island are usually filled with cars, creating slow-moving, frustrating traffic jams. But if you change your focus and concentrate on the scenery, the sunshine, and each other, everything is forgivable.

Besides being the second-largest island in the Hawaiian chain, Maui has the dubious distinction of being considered the island of the well-heeled. There are more millionaires per capita here than anywhere else in the United States. In alliance with that statistic, Maui also has some of the most expensive, prestigious hotel rooms in the world: Two suites at the Grand Wailea go for $10,000 a night. (We won't describe what you get for that; it would only cause you a great deal of envy and potential kissing distress.) Despite the preponderance of expensive properties with stupendous places to stay, there are also many moderately priced places that can feel almost as indulgent and grand.

No matter if you're a first-time visitor to Maui or a seasoned devotee, there are certain tourist activities that are mandatory on any romantic (or nonromantic) itinerary: Climb above the clouds to witness a sublime sunrise or sunset from **HALEAKALA CRATER** or hike through lush **IAO VALLEY STATE PARK** to reach the 2,250-foot rocky spire of **IAO NEEDLE**. If cruising is more your style, drive two and a half hours through tropical rain forest, navigating more than 600 hairpin turns, to the remote, scenic town of **HANA** and the dramatic **SEVEN POOLS** waterfall just outside of Kipahulu. Be sure to witness Maui's underwater world by slipping on some fins and a mask. Two of the best places for smooth and easy snorkeling are **HONOLUA BAY** near Kapalua and off **BLACK ROCK** in Kaanapali. No matter where you end up snorkeling, you're bound to see plenty of colorful marine inhabitants. What else is there to do on Maui?

Stroll through the old whaling village of **LAHAINA**; watch windsurfers skim back and forth over the waves at **HOOKIPA PARK** on the north side of the island; or just sit back and be treated like royalty while enjoying a leisurely Sunday brunch at any of the phenomenal resorts that hug exquisite sections of the island. The best part about most of these activities (except brunch) is that you won't be reaching into your wallet often.

If your vacation budget is generous, consider bicycling down Haleakala on an organized biking trek ($100–$120 per person) or taking a helicopter to Hana (tickets start at $150 per person). There are also boat excursions to the extinct volcanic crater of **MOLOKINI** (see Romantic Warning) or other less public snorkeling spots ($65–$95 per person). For a deeper underwater journey, take the plunge with scuba diving lessons (rates vary widely, but usually fit into the expensive category). Or simply savor a gourmet dinner at one of the island's select romantic restaurants ($100–$150 per couple).

All of the paid-for outdoor activities are well organized and fun, and provide extraordinary experiences in extraordinary places. However, if you have to choose only one, we suggest going on a romantic sunset sail or some type of boat ride that includes snorkeling. For specific information on Maui and all of the activities on the island, call the **MAUI VISITORS BUREAU** (808-244-3530, 800-525-MAUI; www.visit maui.com) to receive a complimentary Maui Vacation Planner. The reviews that follow will help you indulge your romantic inclinations in less touristy, more intimate ways.

Romantic Warning: Snorkeling cruises to Molokini are extremely popular, and the area is packed with people. (Watch out for flailing flippers!) The trip out is wonderful, but the crescent-shaped rocky rim can resemble a parking lot for boats. Last, but not least, the fish are so overfed in these waters that they'll often give you the "fins down" when it comes to your food offerings.

Historical Note: Maui is the name of the Hawaiian deity who created all the Hawaiian Islands. The story goes something like this: At the beginning of time, Maui used his legendary rope to hook and haul up the land submerged under the seas, forming the islands. After accomplishing this mythic feat, Maui then attempted to lasso the sun god, La, to bring light to

Be sure to pack comfortable walking shoes. Sandals may not provide enough traction for the various hikes on each island.

the islands. Their great struggle took place at the top of Haleakala Crater. Maui emerged victorious. In a dire effort to obtain his freedom, the enslaved La promised to travel slowly across the heavens to forever warm the people and their harvests. It is for these benevolent acts that the god Maui came to have an island named after him.

West Maui

Kapalua

Quite literally the end of the road on the westernmost tip of Maui, Kapalua is the last developed place on this side of the island . . . and it's likely to stay that way. You can't exactly call this area remote, but the traffic and the crowds thin out immensely up here, especially compared to other areas on Maui. The West Maui mountains, 23,000 acres of pineapple fields, and a rugged shoreline define this lush, majestic domain.

Among Kapalua's virtues are its truly remote, unmarked beaches (all but three are accessed only by substantial hikes); the incredibly scenic drive (somewhat inaccessible without a four-wheel-drive vehicle) from Honokohau to Kahakuloa; and a welcome feeling of relative seclusion. One minor drawback is that this is one of the wettest places on Maui. What that really means are a few more clouds and a couple extra hours of precipitation during the rainy season, but that's about it. Kapalua's only other potential letdown for some travelers is what makes it wonderful for the rest of us: It isn't the place to catch the action on Maui. Instead, you will find serenity, seclusion, and silence, all of which should lead to a more amorous vacation.

Hotel/Bed and Breakfast Kissing

❧❧❧ **KAPALUA BAY HOTEL, Kapalua** We're happy to report that since our last visit, the Kapalua Bay Hotel has received a much-needed face-lift and has reemerged as a first-class destination resort. Besides the refreshed look and new room upgrades, the hotel's best-selling feature is (and always has been) its oceanside bluff location. The Pacific views from the massive open-air lobby, not to mention from most of the 194 rooms, are postcard perfect. In fact, most everything is as pretty as a picture. Throughout the 18 luscious acres, discover beautiful landscaped gardens, rocky bluffs overlooking the turbulent surf below, and swaying palm trees gracing the grassy lawns.

All refurbished guest rooms are identical in size and layout; only the views differ. View classification is defined by what you can see from the comfort of your bed. (What a great rating system!) Most rooms offer ocean or partial ocean views; on the lower levels you'll look out onto the hotel's well-groomed gardens. Also from your pillow vantage point you'll see the lovely interior of your room. Softened by seven shades of beige, each room features high ceilings, a large lanai, stylish yet simple furnishings, fine linens and artwork, and a large white-tiled bathroom with a soaking tub.

The hotel has several noteworthy restaurants, including the **GARDENIA COURT** and **THE BAY CLUB** (see Restaurant Kissing for reviews of both). Two pools, surrounded by large decks and roomy green lawns, provide plenty of private sunning space. The Kapalua Beach below, rated as one of Hawaii's best, can become overrun by the bikini-clad crowd in the afternoon, but in the morning the surf is gentle and the snorkeling prime. In Hawaiian, *Kapalua* means "arms embracing the sea," a reference to the lava outcroppings that form the surrounding bays. We guarantee you'll find "arms embracing each other" quite easily at this resort. **One Bay Drive; (808) 669-5656, (800) 367-8000 mainland; www.kapaluabay hotel.com; very expensive to unbelievably expensive and beyond; recommended wedding site.**

❧❧❧❧ **THE KAPALUA VILLAS, Kapalua** High atop the scintillating Kapalua coastline, you can dwell in the lap of luxury at any of the 266 units managed by The Kapalua Villas. Stay in one of three separate developments (the Bay, Ridge, and Golf Villas), or rent a stunning Pineapple Hill home if your pockets are deep.

Generally, privately owned condominium units are tricky to recommend, regardless of the property, because individual owners have different tastes and budgets. Such a dilemma does not exist here. Simply stated, those who can afford to purchase a condo in this neighborhood (it features some of the most expensive real estate on Maui) can and do invest in furnishing it beautifully.

Units in the Golf Villas are the lowest priced because the ocean view is distant and interrupted by other properties' rooftops. Still, these lodgings may be the best value because their views aren't unbearable by any means, and the spacious one- or two-bedroom units are well maintained and have designer kitchens. Four pools are shared by guests and tenants, so the chances of having a swimming spot all to yourselves is above average.

Considerably closer to the ocean are the pricey "oceanfront" Bay Villas, set on a hillside overlooking the water, and the "oceanview" Ridge Villas behind them. Interiors of both Bay and Ridge Villas are gorgeous.

With their stylish furnishings, exquisite artwork, expansive lanais, enviable kitchens, vaulted ceilings, loft bedrooms, and walls of windows showcasing views of Molokai and the deep blue Pacific, these are accommodations you won't want to leave.

The private, gated community of Pineapple Hill contains the most exclusive and grandest options. Ample room between each of these homes guarantees supreme privacy. Every house has its own tiled swimming pool or large outdoor Jacuzzi tub, as well as a modern kitchen and bathroom, sumptuous furnishings, and sensational views. Yes, the price tag is steep (and we mean *steep)*, but you won't be disappointed with this once-in-a-lifetime getaway filled with opulent romantic opportunities. **500 Office Road; (808) 669-8088, (800) 545-0018 mainland; www.kapalua villas.com; expensive to unbelievably expensive.**

Romantic Warning: Some units in the Bay Villas and Ridge Villas do not have air-conditioning. Trade winds blow through here on many days, but if you don't want to be at the mercy of Mother Nature, it is essential to request in advance a unit with air-conditioning.

Romantic Note: A free on-call shuttle service can take you wherever you need to go throughout the Kapalua Resort, be it the beach or one of three championship golf courses. Take advantage of this service and be sure to visit the neighboring **RITZ-CARLTON** (see review below). Complimentary use of Ritz facilities is included with your stay.

❀❀❀❀ **THE RITZ-CARLTON, Kapalua** In some ways this is just another Ritz-Carlton, but the name itself says a lot about the kind of elegance you can expect. As you cross the threshold into the impressive lobby, you enter a world where luxury and finesse are paramount. With 50 acres sloping downward to the ocean and 548 rooms on the property, this is the second-largest Ritz in the chain (there are 37 internationally). Does bigger mean better? Not necessarily. However, one thing is certain: No matter how large this place is, it will definitely set the stage for a romantic getaway.

European refinement (a Ritz trademark) is evident in the formal fabrics and gilt-edged furnishings. The rooms, mostly upscale hotel-basic with large marble bathrooms, are filled with light and are more than comfortable. Color schemes vary from subtle rose to pastel blue, and tasteful Hawaiian art adorns the walls. Most of the adequately sized lanais, equipped with wrought-iron railings and patio furniture, look out toward the ocean over the golf course or beyond the three cascading pools; the rest face the emerald Maui mountains.

Amenities such as outstanding restaurants, a day spa, a gorgeous terraced pool, and spectacular sandy **FLEMING BEACH** (see Outdoor Kissing) are all must-sees and must-dos during your stay. As amazing as it seems, *all* of the restaurants here deserve unusually high praise. One of the absolute best dinner destinations on the island is **THE ANUENUE ROOM** (see Restaurant Kissing). For a casual lunch, try **THE BANYAN TREE** (see Restaurant Kissing) or **THE BEACH HOUSE AND BAR** (inexpensive; lunch and appetizers daily). The latter features a varied selection of sandwiches and salads along with plenty of tasty tropical drinks. It's splendidly located directly on Fleming Beach, with comfortable tables and chairs set underneath a canopy of coconut palms.

Another special spot on the Ritz property is the historic **KUMULANI CHAPEL**, built in the 1950s by plantation families as their place of worship. Sunday-schoolers still come here every week, but this charming little white steepled church is a gorgeous site for brides and grooms to make or renew their vows. Helpful wedding and honeymoon planners are on-site, and various wedding packages are available, including one for golf-loving newlyweds. Couples captivated by the tranquillity, warmth, and romance of Maui have made impromptu weddings a fairly common occurrence here.

Whatever you want or need, as a guest at the Ritz-Carlton you won't have to leave the property to get it. **One Ritz-Carlton Drive; (808) 669-6200, (800) 262-8440; www.ritzcarlton.com; very expensive to unbelievably expensive and beyond; recommended wedding site.**

Restaurant Kissing

❀❀❀❀ **THE ANUENUE ROOM, Kapalua** Come early to enjoy the sunset and plan on staying until the stars are high in the night sky. You'll want to savor your time at this fine-dining restaurant. The service is flawless, the formal setting is simply stunning, and the food is some of the most tantalizing and brilliantly presented on the island. There is little to inhibit a leisurely romantic evening. Begin by toasting your love in the stately lounge adjacent to the restaurant, where handsome loveseats and plush armchairs invite you to snuggle close while you listen to live piano music.

The Anuenue Room offers indoor seating, but the majority of seats are al fresco. Sunset views over Molokai steal the show if you sit outside, while warm, formal decor along with contemporary artwork from local artists set the scene inside. Once you are seated for dinner, the menu works its

---

Disposable underwater cameras take surprisingly good photographs. We recommend purchasing one to take along on snorkeling adventures and boat rides so you won't have to worry about getting your nondisposable camera wet.

own seduction. Don't even try to resist the oven-roasted *onaga*, grilled Kona lobster, or glazed rack of lamb. Every dessert is a masterpiece, and the sweet sensations are sheer ecstasy. **One Ritz-Carlton Way, at The Ritz-Carlton; (808) 669-6200; www.ritzcarlton.com; expensive to unbelievably expensive; dinner Tuesday–Saturday; recommended wedding site.**

❀❀❀ **THE BANYAN TREE, Kapalua** For a stylish, relaxed oceanfront lunch, venture from the hot sun into the cool shade of The Banyan Tree. An ornate iron chandelier hangs from the high, beamed ceiling, marking the center of the room. Tables and chairs made of redwood are dispersed throughout the dining area, and a slate floor enhances the casual ambience. The entire restaurant has the potential to be open-air, but winds are usually strong enough to keep the sliding glass doors shut. Tables are also available outside, where glass partitions and canvas umbrellas effectively buffer the wind.

Incredible ocean views from nearly every seat make up for the restaurant's proximity to the bathing-suit crowd lounging around the nearby pool. Tempting lunch entrées, some with a Mediterranean twist, include gourmet thin-crust pizzas, sandwiches, pastas, seafood, and a variety of salads. Pizzas and salads are consistently good, but our Thai chicken sandwich needed some spice. The restaurant is open for lunch every day, and serves *pupus* (appetizers) and cocktails until 4 P.M. **One Ritz-Carlton Way, at the Ritz-Carlton; (808) 669-6200; www.ritzcarlton.com; moderate; lunch and appetizers daily.**

❀❀ **THE BAY CLUB, Kapalua** The sound of the surf accompanies the leisurely meals served at this handsome open-air restaurant, situated on a small bluff just above the water's edge. Decorated in a modest, Hawaiian-style fashion, the open-air dining room offers views of palm trees, the swimming pool below, and Kapalua Bay beyond. Luckily, such vistas take your mind off (but don't compensate for) the very standard seafood served here. We recommend sticking to cocktails or dessert at sunset, when the surf is accompanied by a pianist's soothing melodies. **One Bay Drive, at the Kapalua Bay Hotel; (808) 669-5656; www.kapaluabayhotel.com; moderate to very expensive; reservations recommended; lunch and dinner daily; recommended wedding site.**

❀❀ **GARDENIA COURT, Kapalua** In spite of the big hotel setting, this airy ocean-view restaurant feels surprisingly secluded and quaint. A towering wall of French doors open to let warm tropical breezes caress the interior. Water cascades down one wall of the dining room, trickling into a koi pond and a stream that winds through the restaurant. The menu features

Hawaiian cuisine, reasonably priced and beautifully presented. We particularly enjoyed the fresh Pacific salmon and *ahi* served with wasabi and a red pepper coulis. **One Bay Drive, at the Kapalua Bay Hotel; (808) 669-5656; www.kapaluabayhotel.com; moderate to expensive; reservations recommended; call for seasonal hours.**

❤❤❤ **PLANTATION HOUSE RESTAURANT, Kapalua** Perched high on a hill with breathtaking views of the water, surrounding emerald fairways, and the distant isle of Molokai, this restaurant is romantically recommended for its vantage point alone. Thankfully, the chef makes sure there are plenty of other reasons to come here.

Although the restaurant is set on a golf course, its atmosphere is up to par with our definition of romantic dining. The nicely appointed dining room features teak woods; high, beamed ceilings; upholstered chairs with pineapple-carved backs; a massive two-sided fireplace with marble hearth; and open-air windows. The view, efficient professional service, and attractive interior make kissing inevitable.

Breakfast and lunch tend to be more social and casual than intimate, but don't let this stop you from stealing a smooch or two. Dinner here is a must, especially when the sun is making its daily descent behind Molokai or into the ocean (depending on the time of year). Most of the entrées from the Mediterranean–Pacific Rim menu are excellent. Curried spinach potstickers are a delicious starter, and the catch of the day, available in various preparations, is always fresh and moist. We enjoyed mahi mahi pan-seared in rice wine, topped with macadamia nuts, and accompanied by jasmine risotto and a caramelized chile-sesame sauce. Be sure to stay for dessert, as well as the spectacular show that follows sunset. With no other lights and buildings around, the sheer magnitude of the starry sky will dazzle you. **2000 Plantation Club Drive; (808) 669-6299, (800) 245-4301; inexpensive to expensive; breakfast, lunch, and dinner daily; recommended wedding site.**

Outdoor Kissing

❤❤❤ **THE DRIVE FROM HONOKOHAU TO KAHAKULOA, West Maui** Just north of Kapalua's hotels and condominiums, you'll come to the northernmost section of Highway 30. When you get here, be prepared to take turns driving: The scenery along this minimally traveled road is so spectacular, your natural inclination will be to keep your eyes *off* the road and *on* the unbelievably beautiful surroundings.

Along the way, on the ocean side of the road, you'll find many accessible viewing spots with innumerable photo opportunities of the breathtaking seascape. Waves crash dramatically up against the jagged black rocks, while the brick-red cliffs contrast beautifully with the deep blue water. Stunning vistas of sea and sky unexpectedly appear around every turn. Some homes dot the roadside, but don't expect to see any "gas-food-lodging" signs. Traveling this route is a clear reminder of what Maui was like before it was overrun with hotels, condos, and T-shirt shops.

When you come to the end of the road, you'll know it. Deep potholes and gravel mark the road when the pavement ends. We recommend turning around at this point (although there are brave souls who carry on, even though car-rental places don't allow it). Hopefully, on the return trip you'll get to see the panoramic sunset, which is certainly a celestial sight to behold. *From Kapalua, head northeast on Highway 30. When you come clear of the hotels and see nothing but water and trees, you'll know you're in the right place.*

❀❀❀❀ **FLEMING BEACH, Kapalua** You *must* visit this remarkable stretch of beach. Although it is rather small, it is arguably one of the most beautiful in the world. The silky-soft sand is edged with lava outcroppings, and the coastal hills above resemble rolling carpets of green. Depending on the weather, the surf either comes in like a lion or goes out like a lamb. The Ritz-Carlton's restaurants (see Restaurant Kissing) are close by, so refresh yourself with a mai tai, piña colada, or delicious *pupus* (appetizers) after playing in the rolling waves. *The beach is accessible from Highway 30, north of the Ritz-Carlton, after you've passed the Kapalua sign.*

❀❀❀ **HONOLUA BAY, Kapalua** Cars parked on either side of the road are the only obvious markers at this extraordinary snorkeling bay. Unfortunately, they are also a signal that you won't be alone (which truly would be too much to expect at such a wonderful spot). A short, steep walk through forest brings you to the inviting rocky beach. Swim alongside colorful tropical fish and the large resident sea turtles that live here; it is fascinating to watch these gentle giants swim in and out of their caves. *The beach is accessible from Highway 30, about three miles north of Kapalua.*

Romantic Note: Catamarans can capture the breeze in their sails to whisk you here in style. The Hyatt Regency's *KIELE V* (808-667-4727) offers snorkel tours every day except Wednesday and includes a continental breakfast and deli sandwiches. Kaanapali Kai Charter's *TERALANI* (808-661-0365) features a daily picnic snorkel as well as an evening champagne sunset cruise (without snorkeling). Excursions from both companies depart from Kaanapali Beach, and the price, ranging from $35 to $75 per person, includes snorkel gear plus appetizers, drinks, or lunch on some sails. Dozens of other eager snorkeling enthusiasts will join you, but the trip is a wonderful opportunity to see the island from the water. If you wish to visit Honolua Bay on your own, we recommend arriving before or after the boat excursions (before 11 A.M. or after 3 P.M.).

Napili

Buried between the high-rent districts of Kapalua and Kaanapali, Napili has a plethora of condominium developments and hotels piled one on top of the other, without much breathing room or beachfront. There are some bargains to be found here, but the sacrifice often means no air-conditioning or privacy. This isn't our favorite section of Maui, but it is only a stone's throw from its neighbors' more remarkable beaches and restaurants, and the accommodations won't drain your pocketbook.

Hotel/Bed and Breakfast Kissing

❧❧ **HONOKEANA COVE, Napili** Upon pulling up to this low-rise building, you may be apprehensive; the weathered brown exterior doesn't look very inviting. Fortunately, this is just the back of the building, which gives no indication of the ample space and openness found in the courtyard and 32 units. Beyond the grassy, palm-tree-filled courtyard, you'll find a pool, which sits at the edge of a rocky bluff. Down below is a relatively secluded cove, ideal for snorkeling and swimming. A short walk reveals a sandy beach perfect for sinking those toes into as you stroll along.

The one-, two-, or three-bedroom accommodations have private lanais facing the water; petite, but fully equipped kitchens; nice-sized living rooms with comfortable furnishings; and rather small, lackluster bathrooms. What they don't have is air-conditioning. (Laundry facilities are available on-site, but not in the units.) Some of the furnishings are dated, but the price is right and, overall, the condos are pleasant and well maintained. There is a three-night minimum, and prices get better the longer you stay. **5255 Lower Honoapiilani Road; (808) 669-6441, (800) 237-4948 mainland; www.honokeana-cove.com; inexpensive to moderate; minimum-stay requirement.**

❧❧ **ONE NAPILI WAY, Napili** Put simply, One Napili Way is a clean, comfortable, and affordable option for a romantic retreat. Lacking views but attractively appointed, this unusually small condo complex has only

---

Before flying, be sure both of you are signed up as frequent flyers. Mileage to Hawaii adds up quickly.

14 units. Each features a towering wood-beamed ceiling, contemporary cane furniture, a big-screen TV/VCR, spacious kitchen, an attractive bath with a small whirlpool tub, plenty of windows, and a 150-square-foot lanai. Thankfully, there are ceiling fans in every room to compensate for the lack of air-conditioning. Each unit is decorated the same, so you won't have to worry about the whims of individual owners. These bright, roomy rentals are available with one, two, or three bedrooms. Well-tended gardens and swaying palm trees front the units, and a small crystal-clear pool with an outdoor spa is set out back. It may not be beachfront, but access to Napili Bay is nearby. **5355 Lower Honoapiilani Road No. 101; (808) 669-2007, (800) 841-6284 mainland; www.choice1.com/onenapili.htm; inexpensive to expensive; minimum-stay requirement.**

Kahana

Between the serenity of Kapalua and the madness of Kaanapali resides the residential/condo-filled area of Kahana. There's not much to see here, except these two restaurants, which are worth stopping for anytime.

Restaurant Kissing

❧❧❧ ROY'S KAHANA BAR AND GRILL, Kahana

❧❧❧ ROY'S NICOLINA, Kahana

That's right: Same address, same owner, same lip rating, but these are two separate establishments right next door to each other. What's the difference? It is easier to begin by explaining the similarities. Both restaurants were opened by Roy Yamaguchi, chef and restaurateur extraordinaire; both have an upbeat ambience; both feature out-of-this-world entrées; both have an outstanding waitstaff; and both stick to Roy's original Euro-Asian–inspired dishes. Last, both establishments share the same regular and fixed menu. So what's the difference? Each has different nightly specials, offering inventive and uniquely prepared items, which allow each restaurant's chef to really shine.

For those with romance on their minds, the only drawbacks are the boisterous atmosphere (these dining rooms are always packed) and the roadside shopping center location with parking lot views. But don't worry: Whether you take a table at either Roy's Kahana or Roy's Nicolina, your lips and palate won't be disappointed. **Roy's Kahana Bar and Grill: 4405 Honoapiilani Highway; (808) 669-6999. Roy's Nicolina: 4405 Honoapiilani Highway; (808) 669-5000. www.roysrestaurant.com; expensive to very expensive; reservations recommended; dinner daily.**

Kaanapali

Years ago, the Kaanapali coastline was considered the premier destination on Maui. Two miles of soft, sandy beach with gentle rolling waves made it the most desirable of Hawaiian areas. Unfortunately, the proliferation of high-rise condominiums and mega-resort hotels has changed this once-serene location into a crowded mess. Do not expect calm here, particularly during high season.

Many of the properties in this area boast rooms with either garden or mountain views. You might very well see beautiful gardens and mountains from these rooms, and the prices may even be reasonable, but you will also see (and hear) a barrage of traffic. The noise can be maddening. Of course, the restaurants and the ocean-view rooms are free from this offense, but they carry the requisite high price tag. Please note that all of our recommendations in the Kaanapali Hotel/Bed and Breakfast Kissing section are only in consideration of the location. Even the most beautiful properties and romantic interludes may be marred by slamming car doors and screeching brakes.

Surprisingly, the beach is still radiant, and because the hotel and condominium properties all have great pool areas, it is relatively uncrowded. For swimming and soaking up the sun, this is a great location. For romance—well, you may have to wait until after dark to really be alone.

Hotel/Bed and Breakfast Kissing

❤❤❤ **EMBASSY VACATION RESORT, Kaanapali** Judging from the conspicuous pink exterior and pyramid-like, tiered construction, you would never guess this towering 12-story hotel holds some of the most spacious and attractive suites in town. Every one of the 413 rooms is a large, beautifully appointed suite with over 820 square feet of elbow room. A comfortable sitting and dining area, tiny kitchenette with microwave and refrigerator, and a sizable lanai grace each unit, along with a stereo system and a 35-inch TV/VCR. The bathrooms are surprisingly sensual, with corner bathtubs big enough for two and separate glass-enclosed showers framed in white tile. Some rooms have a cheery feel, with crisp blue-and-white furnishings, while others have a more refined theme, with shell-print fabrics, classic-style furnishings, and elaborate window treatments. In addition to the extra space, you'll also enjoy early-evening cocktail hour and the generous complimentary breakfast buffet served poolside each morning.

A sandy beach with tranquil surf fronts the pool area. All this, plus the open-air lobby and the water views from many rooms, makes the Embassy, to borrow a phrase from the management, one "suite deal." In comparison to other oceanfront hotels and considering the size of the rooms, the prices are downright reasonable. The only drawback is that you'll have to travel off the property for good food; the Embassy's on-site restaurants are a major letdown. **104 Kaanapali Shores Place; (808) 661-2000, (800) 669-3155; www.maui.net/~embassy; expensive to unbelievably expensive.**

❤❤ **HYATT REGENCY MAUI RESORT, Kaanapali** Open courtyards, dense tropical gardens accented with tall palms, and clear-flowing streams are just a few of the wonders that await at this massive hotel. Continue on past the 150-foot lava-tube waterslide and down to the jungle-like pool only steps away from the ocean. Such a grandiose, lush, and beautiful setting makes the Hyatt a fantasy escape unlike any other in Kaanapali.

As hotel rooms go, the Hyatt's 815 rooms rank above average, thanks to stylish bathrooms, king-size beds facing the windows, and classy Asian-style furnishings. With the size of this hotel, all rooms can't be oceanfront, and you may find yourselves looking out onto a shaded parking lot, the mountains, other hotels, a golf course, or a combination of all four. Need we mention that prime ocean views command the steepest prices?

The five restaurants here are all quite good, but only the **SWAN COURT** (see Restaurant Kissing) ranks up there for romance. After dark, the long stretch of sandy beach out front and the trails that wind through the lush landscaping are wonderful places for holding hands and kissing by the light of the moon. **200 Nohea Kai Drive; (808) 661-1234, (800) 233-1234; www.hyatt.com; very expensive to unbelievably expensive and beyond; recommended wedding site.**

Romantic Note: If you're interested in attending a luau, the Hyatt's **DRUMS OF THE PACIFIC LUAU** ($62 per person; reservations required) is considered one of the best on the island. Even if you are not interested, if your room is in the Lahaina Tower you will hear the show every night around 7 P.M., making rest and relaxation nearly impossible. A much more desirable and quieter entertainment option is the Hyatt's **TOUR OF THE STARS** ($15 per guest, $20 per nonguest; reservations required). Head upstairs and onto the hotel's roof where an elaborately assembled telescope enables you to see and learn about the stars. A closer acquaintance with various heavenly bodies could put romantic ideas in your head. If you still need some guidance, have no fear: The Hyatt is prepared with a computer program called **DISCOVERIES IN ROMANCE** to help couples spice things up if you're having trouble deciding what to do with all of this intimate time alone. It's sure to at least provoke some interesting discussions and give you some good ideas of where to go on the island.

❀❀❁ **KAANAPALI ALII, Kaanapali** The first line of Kaanapali Alii's brochure states that there is "no greater luxury than spaciousness." While that's debatable, one thing is certain: Space is in ample supply here. As many savvy travelers have learned, most hotel and condominium properties have extensive grounds and exteriors but small, standard guest rooms. Not so here. Four massive, 11-story buildings envelop Kaanapali Alii's large pool area and palm tree–covered grounds, and all 210 of the one- and two-bedroom units average 1,500 and 1,900 square feet, respectively.

Hardwood-floored foyers in every unit provide a pleasant welcome. Interiors range from Hawaiian wicker and bamboo to white and beige contemporary, and every unit is clean, comfortable, air-conditioned, and (we'll say it again), spacious. Expect a large, fully equipped, tiled kitchen; separate dining and living rooms; an ample lanai; a washer/dryer; and a jetted master bathtub. Compared to what you find in other hotels and condo complexes, this is a real bargain. All the amenities of a big hotel are available except for on-site restaurants, but you won't have to go far for intimate dining: The hotels surrounding this property have enough restaurants to keep you eating well for days. **50 Nohea Kai Drive; (808) 667-1666, (800) 642-6284; www.kaanapali-alii.com; expensive to unbelievably expensive; recommended wedding site.**

Romantic Warning: The size of these rooms makes Kaanapali Alii popular for family vacations (with kids in tow). That's good to know if you're planning to take the little ones, but be forewarned if you're not.

❀ **MAHANA AT KAANAPALI, Kaanapali** On the sunny side of things, every unit in this twin-towered condominium resort is oceanfront, and we *mean* oceanfront—you can't put a building much closer to the water or it would fall right in. There's also a nice pool area, set between the two buildings, which faces the Pacific, and a little strip of sandy beach out front. Now for the downer: Many rooms are severely in need of refurbishment, with their outdated kitchen cabinets and wallpaper, rusty window frames, and worn carpet.

Of the 216 units in the resort, 149 are available for rent. Of these, choose between studios and one- and two-bedroom units, all with full kitchens. The studios feel like standard hotel rooms because the bed is in the would-be living room, but the one- and two-bedroom units are spacious and a relatively good deal (especially for two couples traveling together). Although each condo is decorated differently, you can count on finding pastel tones and Hawaiian-style furnishings such as cushioned rattan or cane couches and chairs. Other amenities include in-room washer/dryers and air-conditioning. If you're the out-and-about type, these condominiums will prove satisfactory for your nightly stopovers. **110 Kaanapali Shores Place; (808) 661-8751, (800) 922-7866 mainland, (800) 321-2558 interisland; www.aston-hotels.com; moderate to unbelievably expensive.**

❀ **MAUI KAI, Kaanapali** Hugging the Kaanapali coastline, this relatively small condominium building features 79 affordable one- and two-bedroom units. The entire place isn't fancy; in some ways it's rather plain, and the concrete brick construction (painted pink) screams "built in the '60s." But unlike many neighboring hotels, all units here are oceanfront with large lanais, ample windows, central air-conditioning, and comfortable (although sometimes dowdy) furnishings. A small fenced-in pool area with accompanying Jacuzzi tub is strangely situated in the parking lot, but the unparalleled views from the units and the sandy beach next door make this a notable romantic option. **106 Kaanapali Shores Place; (808) 667-3500, (800) 367-5635; www.mauikai.com; inexpensive to expensive; minimum-stay requirement.**

❀ **ROYAL LAHAINA RESORT, Kaanapali** A one-lip rating might not seem all that exciting, but the hotel's location at the north end of Kaanapali Beach makes it a viable escape from the town's hustle and bustle. On top of that, the oceanfront cottages are actually quite nice and spacious (and probably deserve another lip or two). Unfortunately, the majority of the hotel and its restaurants are in desperate need of restoration.

Our choice for romance are the cottages, which resemble suburban ranch-style homes à la Hawaiian style. The rest of the standard, worn (but still pricey) units in the tower need help, not to mention soundproofing. If you stay here, delight in three sparkling pools—perfect places to desalinate after a day of ducking in and out of waves. Venture into the heart of Kaanapali or Kapalua for your dining pleasures, because the Royal Lahaina's restaurants are not recommended. **2780 Kekaa Drive; (808) 661-3611, (800) 447-6925; expensive to unbelievably expensive.**

❀❀ **THE WESTIN MAUI, Kaanapali** If only more of The Westin's lower-priced rooms (still in the very expensive range) weren't so disappointing, this would be a remarkable place to stay. The splendor of the lobby quickly draws you into the hotel and embraces you with luxury. An exceptionally delightful multilevel pool area, complete with slides, waterfalls, and grottos, borders exquisite Kaanapali Beach. Unfortunately, the 789 guest accommodations don't begin to live up to the gracious common areas. Some rooms could stand a bit of sprucing up; most are simply standard. Many suites offer mountain views compromised by a fairly busy parking lot, something the brochure doesn't mention. A lot of the units with water views are set back from the shore, so the ocean is only visible beyond the green grounds and sparkling pool. The more desirable rooms are in the Beach Tower. These are by far the most attractively appointed, with the best views and the highest tariffs. **2365 Kaanapali Parkway; (808) 667-2525, (800) 937-8461 mainland; www.westin.com; very expensive to unbelievably expensive; recommended wedding site.**

Romantic Note: Ask about The Westin's Romance Package and Wedding Package. The latter includes just about everything you need, including the minister, to get those wedding bells ringing.

Restaurant Kissing

❦❦❦ **SWAN COURT, Kaanapali** One advertisement for the Swan Court proclaims: "We've taken a page from a steamy romance novel and added a dessert tray." Believe the advertising, for just this once. It doesn't get much more romantic than this elegantly appointed dining room. A towering wall of open-air windows look out to a dramatic pond where gracefully poised swans glide by with the ocean in the background, enhancing the elegantly sensuous mood. But, alas: If only the dinners here lived up to the ambience, Swan Court would rate ten lips. The grand menu, highlighting steak, seafood, and pastas, reads like an engaging novel, but the outcome is anticlimactic, lacking seasoning and finesse. However, the plot picks up near the end. The desserts here are perfectly exquisite, particularly the mango soufflé with ginger crème anglaise ladled in the middle. **200 Nohea Kai Drive, at the Hyatt Regency; (808) 667-4727, (800) 233-1234; www. hyatt.com; expensive to unbelievably expensive; breakfast and dinner daily.**

Romantic Note: The Swan Court, like many other hotel restaurants in Hawaii, serves a daily breakfast, but the similarity ends there. This one is truly romantic, excellently prepared, and moderately priced.

Outdoor Kissing

❦❦❦ **KAANAPALI BEACH, Kaanapali** Without question, this magnificent stretch of soft, sandy beach would be the beach of choice on Maui if it weren't for the array of towering hotels and condominiums lining it. The

High season is from mid-December through the end of March. Low season runs from April to mid-December. Not only do rates go down in low season, but business hours may be more limited too.

flip side is that guests of the hotels and condos generally spend time by the properties' luxurious pools rather than the beach, so it is never jam-packed. And at sunset, or even after dark, the beach is superior for long walks and wave dodging. **BLACK ROCK,** at the north end of the beach, is an extraordinary place to snorkel and possibly meet a sea turtle face to face. *Located off Highway 30, just north of Lahaina.*

Lahaina

Founded in the 1600s, Lahaina was once the capital of the Hawaiian Islands. Royalty was the focus of the town back then, with all the commensurate traditions and rituals. Later, from 1840 to 1860, Lahaina was an enterprising whaling port, with rowdy sailors and hundreds of ships coming and going yearly. Today, it is hard to imagine those times as you walk along the crowded, compact streets of this small village. Lahaina's monarchs and mariners are long gone, and the once-quaint community and energetic port is filled with a hodgepodge of T-shirt stores, jewelry boutiques, art galleries, clothing shops, trendy eateries, oceanfront restaurants, and sightseeing boats. Visit anyway: There are several excellent restaurants here, and the sunset-over-the-harbor views are exciting.

Romantic Note: Between December and March, many whale-watching charters depart from Lahaina to witness the yearly migration of the humpback whales. During this time, you're just about guaranteed a sighting, but even if you don't see whales, you're likely to spot dolphins, sea turtles, and other "see-worthy" sights.

Hotel/Bed and Breakfast Kissing

❤❤❤ **LAHAINA INN, Lahaina** The Lahaina Inn demands a little romantic bookkeeping. Debits: Lahaina's hectic town center pulses right outside the door (which prompts our earplug recommendation), you don't even have a glimpse of the ocean, and the nearest beach is several miles up the road in Kaanapali. Assets: Once you enter your room, there is little evidence the outside world even exists, letting you concentrate on each other in luxurious bliss.

Victorian elegance is a rare commodity in Hawaii, but it exists in abundance at the Lahaina Inn. A stunning, authentic renovation has turned this 12-room inn into a fascinating, sumptuous place to stay. Each room is affectionately decorated with period wallpaper, lace draperies, stately antiques, eyelet bedspreads, antique rugs on original hardwood floors, and attractive tile and marble bathrooms. Small, private balconies overlook the bustling downtown or the back parking lot: not exactly romantic, but a fact of life in this area. Some of the less expensive rooms are on the tiny side, and tall/big people should be aware that small beds and low-hanging ceiling fans are common. A simple, continental breakfast is served buffet-style in the common area each morning. Trays are provided so you can take your goodies back to your lanai for a truly intimate repast. **127 Lahainaluna Road; (808) 661-0577, (800) 669-3444; www.lahainainn.com; inexpensive to moderate; minimum-stay requirement on weekends.**

Romantic Note: Downstairs, adjacent to the lobby, awaits one of Maui's best restaurants, **DAVID PAUL'S LAHAINA GRILL** (see Restaurant Kissing). Guests staying at Lahaina Inn receive discounts and preferred reservations at the restaurant.

❀❀ **LAHAINA SHORES BEACH RESORT, Lahaina** If simplicity is all you're looking for in a Hawaiian accommodation—a clean room, waterfront location, and a reasonable price—you're in luck. Sheltered along a sandy beach, this seven-story plantation-style hotel resides just outside Lahaina's town center. Most of the hotel's 200 spacious studio and one-bedroom units are worth your consideration, with towering ceilings, simple but comfortable furnishings, full kitchens, and wide lanais; many feature outstanding ocean views. Even the mountain vistas in the upper-floor units are lush and lovely. Although the outdoor pool resembles a lap pool and the surrounding area can get crowded with sunbathers, the ocean swimming more than compensates. You won't be living in the lap of luxury at the Lahaina Shores, but its relative privacy, affordability, and oceanfront location render it lip-worthy. **475 Front Street; (808) 661-4835, (800) 628-6699; www.lahaina-shores.com; moderate to expensive.**

❀❀❀❀ **THE PLANTATION INN, Lahaina** This elegant, sparkling-clean, plantation-style bed and breakfast is an utterly refreshing place to stay. All 19 rooms have sensuous, plush furnishings and fabrics, stained glass windows, bay and French windows, a private veranda, a canopy bed, a VCR, daily maid service, and central air-conditioning. Several rooms also have oversize Jacuzzi tubs.

Attention to service is evident in the immaculate surroundings and in the care the staff takes to attend to your every need. Within a private courtyard, you'll find a lovely tiled pool and Jacuzzi tub, an immaculate garden area, and a common patio where a generous full breakfast is served to guests each morning. We have only one complaint with this wonderful inn: The maintenance man came into our room at 9 A.M. despite the posted "Do Not Disturb" sign . . . a major no-no at any hotel. We only hope it was an isolated incident. **174 Lahainaluna Road; (808) 667-9225, (800) 433-6815; www.theplantationinn.com; moderate to expensive.**

Romantic Suggestion: You'll want to plan at least one dinner at GERARD'S (see Restaurant Kissing), the hotel's lovely dining room. Special prices on meals are offered for guests.

❤❤ **WAI OLA VACATION PARADISE, Lahaina** Inexpensive *and* romantic accommodations are few and far between on the Hawaiian Islands, so we always get excited when we find a place we can enthusiastically recommend. Wai Ola is a private home, set in an unassuming residential neighborhood, just two blocks from Wahikuli Beach. Designed with privacy in mind, all three guest units have a private entrance, a private bath, and a telephone with answering machine. The two recently redecorated apartment units are adorned with Pegge Hopper prints and bright, new furnishings. Both have a fully equipped kitchen. If you don't need to cook, the new Kuuipo Room is the best option for a romantic getaway. Named for the Hawaiian word for "sweetheart," this room has many amenities to sweeten your stay, including a king-size bed, private bath, refrigerator, and the only full ocean view in the house. Breakfasts aren't served here, but coffee beans and accompanying coffee pot are supplied to help you get your day going. No matter which room you choose, all are kissing bargains! **(808) 661-7901, (800) 492-4652; www.maui.net/~tai/WaiOla. html; inexpensive to moderate; minimum-stay requirement seasonally.**

Restaurant Kissing

❤❤◖ **AVALON RESTAURANT, Lahaina** Set at the back of a small brick courtyard, somewhat away from the jam-packed main street of Lahaina, this casual oasis serves up Hawaiian and Asian cuisine in a charming setting. It isn't far enough away from the mainstream to be considered intimate, but the food and the setting are delightful and the savory offerings worth the culinary diversion from true romance. The mix of shellfish and fresh island fish in the tossed Asian pasta are delicious; the whole fresh *opakapaka* is beautifully presented; and the salmon tiki salad layered with potatoes, seared salmon, and eggplant is distinctive. For those who have a terrible time deciding which dessert to order, the decision has already been made. Your only dessert option is caramel Miranda, a plate of various tropical fruits baked atop a pool of caramel sauce, then topped with macadamia nut ice cream. Luscious! **844 Front Street; (808) 667-5559; www.maui. net/~eatmaui; moderate to expensive; lunch and dinner daily.**

❤❤❤ **DAVID PAUL'S LAHAINA GRILL, Lahaina** Count on friendly, attentive service and superior, creative cooking at this sleek, bistro-style restaurant. The bold black-and-white-tiled floor, colorfully painted plates, and cozy tables draped in white linen fill the bright dining room with drama. Some tables are set close together, so if privacy is important request tables No. 45, 28, 29, or 34, which are all tucked into a back alcove.

The varied menu will wow the taste buds with such starters as luscious corn chowder or spicy shrimp atop blue-corn cakes. Other dazzlers include seared mahi mahi spiced by a Southwestern beurre blanc or the divine beef filet accompanied by stuffed poblano chiles and lobster polenta. Java fans may want to order the unique and delicious roasted rack of lamb marinated in Kona coffee and served with a hearty Kona coffee–port wine sauce. Finish off your meal with the prickly pear cake and sorbet (if available), carefully made from cacti harvested on Maui's dry side. **127 Lahainaluna Road, at the Lahaina Inn; (808) 667-5117; www.lahainainn.com; expensive; dinner daily.**

❤❤❤ **GERARD'S, Lahaina** Petite, quaint restaurants are hard to find in Hawaii: Among the affluence and grandeur of the large-scale hotels, Gerard's is a breath of fresh air. Relax in the cozy dining room or outside on an old-fashioned veranda, replete with white wicker furnishings, while enjoying a cornucopia of savory delights—a perfect end to your perfect day on Maui. The menu is decidedly French, but the chef cleverly incorporates Hawaiian ingredients to create the freshest and most delicious meals possible. You won't be disappointed with any of the selections. Grilled rack of lamb with mint crust, and roasted Hawaiian snapper with an orange and ginger butter sauce are both absolutely wonderful. Prices are high, but you are encouraged to linger, enjoy soft guitar melodies, and savor every moment (and bite). Service is excellent, and, due to space constraints, reservations are a must. **174 Lahainaluna Road, at The Plantation Inn; (808) 661-8939; www.theplantationinn.com; expensive to very expensive; reservations recommended; dinner daily; recommended wedding site.**

❤❤ **KIMO'S, Lahaina** Located in the heart of Front Street's commercial hustle and bustle, Kimo's lower dining room and bar resemble a crowded steak house—clearly not the most romantic of settings. Fortunately, crowds thin out in the upstairs open-air dining room, accented with beamed ceilings, Oriental carpets, high-backed Colonial-style chairs, and riveting views of the ocean and crashing surf. Kimo's casual menu features generous, well-prepared portions of steak and extremely fresh seafood. The catch of the

All beaches in Hawaii are public. As long as you can find public access, you are welcome to enjoy the beaches everywhere.

day can be prepared several ways, including Kimo-style (baked in a garlic–lemon–sweet basil sauce), teriyaki style, or sautéed and topped with a lemon-caper butter. If you're worried about squeezing into that swimsuit, try the grilled fish with tropical salsa. For more Polynesian-style specialties, opt for the delicious Kula pork ribs. All meals come with a Caesar salad, carrot muffins, and herb bread. You won't be walking out of here hungry. **845 Front Street; (808) 661-4811; inexpensive to moderate; reservations recommended; lunch and dinner daily.**

❀❀❀ **PACIFIC'O, Lahaina** Nothing compares to oceanfront dining (except maybe oceanfront kissing, but you have to eat sometime). The sound of the surf, the scent of the salt air, and the sight of rolling turquoise waves remind you just how blessed you are to be in the Hawaiian Islands. From the casual outdoor deck of Pacific'O, you can appreciate all these sensations, along with inventive Pacific Rim cuisine and a relaxed tropical atmosphere. Inside, where there is open-air seating with green-and-white accents and pretty tiled floors, you can still experience the ocean's breezes and beauty.

Begin your meal with a tasty appetizer like shrimp wontons: whole shrimp wrapped in a basil leaf and a wonton wrapper, then served with a spicy sweet-and-sour sauce and Hawaiian salsa. For an entrée, consider trying the coconut–macadamia nut–crusted catch of the day. The menu is truly imaginative and changes daily, and the attentive staff can answer any questions you may have.

Lunchtime is extremely casual, with bikini-clad bodies wandering by as you dine, but at night, when the beach traffic slows down, Pacific'O turns exceedingly demure and romantic. Soft jazz accompanies your evening meal on Thursday, Friday, and Saturday nights from 9 P.M. until midnight. **505 Front Street; (808) 667-4341; www.maui.net/~pacifico; moderate to expensive; reservations recommended; lunch and dinner daily; recommended wedding site.**

Romantic Note: When we visited, a new restaurant called I'O (505 Front Street; 808-661-8422; expensive to very expensive; dinner daily) was being constructed alongside Pacific'O. Smaller than its neighbor, I'o features an open kitchen shielded by glass, which allows you to watch the chef preparing new Pacific cuisine, without being distracted from more intimate conversation.

Kihei

Kihei is a vivid example of what can happen to paradise when it's developed without consideration for the natural beauty of the area. One high-rise condominium complex after another continues to sprout up along a once-spectacular sweep of beach. Actually, the beach is still magnificent, but the landscape has been indelibly changed and the traffic through town can be a nightmare. Most of the properties in Kihei are mediocre, outdated condo units—some with views, many directly on the beach, all with pools, and most without air-conditioning. Some of the best bargains around are located in this part of the island, so as long as you stick to our recommendations, a romantic Hawaiian respite is possible in this busy neighborhood.

Romantic Note: Luckily for sun worshippers and golfers, Kihei is located on Maui's southwest side—one of the island's drier areas. In a typical year, only ten to 15 inches of precipitation falls in this region. The arid conditions contribute to the barren landscape, but mean fewer days spent indoors during the rainy season.

Hotel/Bed and Breakfast Kissing

❂❀ **MANA KAI MAUI RESORT, Kihei** At the southernmost end of Kihei, looking out to the idyllic beaches of Wailea and Makena, this high-rise condominium building is an inexpensive place to enjoy great views and a sweeping sandy beach. Just don't let the hotel's drab lobby—in pressing need of renovation—detour you from checking out the one- and two-bedroom rooms, which have been recently upgraded.

For incredibly low prices, this hotel provides the basics for a romantic tropical interlude, including full kitchens and small but functional lanais with stellar views of the water and Haleakala. Each guest room has the option of being a one-bedroom unit with kitchen, a two-bedroom unit with kitchen, or simply a one-bedroom unit. How so? Depending on what you request, the management locks or unlocks the door to the other rooms. For the best kissing bargain, choose the one-bedroom, ocean-view unit with a kitchen, where you'll awake to the sea shining right outside your bedroom. If you choose to book the one-bedroom unit without kitchen, be forewarned. While it's inexpensive, you don't have a kitchen or a view and, overall, these rooms feel too claustrophobic for true romance. **2960 South Kihei Road; (808) 879-2778, (800) 367-5242 mainland; www.maui.net/~crh/unit_manakai.html; inexpensive to expensive.**

Romantic Suggestion: Resting just above water's edge, the **FIVE PALMS BEACH GRILL** (808-879-2607; moderate to expensive; breakfast, lunch, and dinner daily) is the hotel's casual and colorful beachfront restaurant, offering terrace seating with beautiful ocean views. Service is friendly and the kitchen serves up standard, hearty breakfasts, salads and sandwiches for lunch, and steak and seafood for dinner. The closer you sit to the beach, the better off you are here.

❤❤❤ **MY WAII BEACH COTTAGE, Kihei** Have it your way at My Waii, a small yellow beach house that has what few accommodations in Maui can offer: your own large grassy yard, your own private sandy beach bordered by lava outcroppings, and plenty of privacy. Situated next to the owner's well-kept home, the cottage has everything necessary for romantic comfort, including a king-size bed, all the usual electronic entertainment equipment, a fully equipped kitchen (bring breakfast provisions), and a large walk-in shower. But best of all is the location. On one side is a neighborhood; a few hundred feet away is a park; and in front, it's all green and blue. Underneath the covered lanai, you'll have all the privacy you need to kiss and kiss and kiss. If you want company, walk a few blocks to the popular Kamaole Beach nearby. **2128A Iliili Road; (800) 882-9007; www.wwte.com/hawaii/maui/mywaii.htm; moderate.**

❤ **SUGAR BEACH RESORT, Kihei** Located between a high-rise hotel and a small strip mall, this mustard-colored low-rise condominium complex feels a bit cramped. The saving grace here is the five-mile stretch of soft, sandy beach directly in front of the building, just over a gentle grassy knoll. Soothing sounds of the waves help drown out the less soothing sounds of car engines and screaming kids playing in the pool area.

Sugar Beach is a good, affordable place to stay right on the beach. Every unit is air-conditioned and has a full kitchen and standard bathroom, and all oceanfront rooms have stunning views of the tranquil Pacific. However, the lack of affectionate ambience is disappointing. Some of the bedrooms face the parking lot (not the first thing you want to see in the morning). Decor in the privately owned condos can vary considerably from unit to unit, so be sure to ask how the condo rates when you call. Some have a rustic feel, with personal knickknacks, outdated carpeting, and old hide-a-beds that could use reupholstering. Others have more of a hotel look, with matching wicker furniture, tidy kitchens, and attractive floral linens. Units above the first floor that end with the number "35" have incredible views of the ocean and West Maui Mountains and are the furthest from the pool commotion. While Sugar Beach isn't overflowing with sweet, romantic ambience, the money you'll save can be spent on luscious treats elsewhere. **145 North Kihei Road; reservations through Maui Condominium Rentals and Home Realty, (808) 879-5445, (800) 822-4409 mainland; inexpensive to expensive; minimum-stay requirement.**

Restaurant Kissing

❤❤ **A PACIFIC CAFE, Kihei** Many island restaurants rely on oceanfront settings and tropical splendor to keep their patrons happy, but not this café. Because it is located in a nondescript shopping center, you may decide that the destination is not Hawaiian enough to meet your tropical expectations. Be patient: The expansive dining room is striking, and truly complements the chef's culinary skill. Creative architectural touches, colorful artwork, vaulted ceilings, and warm terra-cotta–colored walls give distinction to the two separate dining rooms. Bamboo chairs with muted floral cushions and tables without tablecloths contribute to the casual but upbeat atmosphere.

Food is where A Pacific Cafe gets serious. What to choose? A world of Pacific Rim flavors awaits, from the tender Mongolian barbecued lamb rack to the *ono* in a candied peanut crust served with Indonesian sticky rice. During our visit, locally grown asparagus was in season and the chef made a masterpiece out of this vegetable with the help of the grill, goat cheese, and a walnut oil vinaigrette. Each dish was beautifully presented and perfectly prepared. Our only complaint was the dessert: a bland coconut tapioca pudding. Try something else to end your evening on a sweet note. **1279 South Kihei Road, Suite B-201; (808) 879-0069; moderate to expensive; dinner daily.**

Romantic Note: We came too early to see the opening of the new A Pacific Cafe in Honokowai, Maui (3350 Lower Honoapiilani Road, Building 7; 808-669-2724; moderate to expensive), also located in a strip mall. While all six cafés in this chain differ somewhat in atmosphere, the food is always up to the same high standards.

Wailea

In many ways, Wailea is the premier destination on Maui. Unlike the developments at Kaanapali, which are squished together with no elbow room, Wailea's series of prestige hotel and condominium developments are quite spread out. You couldn't say that it isn't crowded here, and the shore is indeed obscured by these super resorts, but it isn't anywhere near as dense as Kaanapali. Plus, the resorts are absolutely some of the sexiest places to stay on the island, and the beaches are simply sublime. The major

---

Sunscreen of at least SPF 15 is essential and must be applied 20 minutes before going outside. For both UVA and UVB protection, make sure the active ingredients on the label include one of the following: titanium dioxide, zinc oxide, or avobenzone.

hotels in this area line up along a mile of premier beachfront like five sisters posing for a picture: Kea Lani, Four Seasons Resort Wailea, Aston Wailea Resort, Renaissance Wailea Beach Resort, and the biggest sibling, Grand Wailea. It is hard to imagine being disappointed with any of them.

Those who have golf clubs or tennis racquets in hand can try to reserve time at the famous **WAILEA GOLF COURSE** (808-875-7450, 800-332-1614; www.wailea-resort.com.) or the 14-court **WAILEA TENNIS CLUB** (808-879-1958, 800-332-1614; www.wailea-resort.com). No matter where you stay in Wailea, the entire area is one big playground for those who can afford to play.

Romantic Note: The beaches here are among the most beautiful on Hawaii. They are somewhat difficult to reach around the massive hotels, but they are accessible (look for the beach access signs) and usually have public rest rooms, showers, and a parking lot. Remember, all beaches in Hawaii are available for use by the public.

Hotel/Bed and Breakfast Kissing

❤❤❤ **ASTON WAILEA RESORT, Wailea** The 22-acre Aston Wailea Resort was the first hotel property built on the Wailea beach strip and it is the closest to the water's edge, thanks to less stringent building codes back then. Such a prime location, along with comparatively moderate prices and the widespread distribution of its 516 rooms, make it an ideal find. Although the Aston's age shows in some public areas, such as the lobby, many of the guest rooms have been generously upgraded. (Continuous upgrading will also take care of the lobby, too.) In addition to their great views, these refurbished rooms now sport Berber rugs, neutral beach tones, and attractive wicker furniture. As for the remaining rooms, though more affordable, they are sorely in need of renovation and cannot be romantically recommended until major improvements are made.

All of the amenities are here: an expansive pool area, sandy beach, rather good restaurants, and attentive service. The Aston Wailea Resort may not be as elegant as its ritzy neighbors, but it is still worth your affectionate consideration. **3700 Wailea Alanui Drive; (808) 879-1922, (800) 367-2960; www.aston-hotels.com; expensive to unbelievably expensive; recommended wedding site.**

❤❤❤❤ **FOUR SEASONS RESORT, Wailea** How does one describe one of Maui's finest resorts? Let us count the ways: palatial in scope, intimate in detail, elegant without pretension, and beauty at every turn. Simply stated, the Four Seasons at Wailea will meet your every expectation for romantic ambience.

Expectations, in fact, are soon surpassed once you set eyes on one of the 380 guest rooms and suites. Decorated in refined shades of pale green or peach and appointed with spacious marble bathrooms, soaking tubs, and separate glass showers, the rooms are ideal for romantic escapes. As you'd expect, the oceanfront rooms are prime, but since the property is set away from the water's edge, the views aren't surfside. Still, the surroundings are outstanding, beautifully manicured, and worth your wholehearted consideration. A fabulously elegant pool area with a fountain and private cabanas lining the edge is undeniably one of the best places to kiss. In addition, the Four Seasons' restaurants, particularly **FERRARO'S** and **SEASONS** (see Restaurant Kissing for reviews of both), burst with romantic flair. **PACIFIC GRILL** (expensive to very expensive; breakfast and dinner daily), serving a bountiful breakfast buffet and casual dinner fare, is also first-rate. **3900 Wailea Alanui Drive; (808) 874-8000, (800) 334-MAUI; www.fourseasons.com; very expensive to unbelievably expensive and beyond; recommended wedding site.**

Romantic Suggestion: The various romance/honeymoon packages offered by the Four Seasons Resort are worth asking about. Any romantic detail you may have forgotten, they will remember.

❤❤❤❤ **GRAND WAILEA RESORT, Wailea** There is little argument that the Grand Wailea is the ultimate resort spa in Hawaii—and possibly the world. This might sound like an exaggeration, but in fact it may be an understatement. Six hundred million dollars' worth of sheer opulence and grandeur dazzle you at every turn.

Flowers, waterfalls, reflecting pools, trees, sounds, lights, and art have been utilized as design elements in 40 acres of sumptuous, tropical surroundings that will exceed your wildest fantasies. The 2,000-foot-long activity pool, better known as the Wailea Canyon, features water slides, waterfalls, caves, rapids, a Jacuzzi tub, and a sauna. It even has the world's only water elevator, which lifts you back to the top once you've completed your slippery journey down the slides. A second, more formal pool features a spouting water fountain and a stunning hibiscus mosaic on the bottom. You can also take advantage of the scuba-diving pool (lessons are available for a fee), racquetball courts, aerobics room, game room, and weight-training facilities. Thoroughly exhausted after a day of play? Pamper yourselves at the Grand Wailea's world-class **SPA GRANDE** (see Miscellaneous Kissing), which offers every conceivable therapy for the body and mind.

When you first arrive, be sure to get specific directions to your room; it's very easy to get lost in the resort's maze of six independent guest-room wings. Sumptuously appointed in an upscale hotel style, all rooms are lovely and overflow with amenities, although some rooms still retain a basic hotel feel. Ocean-view rooms look out over the pool, and are the most coveted and expensive in the resort. Actually, the Grand Wailea holds one of the most expensive suites in the world. For $10,000 a night, you can live in the lap of luxury, but only if a sultan or celebrity hasn't beaten you to the punch. As if this weren't enough, each floor has its own butler on call. And for a real splurge, you can even order an extremely private multicourse dinner served by your own personal waiter on your lanai. Now that's romantic!

Appropriately, there's also an utterly quaint wedding chapel, set on a small island in the middle of a freshwater pond. Its stained glass windows, depicting handsome Polynesians in repose, radiate golden light with the movement of the sun. As many as 60 weddings a month take place here. If this is where you'd like to exchange your vows, the Grand Wailea's wedding director can help create the wedding of your dreams.

As you might expect, dining at this palace is a lavish experience. A near-legendary Japanese restaurant called **KINCHA** (unbelievably expensive; dinner Saturday–Thursday) has incorporated more than 800 tons of rock from Mount Fuji in its foundation and surrounding gardens. With its soaring ceilings, open-air dining room, and 40-foot-high murals, the **GRAND DINING ROOM MAUI** (expensive; breakfast daily) is literally sublime. The thatch-roofed **HUMUHUMUNUKUNUKUAPUA'A** (expensive to very expensive; dinner daily) dishes up a long name along with plenty of fresh fish entrées in a casual, open-air restaurant. Surrounding the restaurant is a massive saltwater lagoon where tropical fish swim in peace. There's lots more to see at the Grand Wailea, but this listing would go on forever if we mentioned everything. Go see the splendor for yourselves. **3850 Wailea Alanui Drive; (808) 875-1234, (800) 888-6100; www.grandwailea.com; unbelievably expensive and beyond; recommended wedding site.**

Romantic Note: Children in tow rarely make for a romantic escape, but if you happen to have the little darlings along, the Grand Wailea offers **CAMP GRANDE.** A computer room, theater, soda shop, arts-and-crafts room with pottery wheels, video-game room, infant care center, and a wonderful outdoor playground with a whale-shaped pool provide supervised fun for the younger set.

❀❀❀❀ **KEA LANI HOTEL, Wailea** Twenty-two acres of palm trees, lily pad–laden lagoons, and tropical landscaping encompass this Mediterranean-style white stucco hotel. You will feel as if you have been transported to Greece, where scintillating white archways, alcoves, balconies, and footbridges contrast with the azure ocean. Inside, however, the interior decorations have little hint of Mediterranean flair. Instead, Asian antiques and statues, bamboo forests, and koi ponds set the stage for romance.

All of Kea Lani's 413 rooms are impressive one-bedroom suites, beautifully designed with curved doorways, plush white fabrics and linens, and lovely wood antiques. Oversize marble bathrooms offer deep soaking tubs, dual pedestal sinks, and walk-in showers for two, while the double lanais outside enhance the spacious feeling of each suite. Amenities include full entertainment centers (two TVs, a stereo, VCR, and CD player), plus a microwave, refrigerator, and coffeemaker. For an extra splurge, reserve an even larger, more extravagant beachfront villa, replete with a full kitchen, two full bathrooms, laundry facilities, a home entertainment center, and a private plunge pool on the patio.

With or without a private pool, you are certain to enjoy splashing around in the splendid lagoon-style pool and sliding down its 140-foot water slide. Those who crave calmer waters can dip into the European-inspired lap pool (for adults only). Private poolside cabanas surrounding the lagoon pool are always perfect places to take a nap or kiss undercover. Besides the pool picks, the Kei Lani has an enticing new spa in which to pamper yourselves, a wonderfully silky-sand beach, excellent outdoor dining, and superior service. Without a doubt, this hotel easily rates as one of Wailea's premier destinations. **4100 Wailea Alanui Drive; (808) 875-4100, (800) 882-4100; www.kealani.com; very expensive to unbelievably expensive and beyond; recommended wedding site.**

Romantic Suggestion: You don't have to walk far to find excellent cuisine at the Kea Lani Hotel. Dinner is served in the open-air restaurant called **NICK'S FISHMARKET** (see Restaurant Kissing). Although it doesn't sound romantic, you'll change your mind once you set your eyes on it. **CAFFE CIAO** (inexpensive to moderate; breakfast, lunch, and dinner daily), the Kea Lani's casual and less expensive dining option, is a delightful deli and bakery with elegant Corinthian columns, marble floors, and a small handful of wrought-iron tables. Fuel up with a frothy cappuccino or iced latte and a mouthwatering pastry. If you're planning to be out and about, pick up the makings of a gourmet picnic lunch and then dash off to kiss. And let us not forget to tell you that the wine selection is excellent.

❤❤ **MAKENA SURF, Wailea** These townhouse-style condominiums scattered around the Wailea beachfront aren't grand by any stretch of the imagination; however, the attractive array of units provide a welcome alternative to the excesses of Wailea's huge hotels. Each one-, two-, and three-bedroom unit is decorated differently, but all feature central air-conditioning, a spacious lanai with partial or full ocean views, and a full kitchen. The only drawbacks are a somewhat cramped feeling, with front doors or lanais facing one another, and the rather small pool areas. Still, the relaxed surroundings make this a quiet and enjoyable place to stay 'n' smooch. **3750 Wailea Alanui Drive; reservations through Destination Resorts, (808) 879-1595, (800) 367-5246 mainland; www.destination resortshi.com/makena.htm; very expensive to unbelievably expensive; minimum-stay requirement.**

❤❤ **MAUI PRINCE HOTEL, Wailea** Referred to as Wailea's last resort, the Maui Prince is far removed from Wailea's other hotels, and is surprisingly modest compared to its competition. An expansive, nondescript lobby encircles a small open-air courtyard filled with miniature waterfalls and a koi pond. The hallway decor is somewhat sterile and out of touch with the times, a trend that spills over into many of the hotel's 310 guest rooms. However dated they are, each room is reasonably attractive and comfortable, appointed with Pegge Hopper Hawaiian prints, white linens, and Hawaiian-quilted pillows. Spacious lanais face the ocean and the circular swimming pools. If outdoor activities are high on your priorities (second, of course, to kissing), you won't be disappointed with the Maui Prince's options: golf, snorkeling, tennis, swimming, scuba diving, boogie boarding, volleyball, and sailing, to name only a few. While the Maui Prince lacks the upscale feel of neighboring resorts, it can still provide you with all of the ingredients for a blissful tropical getaway—at a much better price. Be sure to ask about the hotel's excellent package deals, which allow you to save money rather than kiss it goodbye. **5400 Makena Alanui; (808) 874-1111, (800) 321-MAUI; www.westin.com; expensive to unbelievably expensive; recommended wedding site.**

Romantic Suggestion: Although dining options are vast at the Maui Prince, they aren't necessarily romantic. **HAKONE** (expensive; dinner Monday–Saturday) serves excellent Japanese cuisine in a somewhat stark atmosphere, while the **PRINCE COURT** (expensive to very expensive; dinner daily, brunch Sunday) focuses on Pacific Rim delicacies.

❤❤❤ **RENAISSANCE WAILEA BEACH RESORT, Wailea** Set down your suitcases for a moment and breathe in the fresh ocean air that flows freely through this grand open lobby. Water fountains border the entrance hall and exotic flower arrangements add splashes of red, orange, and green to the gold-colored interior. From the lobby, look out upon 15 and a half acres of mature tropical gardens where winding pathways lead down to the lovely pool and pristine Mokapu Beach.

After soaking in the introductory sights, you'll be escorted to your stately, sizable room, which is attractively decorated in soft beige and taupe tones, and appointed with wicker chairs, a cane coffee table, TV/VCR, a large lanai with cushioned wrought-iron chairs and table, and pretty tiled bath. Unfortunately, because of the way the property is situated, the ocean-view rooms have poor visibility out to the magical waters of the Pacific. This is one of the few places where a water-oriented room may not be the prize of the resort, but luckily the rich tropical vistas from many of the rooms are outstanding. If you seek to escape the crowds by the pool, journey down to the beach, which has enough sandy space to satisfy your kissing needs. **3550 Wailea Alanui Drive; (808) 879-4900, (800) 992-4532; www.renaissancehotels.com; expensive to unbelievably expensive; recommended wedding site.**

Romantic Note: The Renaissance no longer has a fine dining establishment, but the **PALM COURT** (moderate to expensive; breakfast and dinner daily) will do just fine for casual dining throughout the day. The poolside **MAUI ONION** (inexpensive; lunch and appetizers daily) lives up to its reputation for having the best onion rings and fruit smoothies around. Be sure to indulge at least once during your stay.

Restaurant Kissing

❤❤❤❤ **FERRARO'S, Wailea** By day this poolside restaurant caters to the casual, lunch-seeking sunbathers, but come sunset, it is transformed into one of Maui's most romantic restaurants. Maximize sunset viewing by requesting a table on the terraced patio, or, for more sheltered surroundings, sit underneath the large pavilion and admire its painted ceiling. The tables, set simply with beautiful plates and elegant silverware, are spaced well enough apart so you won't overhear your neighbors' conversation. As the sun begins to set, tiki torches begin to glow, soft breezes warm the evening, and the sultry sounds of *Casablanca*'s theme song "A Kiss Is Just a Kiss" are played by a string duet. Trust us, this is a place where a kiss can be more than just a kiss . . . and we haven't even mentioned the food. Let's just say Ferraro's Mediterranean menu will fulfill your other appetites. **3900 Wailea Alanui Drive, at the Four Seasons Resort; (808) 874-8000; www.fourseasons.com; expensive; lunch and dinner daily.**

Never take the ocean for granted; a calm-looking surface can be deceiving. Strong undercurrents or rogue waves may be only moments or steps away.

❀❀❀ **NICK'S FISHMARKET, Wailea** Despite the grocery store–sounding name, Nick's Fishmarket is the Kei Lani Hotel's offering for upscale and romantic dining. Try arriving somewhat early to watch the setting sun and glowing tiki torches play off the butter-colored walls. Ask for one of the crescent-shaped booths in the main dining room, which sets you apart from the rest, and savor the beautiful grounds and colorful Hawaiian sky. Enjoy fresh salmon with a raspberry beurre blanc, fresh *opah* baked in phyllo, or classic dishes such as lamb chops, filet mignon, or Maine lobster. The staff's attention to detail, an appealing menu, and irresistible desserts all make a pleasant prelude to romance. **4100 Wailea Alanui Drive, at the Kea Lani Hotel; (808) 875-4100; expensive; dinner daily.**

❀❀❀ **THE SEA WATCH RESTAURANT AT WAILEA, Wailea** Because of its advantageous hillside setting, the casually elegant Sea Watch Restaurant boasts views of the glistening green fairways, Molokini Crater, and the vast blue Pacific from every table. However, there is more than just sea watching to appreciate at this golf-course dining room. Superior Pacific Rim cuisine, featuring the freshest ingredients, is the specialty of the house, and each dish is presented with polished finesse. At the noon hour, cool off with a fresh crab and papaya salad and iced tea. When the golfers start heading home, stick around and try the grilled chicken breast in a guava-sesame sauce or any of the fresh fish selections prepared a different way each evening. Dessert decisions are easy: You simply can't go wrong with anything, especially the mango mousse or gigantic brownie sundae. **100 Wailea Golf Club Drive; (808) 875-8080; www.bestofmaui.com/ seawatch.html; moderate to expensive; breakfast, lunch, and dinner daily; recommended wedding site.**

❀❀❀ **SEASONS, Wailea** Fine food, soft music, low lighting, and a view of the resort and ocean—what more could you ask for? Not much. The Four Seasons Resort's signature restaurant offers extraordinary cuisine, elegant ambience, and exemplary service. Varying shades of taupe and pale wood accents fill the dramatic dining room. Outdoor seating, surrounded by glowing torches, is slightly more casual, but every detail here is polished and refined. The cuisine incorporates locally grown produce and fresh Hawaiian ingredients into savory dishes such as breast of pheasant or *onaga* baked in a Hawaiian salt crust. Fresh-from-the-ocean fish entrées are always excellent. Presentations are works of art, which explains the unbelievably high prices. **3900 Wailea Alanui Drive, at the Four Seasons Resort; (808) 874-8000; www.fourseasons.com; very expensive to unbelievably expensive; dinner Tuesday–Saturday; recommended wedding site.**

Romantic Option: For $650, you can arrange an ULTIMATE RO-MANTIC DINNER. The price tag includes a private table on the grassy lawn fronting a koi pond and overlooking the ocean. Tiki torches are lit all around, and your table for two is set with fine china, crystal, silver, crisp white linens, and fresh flowers. Chilled champagne and an exquisite dinner (individually designed for your tastes and preferences) is served by a personal waiter. This indulgence goes way off our cost rating chart, but for a special occasion, it just may be worth it. Let your credit limit be your guide.

Outdoor Kissing

❀❀❀ **WAILEA BEACH/POLO BEACH WALK, Wailea** Can a beach walk be romantic if there isn't soft sand to sink your toes into? After wandering along the rocky stretch of shoreline between Wailea and Polo Beaches, you will be convinced that romance is absolutely possible on a beach without sand.

Native plants line the paved walking path, and there are numerous places to stop, sit, smooch, and just savor the beauty around you. One of the most striking sites is **WAILEA POINT**, where furious waves crash into the island's volcanic edge (a Kodak moment if we've ever seen one).

Don't make the mistake of thinking this beach walk is reserved only for paying guests at the neighboring exclusive hotels. We've said it before, but it's worth saying again: The beauty about Hawaii is that there is no such thing as a private beach. After finding the public right-of-way path, it's just a matter of minutes before you'll be strolling hand in hand along this seaside lover's lane. *These beaches are in front of the Grand Wailea Resort, Four Seasons Resort, and Kea Lani Hotel. Look for signs to either beach.*

Miscellaneous Kissing

❀❀❀❀ **SPA GRANDE, Wailea** Imagine having two massage therapists working on your weary body at once or, more in keeping with the romance theme, being massaged side by side with your beloved, followed by a relaxing private herbal bath *à deux*. Body facials, all forms of hydrotherapy, and total beauty treatments are performed in an amazing marble-ensconced forum. Here you can try the extraordinary "Terme Wailea" (women and men have their own separate areas for this one): Begin with a Japanese-style bath or a loofah scrub, plunge into a hot mineral tub, then a cool one, followed by steam, sauna, a waterfall shower, a unique herbal bath, and then a seemingly jet-powered shower. For the mind, the spa offers a variety of health and wellness sessions, including meditation instruction and yoga. Treatments and combinations thereof can total into the hundreds of dollars, depending on which indulgences you choose. You won't have the energy to kiss after this spa experience, but holding each other close for hours afterward will be sheer bliss. **3850 Wailea Alanui Drive, at the Grand Wailea Resort; (808) 875-1234, ext. 4949; www.grandwailea.com/spa/spa1.html; services range from $25 to $360, nonguests pay a $30 surcharge; open daily.**

North Shore

Wailuku

Those planning to visit **IAO VALLEY STATE PARK** for more than a day should consider basing themselves in the town of Wailuku just five minutes away. Set among the green hillside, this town features numerous historical buildings, not to mention a more hometown feel than that of neighboring Kahului.

Hotel/Bed and Breakfast Kissing

❤❤❤❤ **OLD WAILUKU INN, Wailuku** The *aloha* spirit has never left this 1924 Craftsman-Plantation–style home located in the historical district of Wailuku. There's an intimacy with the past here, from the living room's antique art pieces to the classical handmade Hawaiian quilts in each bedroom. Allow the innkeeper's intuition to select a room that's right for you (she does a good job, trust us). Whichever room you choose, your romantic interlude will be maximized by her applied *feng shui*. Each of the seven rooms are designed to enhance the comfort and serenity of the guest. Some have a private lanai or Jacuzzi tub, and others offer total immersion into the interior of the stately home. While historical in style, all rooms have modern comforts such as air-conditioning, TV/VCR, voice mail/telephone as well as private bathroom with an ample selection of Aveda products. Attention to detail is not only evident in the lovely appointments throughout the home, but also in the elaborate breakfasts served in the dining room. Change awaits every day as the innkeeper brings such treats as banana *lumpia* with passion-fruit dipping sauce, French toast, or breakfast enchiladas to the table. The only *feng shui* problem (if there is such a thing) is the inn's proximity to a nearby road. However at night the traffic noise calms down and you'll sleep soundly in this grand old home. **Reservations through Hawaii's Best Bed and Breakfasts, (808) 885-4550, (800) 262-9912 mainland; www.travelguides.com/inns/full/HI/3605.html; moderate.**

Paia

Paia is the last official-looking town you'll pass before venturing along the road to Hana. Stop for a while (or stay a day), since Paia has plenty of shops and restaurants located along its main street. It's also your last chance for gasoline until you hit Hana.

Hotel/Bed and Breakfast Kissing

🌺🌺🌸 **MAMA'S BEACHFRONT COTTAGES, Paia** Sooner or later, most everyone hears about **MAMA'S FISH HOUSE** (see review on page 103) while visiting Maui. It's a popular North Shore eatery and a must-stop-'n'-eat location as you travel along the Hana Highway. But did you know you can stay at Mama's too? You'll find Mama's Beachfront Cottages hidden alongside the restaurant in a quiet cul de sac. The two-story green-shingled duplex offers two suites, both facing the Kuau Beach, a favorite sunning spot for Maui residents. Perhaps this location is why these units command such a high price. Identical in layout, each floor has two bedrooms, a well-appointed living area, and a full kitchen (no breakfast is provided). Upstairs, of course, has the better view, but downstairs has immediate access to the beach via the front lanai. As an incentive to try Mama's Fish House, guests are offered a 20 percent discount on all meals. **Reservations through Hawaii's Best Bed and Breakfasts, (808) 885-4550, (800) 262-9912 mainland; www.maui.net/~mamas; very expensive.**

Romantic Note: Another of Mama's cottages next door is equally as nice, but more geared for families.

Restaurant Kissing

🌺🌺🌺 **JACQUES BISTRO, Paia** Jacques, a French bistro with a *Casablanca* ambience, expands the variety of eating experiences in the Paia area. There are plenty of coffee shops and cafés, but few fine dining restaurants catering to the romantically inclined. Uncomplicated stucco walls illuminated by candlelight, ceiling fans whirring above, and 1940s music set a some-

Unless you're on the dry side of the island, always be prepared for a tropical downpour.

what nostalgic mood for an amorous evening here. A small courtyard—where tiki torches are aglow and ocean breezes cool things off—may also appeal to your dining pleasure.

The straightforward menu combines French bistro favorites with local ingredients. Grilled Mediterranean mahi mahi, smoked salmon with angel-hair pasta, and bouillabaisse with a Hawaiian touch should satisfy. Ample portions, attentive service, and a fine house wine provide all the necessities needed for an evening to remember. **89 Hana Highway; (808) 579-6255; moderate; dinner daily.**

Huelo

Huelo is less a town than a residential area, populated with many bed and breakfasts and spread out along the Hana Highway. However, as you drive along, you won't see any of the homes, bed and breakfasts, and vacation rentals. Camouflaged by the lush countryside, they are hard to find and sometimes tricky to get to, but perfect if you're seeking seclusion.

Hotel/Bed and Breakfast Kissing

❤❤❤❤ **A'APALI CLIFFHOUSE AT PALI ULI ESTATE, Huelo** A 150-foot-high waterfall slicing through the dense forest of green is all yours to savor from the patio of this spectacular, secluded vacation home. Yet the breathtaking waterfall is just part of the beauty here. The owners spend much time in Bali, so everything speaks of their love of Indonesian decor, from the magnificent stone statues guarding the gate to the Balinese art inside the one-room Cliffhouse.

Enter through a magnificent Balinese door into a private outdoor courtyard replete with a small lap pool guarded by a sphinx statue. At the far end of the courtyard awaits the first of two separate living quarters that comprise this compound-style home. Inside, a skylight ceiling sheds ample light upon a large, built-in, cushioned sofa surrounded by marble and volcanic-rock floors and accents, a fireplace, and a kitchen made of marble. (Bring your own A.M. fixings, since breakfast is not provided.) Come nighttime, walk through the courtyard and past the pool to the second living space—a detached, octagon-shaped room that holds your bed.

Red ginger and Japanese irises hide the fantastic outdoor shower—a Balinese stone maiden with water pouring from her urn onto you. Dry off on the private cliffside patio with Hanehoi Falls and the green, rugged hillside as the backdrop. Later, venture down a cobblestone path to the hot tub overlooking a lily pond and private garden with a magnificent Buddha statue. At every turn, this Balinese hideaway is a work of art and, for a couple in love, it's the perfect place to practice the art of romance. **(808) 573-0693, (800) 861-9566; www.maui.net/~paliuli; very expensive; minimum-stay requirement.**

❧❧❧ **HONOPOU LODGE, Huelo** "Upscale" and "affordable" are two words not often spoken in the same sentence when it comes to Hawaii's accommodations. Luckily, the two descriptions flow freely from your lips at Honopou Lodge, a new bed and breakfast overlooking Maui's north shore. The 4,000-square-foot, architecturally stunning home makes for an engaging and private place to stay. Three separate guest rooms, each with a kitchenette and luxurious private bath, are decorated with an interior designer's touch and attention to detail. The studio we stayed in overlooked the pool and had a large walk-in shower and Jacuzzi tub. Unfortunately, the bathroom windows open up to the carport used by guests, which reduces the privacy factor a bit. The other two rooms are equally as nice, although the bathrooms differ in size and amenities.

A continental breakfast consisting of eggs, cereal, juices, fruit, and coffee can be savored in-room at a bistro-style table or on the wraparound lanai. After a day out, return to the Lodge for a dip in the lap pool or adjoining Jacuzzi tub. If you'd rather enjoy Mother Nature's swimming spots, take a stroll to nearby waterfalls and freshwater pools for a cool treat on a hot, humid day. **Reservations through Hawaii's Best Bed and Breakfasts, (808) 885-4550, (800) 262-9912 mainland; inexpensive.**

❧❧❧ **HUELO POINT FLOWER FARM, Huelo** This two-acre oceanfront estate, set on the edge of a 300-foot sea cliff, is truly an amazing spot. Below are breathtaking views of Waipio Bay, and surrounding you are lush jungle, a wonderful tropical garden, and a 50-foot-long swimming pool with a waterfall and hot tub. There are four accommodations on the property, ranging from an intimate gazebo to an architecturally stunning home. Of the foursome, we recommend The Gazebo, located right on the cliff's edge. Open the glass doors of this one-bedroom wonder and all you'll see is sea. Koa-wood accents, a queen-size bed, TV, CD player, mini-kitchen, private bath with an outside shower, and tiled private patio make this a romantic outpost. We also like the larger Guest House, a stunning, modified A-frame with a dramatic second-floor loft bedroom (ignore the ugly carpet); large, tiled kitchen; beautiful patio; and all the other necessities you'd find in an upscale home. For those who want to go all out, the exquisite and large Main House should satisfy. The Carriage House, while comfy, lacks romantic charm and coziness.

Breakfast is a buffet that you pick and prepare yourselves. Venture into the field of tropical fruit trees and select what you'd like for the day.

While you're out and about, be sure to ask to see the Wishing Tree. Make a wish underneath this special palm, and who knows? Maybe all your romantic dreams will come true. You've certainly found the right place to start turning dreams into reality. **Huelo Church Road; (808) 572-1850; www.maui.net/~huelopt; inexpensive to very expensive; minimum-stay requirement.**

❧❧❧ HUELO POINT LOOKOUT—A ROMANTIC RETREAT, Huelo If

you think the road to Hana is tricky, just wait until you drive the mildly adventurous dirt road to this bed and breakfast. Yet the rewards for reaching Huelo Point Lookout are its truly charming accommodations.

Nestled on two soft green acres, not far from the ocean cliffs of Waipio Bay, this property enjoys views of the distant ocean, fertile surrounding fields, and Haleakala when the clouds cooperate. Weather is nothing less than epic here. In a matter of minutes it can go from sunny and silent to windy and violent to cool and rainy, then back to sunny again. At some point in this tropical drama, rainbows usually pass right overhead. An outdoor Jacuzzi tub set in the front lawn (available to all guests) is a wonderful place from which to witness all of this firsthand while soaking in swirling, steamy waters. If things get too hot, cool off by jumping into the adjacent pool.

Three cottages are available, or you can rent the entire main house, which we found too big to be cozy. By far the most romantic of all is the Rainbow Cottage. Witness the surrounding beauty in all its glory through the cottage's tall windows. Truly a work of art, the mahogany-wood spiral staircase leads to the bedroom and a blue-tiled bathroom with a glass roof and double shower. Outside on a private patio, enjoy simmering in your own private hot tub right next to the nautilus-shaped outdoor shower.

Star Cottage, also one of our favorites, is set far enough away from the main house to ensure privacy. Upstairs is a loft-style bedroom (watch your head on the stairs), while downstairs awaits a full-size kitchen and a pleasant sitting area with expansive windows. Other features include a private outdoor shower and decks facing nature's surrounding grandeur. Finally, a tropical garden surrounds the petite Haleakala Cottage, a simple but sweet studio unit with a king-size bed, kitchenette, and view of the famous volcano (weather permitting). Vivid colors and striking floral prints tastefully abound in every unit. A Maui-style continental breakfast of fresh tropical fruits, pastries, and Kona coffee is left in each unit's fridge for guests to enjoy at their leisure. **(808)573-0914, (800) 871-8645; www.maui vacationcottages.com; inexpensive to very expensive; minimum-stay requirement.**

Romantic Warning: The jungle is full of critters, and the owners do not use pesticides. That's wonderful for the environment, but may not be for you if having ants around the house are bothersome.

☙☙☙ **MALUHIA HALE, Huelo** Gossamer curtains billowing in the wind, crisp white rooms with antique linens, floor-to-ceiling windows, and iron beds, combined with the owner's beautiful sense of style, merge to create a dream-like oasis on this lush, emerald-green hillside. *Maluhia Hale* means "peaceful home," and once you set eyes on this spot, there will be no disputing that this name perfectly defines the two accommodations here.

Both the in-house suite and the private cottage are equally lovely, so deciding on one of them can be difficult. Only a few steps from the main house, the old-fashioned cottage features a screened-in sunporch, a kitchenette, and a bathroom with an antique claw-foot tub, tiled shower, and plenty of ferns for that tropical touch. Inside the main house, but with its own separate entrance, is the large, light suite. Here you'll find a king-size bed, private bath, and French doors opening to your own little lily pond. No matter which accommodation you choose, a light breakfast is left in your fridge for you to enjoy together as you relish panoramic views of the Pacific, the rolling green countryside, and majestic Haleakala. **Reservations through Hawaii's Best Bed and Breakfasts, (808) 885-4550, (800) 262-9912 mainland; inexpensive.**

☙☙ **TEA HOUSE COTTAGE, Huelo** They say happiness is a journey, but in this case, it's the destination. Drive down a rough, remote dirt road, then hike along a jungle trail (Hint: Keep your luggage light) until you reach your private cottage hidden among the dense tropical trees. Asian simplicity harmonizes with rustic charm in this one-bedroom cottage decorated in a plain but comfortable style. A private outdoor bathhouse, situated a few steps from the screened-in front porch, may enchant you with its uniqueness, or may discourage you from taking that nightly trip to the loo.

Every day the owner, who lives close by, prepares delicacies and delivers them in a basket. After your morning repast, venture along a jungle pathway until you come across one of Maui's more interesting and unexpected sights: a massive Tibetan Buddhist *stupa* out in the middle of nowhere. **(808) 572-5610; www.maui.net/~teahouse; inexpensive; minimum-stay requirement.**

Many restaurants offer early-bird dinner specials, which often include soup/salad, entrée, and dessert. Inquire at the restaurant of your choice and then dine early. You can usually catch the sunset too.

Upcountry

On the northeastern slopes of Haleakala, a different facet of island life is on display for those who can bear to leave the beach. Upcountry is where you'll find the last remnants of true "local" life on the islands.

As you drive farther away from the crowds, you climb up undulating hills covered with emerald green fields and dotted with patches of chaparral. Horses, cattle, and farm crops thrive here. At the end of the road is **TEDESCHI VINEYARDS** (Highway 37 on Ulupalakua Ranch, Ulupalakua; 808-878-6058; www.maui.net/~winery), the only commercial winery on Maui. Tours (9:30 A.M.–2:30 P.M. daily) and wine tastings (9 A.M.–5 P.M. daily) are available. The famous pineapple wine is as sweet as it sounds, and the mature landscape, complete with 100-year-old trees and renovated old buildings, is lovely. Try arriving early before busloads of visitors come for a taste of the tropics.

As the two of you venture forth, be aware that upcountry weather is entirely different from that of the coast. In the winter, evening temperatures can drop into the 40s and rain can be persistent. Dress accordingly. But, on the bright side, the views are spellbinding and the country calm is superlative. No high-rise or condominium developments exist for miles around. If Maui's overdeveloped beaches feel like paradise lost, this may just be paradise found.

Haiku

Hotel/Bed and Breakfast Kissing

❀❀❀❀ **ANUE NUE, Haiku** You'll be amazed and thoroughly impressed with the quality and radiance of Anue Nue ("the Rainbow House"). The sprawling, U-shaped, cedar structure sits on six acres of beautifully landscaped grounds with distant views of the Pacific. The property consists of two self-contained pavilions (one at each end) and a main house at the center. The main house wraps around a tropical courtyard with Japanese gardens and a koi pond. Although each unit has its own entrance and is extremely private, long, covered walkways between the pavilions and the main house make it possible to rent and share the entire building—perfect for a wedding party or if you are traveling in a group.

The two intimate pavilion units each have a queen-size bed, fully equipped kitchen, washer/dryer, charming terra-cotta–tiled bath, and designer decor with vivid French art, crisp linens, and hardwood floors. The main house boasts a similarly bold but plush interior and comfortable amenities, but it has much more space and can be rented as either a two- or three-bedroom unit. Champagne, a fruit basket, and tropical flowers welcome you to your room, and a breakfast basket is left in your refrigerator to prepare at your own morning pace.

Calling Anue Nue a vacation rental doesn't seem appropriate, but it really isn't a resort or a bed and breakfast either. Instead, it offers the best of both worlds: resort-like amenities (a pool, tennis courts, and spa services), along with the coziness and individuality of an exclusive bed and breakfast. Whatever you call it, this unique retreat is just the kind of tropical therapy the doctor ordered. **110 Kane Road; (808) 572-7586; moderate to unbelievably expensive; recommended wedding site.**

Romantic Option: There is also a lower-floor apartment available in the innkeepers' separate home. It is a little too mismatched to be a preferred romantic suite, but it does have character and is the only unit that falls into the inexpensive category.

❦❦ **GOLDEN BAMBOO RANCH, Haiku** Wind blowing through the trees, birds chirping, and the occasional whinny of a horse are about the only sounds you'll hear at this quiet little ranch. A wide variety of tropical fruit trees, flowers, and plants share the property with the friendly innkeepers and three resident horses. Needless to say, the pace at Golden Bamboo Ranch is relaxed and the atmosphere unpretentious. Three private little apartment-like units are available in one building, each with a private bath, California king-size bed, kitchenette, cable TV, and patio. An individual cottage right next door is the most spacious and cozy of the accommodations. Inside you'll find a king-size bed, standard bath, a large kitchen decorated with local artwork, and, last but not least, a bright sunporch with a futon and white-washed pine floors. In all units, simple breakfast fixings are left in your fridge to enjoy in your own sweet time. Best of all, the innkeepers will do your laundry, so you won't waste your romantic time waiting for the wash cycle to finish. **Reservations through Hawaii's Best Bed and Breakfasts, (808) 885-4550, (800) 262-9912 mainland; www.maui.net/~golden; inexpensive.**

❦❦❦❦ **MAUI TRADEWINDS, Haiku** Upstairs, downstairs: There's no "class" difference here. Both accommodations in this contemporary wooden home are first-class in decor, spaciousness, and attention to detail. Set high on the slopes of Haleakala, the home is the perfect place from which to watch the day go by. Bask in the hot tub and watch the rainbows below or just enjoy the refreshing mountain breezes on the 1,500-square-foot lanai.

The upstairs suite, the more expensive and luxurious of the two, mesmerizes with a 200-gallon aquarium, a museum-quality rock and mineral collection highlighted by halogen lights, and a kitchen worthy of the finest gourmet. The marble and tiled bath is a triumph of design and luxury, with a window-enclosed Jacuzzi tub and glass shower built for two. Downstairs awaits an equally elegant but more casual and less expensive suite, with a gorgeous full kitchen, private lanai, and king-size bed. Breakfast is not provided, but both kitchens are so large and lovely you won't mind staying inside to cook. Prices of both suites become less expensive the more days you stay . . . and trust us, you'll want to stay several. **Reservations through Hawaii's Best Bed and Breakfasts, (808) 885-4550, (800) 262-9912 mainland; inexpensive to unbelievably expensive.**

❤️❤️❤️ **PILIALOHA, Haiku** We never promised you a rose garden, but here it is. This charming cottage, surrounded by some 200 rose varieties, crowns an acre of green lawn bordered by thick evergreen and eucalyptus forests. The only nearby home belongs to the owners and matches the cottage in color and design. Everything at Pilialoha is immaculate, totally private, and affectionately decorated, with modest yet comfortable furnishings and a beautifully stocked kitchen filled with breakfast goodies (replenished daily). Beach chairs, picnic coolers, snorkeling equipment, and blankets are available to make your trip to the beach, up to the crater, or out to Hana hassle free. **2512 Kaupakalua Road; (808) 572-1440; www. pilialoha.com; inexpensive; minimum-stay requirement.**

Restaurant Kissing

❤️❤️❤️ **TRATTORIA HAIKU, Haiku** Is it our imagination or do many of Hawaii's best restaurants reside in boring strip malls? (Read through this book and you'll see what we mean.) Trattoria is no exception, although it distinguishes itself from its bland surroundings by an old-fashioned storefront facade. Built in 1921, the restaurant was formerly the eatery for all the cannery workers and builders in the area. Today, in a softly lit dining room, it dishes up succulent and classic Italian specialties to those working on love. A light breeze cools off the main dining room where a handful of linen-covered, candle-lit tables await. An attached screened-in porch, adorned with a few tables, white holiday lights, and a bubbling water fountain, hints at casual dinner affairs rather than affairs of the heart.

House specialties are all richly flavored and generous beyond belief. Both chicken parmigiana and grilled *ahi* rolled in Mediterranean spices delight the palate. However, true love is found in a spoonful of zabaglione, touched ever so slightly with macadamia nut liqueur. Now that's Italian in the heart of the jungle. **810 Haiku Road, at the Haiku Marketplace; (808) 575-2820; moderate to expensive; dinner Tuesday-Sunday.**

Haliimaile

Restaurant Kissing

❧❧ **HALIIMAILE GENERAL STORE, Haliimaile** Don't miss Haliimaile's old-fashioned general-store-turned-restaurant on your way through the upcountry region. This historic landmark has been tastefully transformed into a very casual, somewhat whimsical restaurant and café. Colorful tropical-fish sculptures hang from the high ceilings, and upbeat modern art graces the peach-colored walls. Along the back wall on ceiling-high pine shelving sits colorful ceramicware for sale. Light floods into the front dining room through large windows that look out onto the wraparound veranda, where you can sit outside and enjoy the upcountry breezes.

A must-try on the menu is the rock shrimp–crab *lumpia*, a lighter version of the spring roll that captures the flavors of the sea perfectly. Our coconut seafood curry proved average, but the special of the day, a well-seasoned macadamia nut–crusted *onaga*, wowed us. Tropical tastes take over in such worthy desserts as piña colada cheesecake, mango/blackberry cobbler, and chocolate–macadamia nut pie. The ride back to civilization is a long one, so stay a while at this upcountry restaurant and enjoy savoring the sweets. **900 Haliimaile Road; (808) 572-2666; moderate to expensive; lunch Monday–Friday, dinner daily, brunch Sunday.**

Makawao

Little Makawao has slowly (and reluctantly) made the transition from 1968 to the 1990s. An eclectic assortment of restaurants and country shops line the small Western-style main street. Some are strictly Bohemian (but still interesting), while others are urbane enough to sell lattes and designer clothing.

Hotel/Bed and Breakfast Kissing

❧❧❧ **OLINDA COUNTRY COTTAGES AND INN, Makawao** The zigzag road up the slopes of Haleakala may be challenging, but the reward awaiting the intrepid traveler is worth it. At 4,000 feet, Olinda Country Cottages and Inn brings romantic accommodations to new heights. The main home has three pleasantly appointed rooms, each with a private bath and private entrance. But the real payoff for the ride to Olinda is staying in one of the two cottages. If a view is important, The Country Cottage caters to those seeking vistas of the green slopes below. Inside, you'll find a queen-size bed with down comforter, a cozy living room with a brick hearth and fireplace, and a full kitchen. For those seeking extraordinary privacy, the one-bedroom Hidden Cottage is one of our top picks on Maui. Light suffuses the bedroom, kitchen, and living room, and lanais on every side provide a wonderful sense of openness. As an extra bonus, the lanai off the bedroom has a deep soaking tub for two. Every appointment bespeaks the innkeeper's exquisite taste and love of harmony and solitude.

Guests staying in the inn are served a continental breakfast each morning, while those staying in the cottages will find their first morning's breakfast waiting in their refrigerator. Hiking trails abound near Olinda Country Cottages, so bring those boots, or for a more civilized experience, savor the beauty of the innkeeper's protea flower farm. **Reservations through Hawaii's Best Bed and Breakfasts, (808) 885-4550, (800) 262-9912 mainland; www.mauibnbcottages.com; inexpensive to moderate; minimum-stay requirement.**

Restaurant Kissing

❦❦ **CASANOVA, Makawao** It's not easy to accommodate many tastes and styles without appearing confused and awkward, but somehow this attractive Italian eatery pulls it off. The front half of the restaurant is a smoke-filled nightspot where locals hang out while waiting for the music to begin. Anything from traditional folk music to reggae may be the special entertainment for the evening; sets start at 9:30 P.M. and continue into the wee hours. The back half of the restaurant holds a series of snugly grouped tables where you can indulge in appetizing Italian cuisine. Fresh bread, hearty portions, and efficient service are all standard at Casanova. Although the real Casanova had the reputation of being fickle, this namesake is always reliable. **1188 Makawao Avenue; (808) 572-0220; moderate to expensive; dinner daily.**

Romantic Note: A variety of delicious lunch salads, soups, sandwiches, and desserts are served next door in the **CASANOVA DELI** (808-572-0220; inexpensive; breakfast, lunch, and light meals daily). If you're up early, the deli also serves coffee and pastries to help get you going.

Kula

Hotel/Bed and Breakfast Kissing

❦❦ **BLOOM COTTAGE, Kula** Named for the blooming herb and flower gardens that surround it, this charming white cottage with green shutters is straight out of a storybook. Those in search of quiet solitude will appreciate the cottage's semi-remote upcountry location at 3,000 feet on the hushed slopes of Haleakala. Because the two-bedroom cottage is set behind the owner's home just off the Kula Highway, the only potential distraction is the sound of afternoon traffic.

Quaint antiques and knickknacks add touches of country charm to the cottage's lovely interior, fashioned with hardwood floors and high, peaked, white ceilings. When the cool fog rolls down the mountain, you can take refuge by the warm, wood-stocked fireplace or watch classic movies on the provided TV/VCR. Breakfast is your own private affair; the fully equipped kitchen is prestocked with coffee, tea, island fruit and juice, granola, muffins, and breads. If you plan to visit the crater in the early morning, the proprietor provides thermoses and warm jackets—a nice touch considering most romantics don't include these items in their suitcases. **229 Kula Highway; (808) 878-1425; inexpensive; minimum-stay requirement.**

Romantic Alternative: Another overnight option in Kula is the SILVER CLOUD UPCOUNTRY GUEST RANCH (Old Thompson Road; 808-878-6101, 800-532-1111; www.maui.net/~slvrcld; inexpensive to expensive). Also known for its glorious pastoral views and relaxed setting, this quiet nine-acre property once was part of a working cattle ranch. Guests can stay in one of the 12 modestly appointed guest rooms. A full, home-cooked country breakfast, served family-style in the garden sunroom the following morning, is included in the price. The Silver Cloud is a nice option for those who want to get away from it all and soak up the upcountry's carefree, secluded beauty.

Restaurant Kissing

❧❧❧ **KULA LODGE AND RESTAURANT, Kula** As you begin the ascent to Haleakala Crater, you'll stumble across Kula Lodge Restaurant, renowned for its sensational views. At 3,200 feet, the rustic dining room surveys a bit of everything Maui offers, from the residential neighborhoods below to the cloud-covered West Maui mountains, vast green fields, and the ocean beyond. Open for breakfast, lunch, and dinner, this is the ideal refreshment point before or after your day on the volcano.

Two-person tables set alongside the windows enable you to relish the spectacular views firsthand. If you'd rather be outside, try the garden terrace. Modest and relaxed (no linens, no tablecloths, no fancy silverware), the mountain lodge–style dining room features open wood-beamed ceilings, wood sculptures, and leafy plants. Service is friendly and efficient, and the kitchen does a fair job with its selection of Pacific Rim dishes. We especially enjoyed the light Thai spring rolls and the mouthwatering Kula onion and tomato salad. (Bring breath mints!) After you've eaten your fill, wander through the restaurant's expansive herb and vegetable garden, where the chef hand-picks garnishes for every meal. **Haleakala Highway (Highway 377); (808) 878-1535, (800) 233-1535; www.maui.net/~kullodge; inexpensive to moderate; breakfast, lunch, and dinner daily.**

Romantic Suggestion: Kula Lodge also has five rustic overnight accommodations (inexpensive to moderate) that are worth mentioning. Not intended to be fancy, these modestly appointed chalets have private porches and queen-size beds; one even has a fireplace; and some share the restaurant's magnificent view.

Outdoor Kissing

❀❀❀❀ **HALEAKALA NATIONAL PARK, Kula** Extending from the summit of Mount Haleakala ("House of the Sun") eastward to the southern coast, Haleakala National Park links Haleakala Crater and the Kipahulu Coast near Hana. You'll have to reach both of these areas (the crater and the coast) separately since there are no roads linking them. The park was originally created to preserve the spectacular beauty of Haleakala Volcano, but recent land acquisitions have helped to protect the surrounding delicate ecosystems of Kipahulu Valley, the scenic pools along 'Ohe'o Gulch, and the splendid coastline.

Nothing is more spectacular than witnessing sunrise at 10,000 feet from the top of Haleakala Crater. Unfortunately, this is no secret, and everyone else on the island has the same idea (including those on the downhill bicycle excursions). The never-ending line of buses and cars on this windy, fog-shrouded road at 4 A.M. is nothing short of astonishing. This extinct volcanic crater is definitely worth the drive, but there are other, less crowded times to view Haleakala's splendor. Sunset, when the weather is more apt to be clear and the views are endless, is exceptional. Don't forgo a trip to Haleakala if the weather looks stormy—this can be the best and most thrilling time of all to see the crater, mainly because nobody else is on the road and the cloud formations above the crater shroud the area in mystery and beauty. **(808) 572-4400; www.nps.gov/hale; $10 admission fee per car, $5 per person for hikers and bikers for a seven-day pass.** *Call for directions and additional information.*

Romantic Warning: Take your time and drive cautiously up the long, winding road that leads to Haleakala Crater; local ranchers let their cattle graze and roam freely on the mountain's steep, grassy slopes. Cows cross the road at their leisure and don't bother to look both ways. Also, it can get very cold up here at sunrise or dusk; expect (and prepare for) 30-degree temperatures. It does warm up during the day, so wear layers of clothing you can shed as the sun covers the earth.

East Maui

Hana

The road to heavenly Hana has saved this remote section of Maui from becoming overdeveloped—or, indeed, developed at all. More than any other area on the major islands, this is the way Hawaii used to be. The best way to describe the excursion to Hana by car is, "grueling." With more than 600 hairpin turns, blind corners, and falling rocks (and fruit), the journey can test the skills and patience of the driver. The unpredictable road repairs, which cause unbelievable backups, are another hazard, as are the locals who drive right up on your bumper and stay there. (Hint: Pull over and let them pass!) Despite these conditions, almost 2,000 people in hundreds of cars arrive daily, including sightseeing vans by the dozens.

What could be enthralling enough to attract such a caravan? The main highlight is the **SEVEN POOLS** ('Ohe'o Gulch), a freshwater swimming hole with a cascading waterfall and views of the endless Pacific beyond. This is the kind of scenery most of us see only in the movies. Also, the drive itself is a wondrous journey through a rain forest, replete with remarkable panoramas (see Outdoor Kissing).

Is Hana worth the trip? This pristine town of only a few hundred people, with tropical surroundings and staggering views of the countryside and ocean, makes an enchanting backdrop for a heart-stirring getaway. If you come early enough (allow two to five hours for the drive from most points on the island) or late enough in the day and stay at least a night or two, it is more than worth the drive. Besides, there are many other spots to discover in addition to the Seven Pools. **HAMOA BEACH** is a lovely gray-sand beach in the town center; **WAILUA FALLS**, seven miles outside of town, is a cascading waterfall that ends in a clear blue pool. **WAINAPANAPA STATE PARK** offers a black-sand beach, cobalt blue waters, and camping. Here, an ancient footpath winds along the rugged

Watch out for falling fruit when you drive that convertible down the road to Hana. Guava juice takes on a whole new meaning when you're traveling at 30 m.p.h.

coastline, passing blowholes and sea caves. From all perspectives, Hana is probably the most romantic part of Maui.

Romantic Note: Hana doesn't offer much in the way of dining or shopping; the outdoors— and little else—is the attraction here. The only restaurant and major accommodations in town are at the beautiful **HOTEL HANA-MAUI** (see Hotel/Bed and Breakfast Kissing). Other lodgings include home and condominium rentals, and a couple of bed and breakfasts. Bring a picnic with you, as well as towels and swimwear, so you can take a plunge in the waters, both fresh and salt, when the mood hits.

Romantic Suggestion: On your way to and from Hana, consider stopping at the popular **MAMA'S FISH HOUSE** (799 Poho Place, Paia; 808-579-8488; expensive to very expensive) for lunch or dinner. The casual wood interior has an unpretentiousness about it that's refreshing, and the kitchen has consistently served great fresh fish dishes for more than 30 years. The view of the water and nearby rocky beach is dazzling, but you may see stars when the big bill arrives.

Hotel/Bed and Breakfast Kissing

❧❧❧ **EKENA, Hana** A long, steep driveway leads you to the door of this stately contemporary home perched high on a hillside. Nine acres of verdant tropical landscaping enfolds the spacious two-story redwood home, which surveys panoramic 360-degree views of the surrounding emerald hills and the Pacific Ocean in the far distance. Although Ekena can accommodate up to eight people, the first priority here is privacy; the house is rented out to only one party at a time, even if there are only two of you.

Sunshine cascades through skylights in the 2,600-square-foot upper unit, which is slightly more spacious and appropriately more expensive than the smaller, lower unit. Aside from space, the units are almost identical. Both have an abundance of tropical bouquets, plush cream-colored carpeting, very plain but comfortable furnishings, and a wraparound deck that allows you to take full advantage of the breathtaking views. There's also a TV/VCR and washer/dryer in each unit to make you feel at home, as well as a full kitchen (no microwave). Be sure to bring your own food, since Hana doesn't offer much in the way of dining or grocery shopping. **(808) 248-7047; www.maui.net/~ekena; moderate to very expensive; minimum-stay requirement.**

❧❧❧ **HAMOA BAY BUNGALOW, Hana** Follow the Balinese statues and artifacts through the banana trees and palm fronds to find this charming cottage elevated above it all. Built on the site of an ancient Hawaiian village, Hamoa Bay Bungalow retains a "spirit of place" and exudes a meditative ambience. Upstairs, a king-size bamboo bed fits comfortably in the 600-square-foot cottage, which also offers a full kitchen, private bath, TV/VCR, and a discerning collection of movies. French doors open onto a screened porch with a double Jacuzzi tub that overlooks enormous Java plum trees, guava trees, *lau'wae* ferns, papaya and banana trees, and glimpses of the ocean. (Hamoa Beach is a mere five-minute walk through a grove of African tulip trees.) Downstairs, a lovely open-air lounging area (the upstairs section provides the cover) awaits, complete with wind chimes and comfortable furnishings. It's the ideal place to enjoy your breakfast basket of fruits and muffins. **Hana Highway; (808) 248-7884; moderate.**

❤❤❤ **HANA ALII HOLIDAYS, Hana** A handful of tropical vacation rentals, including cottages and homes in a range of sizes and conditions, are available through the Hana Alii Holidays rental service. Be specific about what you're looking for when booking your reservation, because each of these properties is romantic for different reasons: Some have stunning ocean views; others are secluded among palm trees; several even have the luxury of a Jacuzzi tub, kitchenette, TV, and washer/dryer. Set up housekeeping in the property of your choice and soak up Hana's tropical bliss.

We especially liked **HONOKALANI COTTAGE**, a charming wood-frame bungalow with a wraparound deck that takes full advantage of the ocean view and the lush tropical setting. We found the open one-room layout delightful. Another standout is **HALE HANA BAY**, a petite oceanfront cottage with imposing views from the deck and living room. Comfort abounds, and all the amenities are here, including privacy and verdant surroundings. **(808) 248-7742, (800) 548-0478 mainland; www.hana alii.com; inexpensive to very expensive.**

❤❤❤ **HANA HALE MALAMALAMA, Hana** Well-known author Tom Robbins spoke from experience when he described Hana Hale Malamalama as "somewhere between Eden and Paradise." (He's a regular here.) Nestled beside a recently restored ancient Hawaiian fishpond teeming with *awa*, mullet, and koi, Hana Hale Malamalama offers a truly unique experience with three different accommodations. The three-bedroom/three-bath Royal Lodge is situated in a lovely, circular cottage, originally built and designed out of *nara* wood in the Philippines and painstakingly transported and rebuilt in Hana. Surrounded by lush tropical foliage, the lodge is best suited for larger groups, but still delights with Balinese-style bamboo and teak furnishings, private decks, a Jacuzzi tub, and a complete kitchen.

Sheltered by a *kamani* tree and coconut palms, the second accommodation, called Treehouse Cottage, has lovely views of the fishpond and Hana Bay. Pyramid-shaped skylights allow lots of radiant sun into the bedroom and living areas, and a large whirlpool tub designed for two is perfect for couples looking for unrivaled privacy. Similar to the Treehouse is the Pondside Bungalow, which also has a Jacuzzi tub as well as a direct view of the Pacific. Breakfast is not provided with your stay, but the private, fully equipped kitchen in every unit makes it convenient for you to take turns serving breakfast in bed to each other. **Reservations through Hawaii's Best Bed and Breakfasts, (808) 885-4550, (800) 262-9912 mainland; www.maui.net/~hanahale; moderate to very expensive.**

Romantic Alternative: New to the Hana bed and breakfast scene is **THE BAMBOO INN** (reservations through Hawaii's Best Bed and Breakfasts, 808-885-4550, 800-262-9912 mainland; moderate to expensive), an oceanfront accommodation adjacent to **HANA HALE MALAMALAMA** and operated by the same owners. In keeping with its name, The Bamboo Inn offers plenty of bamboo accents from tightly woven matting to the rafters above. Marble baths and kitchens as well as coconut-wood floors further accentuate the natural beauty. Of the three guest rooms available in this home, the Villa has the romantic advantage of a Jacuzzi tub on its deck, as well as a living room and full kitchen. The upstairs Master Suite offers a kitchen, private deck, and a marble-tiled shower. The less expensive of the threesome is the smaller One-Bedroom Studio with a separate entrance and kitchenette. No matter where you stay, new Balinese teak furnishings adorn each room and a continental breakfast is served in the courtyard each morning.

❤❤❤ HANA PLANTATION HOUSES, Hana

Known for its exceptionally discriminating selection of fabulous cottages and homes, Hana Plantation Houses is a reliable rental agency in the Hana area. You can't go wrong with any of the properties, all of which are distinctive and unique. Many of these homes are spacious, with grand views and tropical settings. Fully equipped kitchens, TV/VCRs, outdoor Jacuzzi tubs, cozy living rooms, full baths, and private lanais are some of the amenities available. This company even offers a solar-powered cottage near Hana Bay. **(808) 248-8975, (800) 228-4262; www.hana-maui.com; inexpensive to very expensive; minimum-stay requirement.**

Unrated HOTEL HANA-MAUI, Hana

Undoubtedly, the Hotel Hana-Maui deserves a four-lip rating; however, when we visited, the place was for sale, management was in disarray, and part of the resort was closed down. We suggest you call to see if new owners have taken over.

If not, be prepared for disorganization. In the meanwhile, this review remains unchanged, with the hope that new ownership will only improve upon this fantastic setting.

For all intents and purposes, this is literally the only game in town when it comes to anything in the way of hotel accommodations and restaurants, and it has been that way for years. Inaccessibility is the main, if not only, reason for the lack of competition, because everything else about this area is spectacular.

More than 50 years old, the Hotel Hana-Maui was once owned by millionairess Carolyn Hunt. Her exquisite taste and style is still apparent in the 93 sumptuous bungalows and cottages scattered over 66 acres of lush Hana hillside. Plush oversize furnishings, comfy beds, roomy baths with walk-in tile showers and soaking tubs, and floor-to-ceiling sliding glass doors that open to private patios make this a perfect getaway. Who would have expected such polish and sophistication in remote little Hana? Many of the units also have handsome lawn furniture, views, and a hot tub. Don't search for a TV or radio in your room: You really are far removed from technology here. (There is a phone, but at least some of the potentially intrusive technology is absent.) A wonderful large pool area overlooks rolling lawns and the ocean in the distance.

Isolation, serenity, and unrivaled luxury are what make this place so captivating. You'd be hard put to find anything quite like the Hotel Hana-Maui anywhere else in Hawaii, or anywhere else in the world. **Hana Highway; (808) 248-8211, (800) 321-HANA; unbelievably expensive and beyond; recommended wedding site.**

Romantic Warning: The hotel's only drawback is its dining room, which serves mediocre food at unreasonably high prices. It wouldn't be such a big deal if there were other restaurants to choose from, but this is it. With room rates starting at $395 a night, the Hotel Hana-Maui should try to provide an on-site restaurant that complements the outstanding accommodations.

Outdoor Kissing

❤❤❤❤ **THE ROAD TO HANA, Hana** During your vacation on Maui, you may wonder where all the untouched, lush, tropical landscapes are—the ones that always pop into your mind when you think of the Hawaiian Islands. Wonder no more. Travel on winding Highway 360 (better known as the Hana Highway), on the northern side of the island, and you'll find them.

The road to Hana is one area on Maui where the natural beauty of the landscape rules and commercial development has not yet bulldozed its way through. Depending on the amount of traffic heading to paradise with you (or depending on your desire to stop and study the scenery more intimately), the trip can take between two and five hours. There are more than 100 one-lane bridges, 617 hairpin turns, and too many steep drop-offs to count. Abundant foliage lines the road in a rainbow of greens. Below, the thunderous surf crashes against jet black lava rock. Picturesque waterfalls, freshwater pools (swim at your own risk), and dirt trails that wind under overgrown branches are some of the heavenly sights along the way.

Despite all this surrounding splendor, be forewarned. The big—and we mean *big*—drawback of this daylong excursion is the bumper-to-bumper procession of tour vans and rental cars. With everyone traveling the same road to paradise, the trip can take a lot longer than it should. Also, the actual town of Hana is a bit of a disappointment once you get there, and you may feel let down by the lack of sights, restaurants, and accommodations.

We suggest you not bother to stop in Hana, but instead continue on for about 30 minutes to the stunning **SEVEN POOLS**. These precious freshwater pools are all fed by connecting waterfalls that begin high in the hills of Maui. Each one gently cascades into the one below it, until the last one spills out into the awaiting open mouth of the Pacific. These natural beauties are your true reward for making it this far, and a definite must-see for anyone visiting Maui. Unfortunately, the Seven Pools are also on everyone else's list of sights, so this is not always the best place for undisturbed time together. Nonetheless, the pools are exquisite and undeniably refreshing after the long, hot drive. *Starting at the town of Paia, the Hana Highway (Highway 360) winds 44 miles to the town of Hana.*

"Let him kiss me with

the kisses of his mouth:

for thy love is better than wine."

The Song of Solomon

Kauai

Haena * * Princeville
   Hanalei *
      * Kilauea
         * Anahola
Wailua Homesteads
         *
* Mana   * Kapaa
         * Wailua
      Lihue *
* Waimea
      Poipu
         *

Kauai

It's no wonder Kauai is called the "Garden Isle." Kauai's landscape is sheer poetry, with burgeoning fruit trees of every kind, brilliant tropical flowers, fertile valleys, razor-sharp cliffs, breathtaking mountains and canyons, and pristine sandy beaches. Bougainvillea blooms in colorful abundance along the roadside, palm fronds sway high atop coconut trees, and acres upon acres of sugarcane rustle in the trade winds.

Kauai is a friendly oasis for those seeking refuge from the hectic pace of the real world, while still offering a wealth of activities. This is the island of choice for hikers, bikers, and outdoor enthusiasts of all types and ages. Lovers looking for quiet beauty can kayak through **HANALEI NATIONAL WILDLIFE REFUGE**, while those with more active intentions will appreciate **NA PALI COAST STATE PARK** on the lush North Shore, and **WAIMEA CANYON STATE PARK** and **KOKEE STATE PARK** on the dry, desert-like west side of the island. Treks through these magnificent parks vary in difficulty and range from one or two hours to several days. To obtain maps and information in advance, write the **DIVISION OF FORESTRY AND WILDLIFE** (3060 Eiwa Street, Room 306, Lihue, HI 96766; 808-274-3433). Include a ten-inch-by-13-inch self-addressed envelope with $1.01 return postage for a hiking map of Kauai.

Although many years have passed since that fateful day in September 1992, locals still talk about when Kauai's tranquil island paradise was ravished by the most devastating natural disaster in Hawaii's recorded history: Hurricane Iniki. Just about everyone (and everything) on the island was affected by the storm's reign of destruction. Kauai was literally defoliated in the storm, and nearly 50 percent of the island's homes were damaged, if not altogether destroyed.

Fortunately, Mother Nature and the human spirit are resilient, and within months the flora and fauna, as well as tourists, began to return. Only seven months after the hurricane, Kauai's lush landscape revealed few traces of the hurricane's ruin. Extensive community efforts rebuilt homes and replaced roofs, but not all buildings were so quickly replaced. During our most recent visit, one major South Shore hotel had just reopened and some Poipu bridges still showed signs of destruction.

Don't leave home without insect repellent. Hawaii's trade winds tend to keep bugs on the move, but in the more tropical, jungle-like areas, mosquitoes are a pesky problem.

Hurricane discussion aside, Kauai is truly the island of choice for lovers who want a taste of paradise. Debates continue over which Hawaiian island offers the most romantic opportunities, but in terms of peacefulness, privacy, and natural beauty, Kauai is number one.

South Shore

Kauai's South Shore is famous for its extraordinary sand beaches; sunny, desert-like landscape; and luxury resort hotels. Much of this area was hit hard by Hurricane Iniki, but now most businesses are up and running (although one major hotel has just recently reopened, six years after the storm). Poipu, as you'll quickly discover, isn't short on condominium complexes. Luckily, most here are quite nice and well maintained, unlike some other areas of Kauai. If cuddling in a condo isn't your style, there are also several fancy hotels to choose from, along with some lip-worthy restaurants to try.

Poipu

Hotel/Bed and Breakfast Kissing

❀❀❀ **EMBASSY VACATION RESORT—POIPU POINT, Poipu** Situated on the sunnier side of Kauai, these 217 luxury condo units are, for the most part, run like a hotel. Currently, many of the units are on a time-share plan, and eventually they all will be. This shouldn't be a problem; the management promises that the time-share sales department won't hunt you down during your stay to convince you to buy—that is, unless you want them to.

Unlike condos elsewhere, each one here is decorated similarly, with plush carpets in cream and beige tones, comfy sofas in cool greens and sea blues, extra-large master bedrooms with down comforters in classic prints, and full kitchens with granite countertops. The spacious bathrooms sport double vanities, tiled tubs, and walk-in showers. As an added comfort, each unit also has air-conditioning—a rare find in many condos. Depending on your budget, choose a one- or two-bedroom Garden View, Partial Ocean View, Ocean View, or Oceanfront Room. However, be forewarned that even the lowly Garden View Rooms are in the very expensive price range. For the best water views, request a unit in buildings No. 3, 4, 6, 8, or 9.

The ten buildings that comprise this resort are spread out nicely and surrounded by large, open grounds. While the landscape isn't as mature as some of the area's other hotels, the terraced ponds filled with koi and lily pads, waterfalls descending into clear pools, swaying palms, and numerous pathways are certainly beautiful in their own right. Unfortunately, there's no swimmable beach fronting the hotel; however, the Embassy has done the next best thing by creating an artificial sandy beach next to the large pool and two Jacuzzi tubs. Also, you won't find a restaurant on the property but, again, the Embassy comes through with a complimentary continental breakfast served poolside each morning. Such bonuses continue, too. Around sundown, enjoy a cocktail reception that's on the house. **1613 Pe'e Road; (808) 742-1888, (800) 426-3350 mainland; www. embassyvacationresorts.com; very expensive to unbelievably expensive.**

❤❤❤ GLORIA'S SPOUTING HORN BED AND BREAKFAST, Poipu

Most residents of Kauai, if they were around during 1992's Hurricane Iniki, have a stormy story to recount. Gloria's Spouting Horn Bed and Breakfast was completely demolished by the hurricane's torrential force. Now, after serious reconstruction, a stunning new cedar home proudly stands at water's edge, challenging Mother Nature to blow a furious storm this way again.

Hammocks sway between tall palms in the nicely landscaped front yard, and waves collide with the black-rock shoreline in back. An inviting lap pool also resides next to the beach and is a relaxing spot for lazy, Hawaiian afternoons. All three cozy guest rooms enjoy this magnificent ocean scene. The handsome first-floor suite (appropriately nicknamed the Love Nest) features a grand bent-willow canopy bed and intricate bent-willow furniture. The two suites upstairs have vaulted ceilings and a more traditional flair, with brass headboards and floral linens. Lanais, wet bars, microwaves, small refrigerators, and private baths with deep, Japanese-style soaking tubs in every suite add to the comfort and convenience of your stay. An extended continental breakfast is served in the main living/dining room each morning; trays are provided so you can take your goodies back to your room if the two of you, like most lovebirds, prefer to visit only with each other in the morning. **4464 Lawai Beach Road; (808) 742-6995; www.best.com/~travel/gloria; expensive; minimum-stay requirement.**

❤❤❟ GRANTHAM RESORTS, Poipu

Grantham Resorts is one of the many vacation rental companies on Kauai that offers a varied selection of luxury condominiums and private homes. The casually adorned **WAIKOMO STREAM VILLAS**, the more plush **NIHI KAI VILLAS**, and the elegant

MAKAHUENA, among other condominium complexes managed by Grantham Resorts, are spacious and pleasant. All provide one-, two-, and three-bedroom suites, full kitchens, view lanais, swimming pools, tennis courts, and easy access to nearby golf courses. The only thing missing in most rentals is air-conditioning.

Of the three properties mentioned above, our favorite units are those at the 60-unit Makahuena. These condos feature light, bright interiors; striking decor; and a fabulous ocean bluff location. The more specific you are about requesting a suite with ocean views and attractive decor, the happier you will be once you get there. With prices topping out at $288 for a two-bedroom deluxe oceanfront unit in high season, this is one of the better luxury deals on the island.

If you're in the mood for ultimate waterfront seclusion, consider one of Grantham's vacation homes. The **HALE KAHAKAI PUNAHELE** (very expensive), a two-bedroom oceanfront home, is an ideal choice, but scrap the seclusion part. This blue-and-white, two-story charmer across from Poipu Beach is so delightful that it attracts a lot of looks (not good when you want to smooch on the lanai). Prices of homes vary, depending on the style, amenities, and location. Many of these homes are simply spectacular and couldn't be more ideal for your enamored encounter on Kauai. **3176 Poipu Road, Suite 1; (808) 742-2000, (800) 742-1412 mainland; www.grantham-resorts.com; moderate to very expensive.**

❀❀❀ **HALE NAI'A, Poipu** *Hale Nai'a* means "House of the Dolphins" and, if you're lucky, you may see a few of these gentle creatures from your oceanfront lanai. Even if you don't, just sitting on the private patio with the Pacific only a few feet away is, in itself, a picture of paradise.

Stroll down a quiet residential street to find this new two-story vacation home, complete with blue-tiled ceramic roof, perfectly trimmed lawn, and bountiful displays of white ginger and bird-of-paradise. A concrete pathway, embossed with leaf motifs, leads you into the modestly decorated, Hawaiian-theme interior. Hale Nai'a comes complete with all you need in a home, including two bedrooms, a washer/dryer, a full kitchen, and a garage.

Your biggest decision of the day will be deciding which porch to lounge on. The large upstairs bedroom has a private lanai looking onto the rocky beach, while the covered downstairs lanai faces the backyard lawn and offers instant access to the beach via a private stairway. Well-tended homes border each side, but the residents can't see you, and vice versa. So sit on the porch, sip a cool drink, and kiss your sweetheart while enjoying the surrounding splendor. **Reservations through Places in Paradise, (808) 742-1803, (800) 838-6637 (access code 22); www.kauaiocean front.com; very expensive; minimum-stay requirement.**

❤❤❤ **HALE PILIALOHA, Poipu** This airy Cape Cod–style home, located at the south end of Poipu, is exceedingly charming and romantic. Myriad flowers generously embrace the semiprivate brick patio entrance and most of the home's white exterior. Simply entering and exiting this adorable location is an eye-pleasing experience.

Dark gray slate floors, crisp white-paneled walls, exposed-beam ceilings, and country furnishings fill the spacious interior. Two bedrooms are available, although the master bedroom is clearly the best choice. A king-size four-poster bed with floral linens; a large, white-tiled bathroom; and French doors leading into the backyard deck and garden make the master bedroom thoroughly inviting. Next to the entryway is the second bedroom; it holds twin beds, which makes it decidedly less romantic than the master bedroom. A second full white, tiled bathroom is located off the hallway.

On the other side of the entry is a sitting area with cozy couches and cable TV, and just beyond that lies a full, open, white-tiled kitchen, imparting a fresh look that complements the entire house. Bright colors peek at you through every window here, making this home a highly alluring find. **Reservations through Rosewood Bed and Breakfast, (808) 822-5216; www.rosewoodkauai.com; moderate; no credit cards; minimum-stay requirement.**

❤❤ **HONU KAI VACATION VILLAS, Poipu** Generally the term "villas" conjures up images of regal elegance and expansive plush accommodations. There is nothing remotely resembling that here at Honu Kai; the four units are more suburban townhomes than châteaus or manored estates. That isn't a drawback, just a name clarification. What you can expect are exceptionally spacious rooms with impressive, sparkling ocean views and all the necessities for setting up home for a carefree island holiday.

Four attractively outfitted villas, all with private entrances, surround a small courtyard swimming pool and spa. Each unit is attractively appointed with slate floors, floor-to-ceiling windows, solid koa accents, and comfortable wicker furnishing. Fully equipped modern kitchens, large bedrooms, spacious living rooms, and washer/dryers add up to a convenient home away from home. One-, two-, or three-bedroom units are available; two of the units are roomy enough for six people. With this much elbow room, two romantically inclined couples can travel together and get a real bargain!

A wonderful bonus are the breakfast fixings provided. You will find your unit's kitchen well stocked with cereals, juices, fruits, and muffins. Equally impressive is the property's location across the street from the rocky shoreline of the Pacific, with the very popular and very swimmable **BRENNECKES BEACH** only about 100 yards west of the property. Don't worry about overcrowded conditions at the beach; few people venture down here, so privacy is ensured. While Hona Kai isn't elegant, there are still many refreshing reasons why you may want to call this place home while you're on the island of Kauai. **1871 Pe'e Road; (808) 742-9155, (800) 854-8363; www.honukai.com; moderate to unbelievably expensive; minimum-stay requirement.**

❤❤❤❤ **HYATT REGENCY KAUAI, Poipu** When one speaks of extravagant hotels on Kauai, the Hyatt Regency immediately comes to mind. Grandiose style is guaranteed at this beachfront Poipu hotel, starting with the stunning lobby, where a mini-jungle complete with colorful parrots will capture your attention. Enveloped by 50 acres of lush landscape and fronting a sandy beach, this palatial resort's design is reminiscent of Hawaii in the 1920s, with green-tiled roofs and white stucco walls.

The Hyatt claims that it gets the most sunshine of all the hotels on Kauai, which is a truism for the entire South Shore. Guests who want to take full advantage of the weather can do so in style: The Hyatt offers a five-acre saltwater lagoon, three pools (one winds through the tropical garden landscape while another has slides, waterfalls, and Jacuzzi tubs), a full-service health and fitness spa, a nearby golf course, tennis courts, and riding stables. In the evening, check out the oceanview lounge and restaurants where you can hold hands while watching the waves.

Yes, the Hyatt really is as extravagant as it sounds! You could actually plan a couple of days around the dining options here: Enjoy the incredible breakfast buffet at the **ILIMA TERRACE**; after a day of sunning and swimming, savor sunset and cocktails at the **SEAVIEW TERRACE**; or have a relaxed dinner at **TIDEPOOLS** or the more formal **DONDERO'S** (see Restaurant Kissing for reviews of all).

Six hundred guest suites with tasteful plantation-style furnishings, attractive tiled baths, and muted floral linens provide a luxurious, albeit hotel-style, retreat. Rooms without ocean views are less costly and face the majestic Haupu mountain range, while oceanview rooms survey the sprawling tropical grounds and overlook the sparkling waters of Keoneloa Bay. Without a doubt, the Hyatt is one of Kauai's few full-scale resorts, and certainly a wonderful place to make your romantic dreams come true. **1571 Poipu Road; (808) 742-1234, (800) 233-1234; www.hyatt.com; very expensive to unbelievably expensive; recommended wedding site.**

❧❧ **KAUAI COVE COTTAGES, Poipu** Hidden away on a quiet residential street, these three vacation rental units are clean, bright, and perfectly suited for a couple in love. What more could you ask for? How about two delightful owners who welcome you with a genuine *aloha* spirit not often found in the big hotels and sprawling condo complexes?

The self-contained rooms reside side by side in one long building, each with its separate entrance via a front patio. Each has a fully equipped kitchen for preparing your meals, a queen-size bed, TV/VCR and CD player, dimming lights, a ceiling fan, and a small fenced-in, private lanai out back. Our favorite is the middle unit because of its large, walk-in slate shower that fronts a window looking into your own little backyard. Popular beaches and snorkeling areas are within walking distance, and behind the cottages is an estuary, popular with the local sea turtles. **2672 Puuholo Road No. A; (808) 742-2562, (800) 624-9945; www.kauai cove.com; inexpensive.**

❧❧❧ **KIAHUNA PLANTATION, Poipu** Kiahuna Plantation ranks as one of Poipu's larger condo complexes, with 333 units housed on 35 acres of manicured lawns and gardens. The two-story white buildings, accented by chocolate-colored shutters, offer an array of view choices, ranging from beautiful garden vistas to three types of ocean views. As views differ, so do the rooms. Every comfortably sized one- or two-bedroom unit is decorated to the owner's liking, but most are simply adorned with rattan furniture and pale tropical prints. All feature full kitchens, dining and living rooms facing a garden or ocean view, private lanais, and ceiling fans (but no air-conditioning).

Besides the lack of air-conditioning, the only other disadvantage is that the pool area is across the street, adjacent to the parking lot and tennis courts, far enough away to be a hassle. Fortunately, you can choose instead to visit the great stretch of sandy beach that fronts the property (a much more romantic option). **2253 Poipu Road; (808) 742-6411, (800) 688-7444; www.outrigger.com; moderate to unbelievably expensive; minimum-stay requirement; recommended wedding site.**

❧❧❧ **POIPU KAPILI, Poipu** Poipu may have condos on every corner, but you'll be hard pressed to find many that are as elegant, romantic, and spacious as these. One of our top kissable favorites in town, Poipu Kapili has only 60 condominium units, a number that lends an intimacy to the surroundings and makes for a crowd-free pool. Seven low-rise buildings are designed in the traditional plantation style with double-pitched roofs and white exteriors. Only a road divides the condos from the beach, so most rooms have some kind of water view, be it peekaboo or direct.

All units are extremely spacious (1,200 square feet for the one-bedrooms) and decorated with Hawaiian-style wicker or rattan furnishings. Accents, such as mahogany wood shutters, moldings, and kitchen cabinets, as well as tiled entryways, kitchens, and bathrooms, add a sense of refinement not seen in other condo complexes. Each unit comes with a TV/VCR, stereo, full modern kitchen, and a private lanai. There's no air-conditioning, but trade winds here are quite reliable.

Romantics should request a two-bedroom deluxe oceanfront unit or go all out with an ultraroomy penthouse suite. Uncompromising in space, the two-bedroom penthouse we stayed in (No. 28) just might coax you into staying inside all day with its huge Jacuzzi tub, a double-headed shower, and two lanais the size of most hotel rooms. (There's even elevator access to this suite.) Embellished by manicured lawns and tropical flowers, the five acres of property holds lighted tennis courts, a herb garden for guests' picking pleasure, and a tranquil courtyard pool perfect for reading, relaxing, and romancing. **2221 Kapili Road; (808) 742-6449, (800) 443-7714; www.poipukapili.com; moderate to unbelievably expensive; minimum-stay requirement.**

❧ **POIPU SHORES OCEANFRONT CONDOMINIUMS, Poipu** From its vantage point on a black-lava rock cliff, this relatively small condominium complex offers incredible ocean vistas. The 36 units include one-, two-, or three-bedroom suites, with only two view categories available: oceanfront and deluxe oceanfront (the deluxe oceanfront is roomier). All have a full kitchen, washer/dryer, and TV (which you probably won't watch since the ocean view is so hypnotic). As is the case with so many individually owned condos, each one is decorated differently and some are more stylish than others. Hawaiian-style rattan furnishings and pastel print linens fill some units, while others have a more homespun feel, with the owners' personal knickknacks on display. Hopefully, the wonderful location will detour you from concentrating on the dated exterior, the worn carpets, and the rickety elevator that takes you to your room. There is no direct beach access from the complex, but a lovely pool area overlooking the ocean lets you hear the roar of the surf below. If a direct ocean view is all you need to spark the flames of romance, Poipu Shores Oceanfront Condominiums delivers. **1775 Pe'e Road; (808) 742-7700, (800) 367-5004; www.castle-group.com; expensive to very expensive.**

❤❤ **SHERATON KAUAI RESORT, Poipu** One of the last hotels to reopen after Hurricane Iniki, the Sheraton Kauai has the advantage of being the new kid on the beach. All 413 rooms are fresh and bright with pleasant, comfortable appointments and high ceilings. You'll find the typical array of room amenities, along with air-conditioning, large lanais, and views that range from direct oceanfront to lovely garden vistas. While the Sheraton is quite a nice hotel, its overall look is on the ho-hum side compared to other luxury hotels on the islands. But don't get us wrong: The Sheraton has plenty to offer, including a fantastic waterfront location, two swimming pools with waterfalls, tennis courts, tropical gardens dotted with koi ponds, and a beach activities center.

Five dining options at the Sheraton will keep your stomachs happy. SHELLS (moderate to expensive; breakfast and dinner daily), an expansive, high-ceiling restaurant specializing in continental and Hawaiian cuisine, stands out as the most kiss-worthy. Sit close to the tall windows or on the patio to soak in panoramic views of Poipu Beach and the Pacific. Those celebrating a special occasion can request in advance a Romantic Dinner for Two (expensive). Your own private table, set up on the quiet, oceanfront lawn, allows you to enjoy the Hawaiian evening in relative peace. **2440 Hoonani Road; (808) 742-1661, (800) 782-9488; www.sheraton-kauai.com; very expensive to unbelievably expensive; recommended wedding site.**

❤❤❤❤ **SUNSET MAKAI HALE, Poipu** You will be engulfed by a sense of utter peacefulness and evocative beauty once you set eyes on this creatively designed vacation home. After admiring the Asian-style exterior, venture inside where more beauty awaits. Cedar ceilings and walls are accented with rough ocean-rock columns, and dark brick floors lead from one exquisite room to the next. Tall floor-to-ceiling windows with breathtaking views of the Pacific surround you as you meander through the formal dining room, full kitchen, living room, and two bedrooms on the main floor. Each window is strategically placed so that the water and sky are always in view. Both bedrooms are appointed with plush ivory carpeting, minimalist decor, Asian-style antiques pleasantly mixed with contemporary furnishings, king-size beds, cable TVs, and stereos.

The upstairs bedroom is the most desirable and private of the three, with exposed beams, cathedral ceilings, towering windows on each side of the room, and a bathroom with even *more* windows, which let you feel as though you're bathing in the raging ocean itself. Outside next to the foamy white waves, you'll find a narrow lap pool bordered by a spacious lanai and surrounded by lush green shrubbery, rustling palm trees, and soft grass. **(808) 742-1161; unbelievably expensive and beyond; minimum-stay requirement; recommended wedding site.**

Romantic Note: There is certainly enough space to share this home with one or two other couples, or even the whole family. Without splitting the cost this way, the price really becomes unbearable.

❦❦❦❦ **WHALERS COVE, Poipu** When brochures make much of "oceanfront luxury," we get suspicious. Advertising executives tend to throw this term around rather indiscriminately, and more often than not, the property they are describing is neither oceanfront nor luxurious. The Whalers Cove brochure not only boasts of oceanfront luxury, it also claims to be romantic, unpretentious, and breathtaking—some pretty big britches to fill, in our opinion. Much to our amazement, these stunning two-bedroom condominiums offer all that, in addition to being tranquil, private, and absolutely gorgeous!

Fourteen million dollars were spent on renovating and refurbishing the two curved buildings that hold 39 condominiums units (23 of which are available for rent). Many of the guest rooms look as if they dropped directly off a page of *House Beautiful* or *Architectural Digest*, with marble floors, high ceilings, sumptuous decorator furnishings, Jacuzzi tubs, bathrooms as big as bedrooms, gourmet kitchens, and beautifully framed art. Others are more simply adorned in white to capture the colors of the setting sun. Nonetheless they are all stylish and sophisticated, from the koa wood–trimmed kitchen cabinets to the spacious, private, tiled lanais. Just as the brochure promises, every unit truly is oceanfront, so you can enjoy the sight and sound of the waves crashing against the black-rock beach below. Some units also overlook the attractive seaside pool and Jacuzzi tub, so if you want direct oceanfront, request a room in Building 1. The majority of condos have no air-conditioning since ocean breezes keep temperatures just right.

Now for a reality check. All of this loveliness doesn't come cheap (rooms start at $295 a night in the low season). But compared to what other nearby resorts and condominium properties charge for accommodations that are a lot less elegant, the price is relatively reasonable. Whalers Cove is a truly romantic getaway on this magical isle. **2640 Puuholo Road; (808) 742-7571, (800) 225-2683; www.whalers-cove.com; very expensive; minimum-stay requirement; recommended wedding site.**

Be sure to pack comfortable walking shoes. Sandals may not provide enough traction for the various hikes on each island.

Romantic Note: When booking your reservation, be specific about what you want in terms of decor and size (units range from 1,400 to 2,500 square feet). Also mention if you want the master bedroom facing the water. Specific units can't be held in advance, but if the gracious staff can get an idea of your taste and style, they should be able to place you in a room that will make the two of you as happy as clams.

Restaurant Kissing

❦❦❦ **THE BEACH HOUSE, Poipu** A beautiful location, by itself, is not enough to stir the heart or the palate. Thankfully, the Beach House restaurant combines a majestic setting with remarkable cuisine, creating one of the most satisfying dining experiences Kauai has to offer. The location is sheer bliss: Nestled on the sand, with the pounding surf only a few feet away, this window-clad restaurant offers stellar views of Hawaii's mesmerizing sunsets. Hold hands as you watch the fiery globe slip into the sea.

Once your meal arrives, however, your attention will be drawn to the culinary delights before you. Curried pumpkin bisque with cheese crisp and chive crème fraîche is sensational. Salmon with saffron-cilantro sauce over savory black lentils is brilliantly prepared, and linguine with roasted clams, asparagus, and Tuscan beans is exceptional. All your senses will be thrilled you came to this spot, especially if you make it in time for sunset. **5022 Lawai Beach Road; (808) 742-1424; moderate to expensive; dinner daily.**

❦❦❦ **DONDERO'S, Poipu** It's no surprise that Dondero's is full of intricate marble flooring, lovely green tilework with inlaid seashells, and colorful murals of the Mediterranean countryside. This level of opulence is typical of the incredible **HYATT REGENCY KAUAI** (see Hotel/Bed and Breakfast Kissing). Although prices are steep, the service at Dondero's is efficient, and you'll thoroughly enjoy savoring Kauai's finest Italian cuisine. Start off your meal with a delicious Gorgonzola, walnut, and apple salad; then move on to sautéed shrimp with lemon over spinach pasta, or sautéed chicken breast with Marsala and grapes. Top it all off with one of Dondero's scrumptious desserts, and you'll have a meal made in heaven. **1571 Poipu Road, at the Hyatt Regency Kauai; (808) 742-1234; www.hyatt.com; expensive; dinner Monday–Saturday.**

❦❦ **THE HOUSE OF SEAFOOD, Poipu** *Papio, a'u, moi, uhu.* No, it's not an ancient Hawaiian chant but, rather, some of the interesting fresh fish that appear on this restaurant's ever-changing menu. We give The House of Seafood extra credit for bringing hard-to-find Hawaiian fish to the table;

we only wish the presentation, accompanying sauces, and side dishes had more pizzazz and flavor.

Luckily, the open-air interior has some romantic flair with its soft, candlelit glow, vaulted ceilings (complete with a suspended outrigger canoe), lush plants hanging from the rafters, and tables set beside open windows. (However, the views of the tennis courts and condos below don't win any prizes.)

If you want to venture beyond ubiquitous mahi mahi, this is the place to do so, but stick to the simple preparations. If you'd rather stay with the familiar, choose between several surf 'n' turf combos, cioppino, seafood pastas, and tableside-prepared Caesar salad. Many desserts, such as bananas Foster or the chocolate delight, are made especially for two, so be sure to share in this sweet ending. **1941 Poipu Road; (808) 742-6433; expensive; dinner daily.**

❤❤ **ILIMA TERRACE, Poipu** At this al fresco restaurant, there's one cuddling couple you can't miss. On the large koi pond bordering the restaurant, a pair of mute swans swim, sun, and snack together, oblivious to the world around them. Watch as they go about their avian activities, while you and your sweetheart enjoy a bountiful breakfast, relaxed lunch, or romantic dinner.

Bird-watching isn't the only attraction at the Ilima Terrace (although birds are everywhere here). Spectacular ocean views are a selling feature of this breezy, open restaurant. High ceilings, weathered brass chandeliers, floral tablecloths, and wicker chairs set the mood for fresh, casual dining. The breakfast buffet is a cornucopia of tropical delights, and the lunch and dinner menus offer light and healthy dishes as well as unusual island treats. Try papaya and smoked tuna salad, or choose salmon broiled and simmered in sake and soy sauce. Top off your meal with a slice of coconut cream pie, and then make like two lovebirds and give each other a peck on the cheek. **1571 Poipu Road, at the Hyatt Regency Kauai; (808) 742-1234; www.hyatt.com; moderate; breakfast, lunch, and dinner daily.**

❤❤❤ **PIATTI RESTAURANT AND BAR, Poipu** Some of the most exquisite Italian cuisine on Kauai is set in the grace and splendor of the original Kiahuna Plantation manor house. A winding stone path enveloped by opulent tropical gardens leads up to this handsomely refurbished home-turned-restaurant. Wraparound floor-to-ceiling windows reveal an attractive, simply adorned series of dining rooms. Before going inside, venture to the back of the property, where the chef's gardens bloom with exotic herbs and succulent vegetables. This is the source of the kitchen's seasonings and bountiful array of vegetables that accompany every meal.

While the gardens are exemplary, the food surpasses any Italian yearnings you may have. Don't miss the generous portion of risotto simmered in veal stock with roasted chanterelle, shiitake, oyster, and porcini mushrooms, and topped with white truffle oil and shaved *grana padano*. Try the incredibly tender filet mignon wrapped in prosciutto, grilled and served with a red wine jus. Roasted marinated duckling with tangerine chutney, steamed jasmine rice, and vegetable spring roll is another delectable option. An evening at Piatti truly defines romantic bliss. **2253 Poipu Road; (808) 742-2216; moderate; dinner daily.**

❦❦ ROY'S POIPU BAR AND GRILL, Poipu Roy's restaurants have spread like wildfire over the Pacific Islands and beyond to the mainland. As at all the other locations, Roy's on Kauai showcases a casual but striking atmosphere, with marble-topped tables, shiny dark brown rattan chairs, track lighting, and bright artwork. Although the location in an outdoor shopping mall is less than amorous, once you have experienced the excellent service and delectable cuisine, you will see why Roy's restaurants have gained such popularity.

When it comes to the cuisine, each dish is a group effort, geographically speaking. Foodstuffs are from Hawaii, seasonings have Asian backgrounds, and the cooking technique is impeccably French. Everything on the menu looks so delicious, you'll want to order at least two appetizers, an entrée for each of you, and, of course, two desserts. Ordering just one item and sharing it can be fun at some restaurants, but that's hard to do at Roy's. Just sample the lemongrass-crusted fish satay served with a Thai peanut sauce, or spinach and shiitake ravioli in a sun-dried tomato and garlic cream sauce, and you'll want more. Roy's signature dessert, a rich chocolate soufflé, always guarantees a sweet ending. **2360 Kiahuna Plantation Drive, at the Poipu Shopping Village; (808) 742-5000; www.roysrestaurant.com; moderate to expensive; reservations recommended; dinner daily.**

❦❦ SEAVIEW TERRACE, Poipu You'll be impressed by the Hyatt's prodigious grounds, and one of the best places to behold them (and the vast Pacific) is from the deck of the Seaview Terrace. The view from up here is truly spectacular, and the atmosphere is relaxed enough that you can take your time absorbing it all as you indulge in cocktails and appetizers. The ideal time to come is when the sun sets. Watch the pounding surf roll in, and admire the palms silhouetted against the colorful sky; then, after dark, witness a whole new tropical world emerge as tiki torches light up the landscape. Hawaiian music is played from 6 P.M. to 8 P.M. nightly, amplifying the already romantic mood. **1571 Poipu Road, at the Hyatt Regency Kauai; (808) 742-1234; www.hyatt.com; inexpensive to expensive; breakfast, appetizers, and cocktails daily.**

Romantic Suggestion: If you're up with the sun, why not try a light romantic breakfast here? In the morning, coffee drinks, fruit juices, and baked goods are served on the Seaview Terrace, and, best of all, the people-factor is substantially lower than in the evening.

❤❤❤ **TIDEPOOLS, Poipu** Tidepools is the Hyatt's casual (but still intimate) dining alternative for those who want sunset views but don't want to see stars when the bill arrives. Guests dine in romantic grass-thatched Polynesian huts surrounded by lovely ponds populated by huge and hungry koi. Stone floors, rattan chairs, and little glowing lamps at every wooden table enhance the warm Hawaiian mood. The beautiful surroundings and relatively moderate prices are the best aspects of Tidepools. The Hawaiian-inspired dishes, while generous in portion, are rather uneventful, including the house specialty: macadamia nut–crusted "fish of the day" with lime-ginger butter. With that in mind, a nice alternative is simply enjoying a Hawaiian tropical drink and *pupus* (appetizers) in the adjacent lounge. Unwind in a large thatched hut while taking in the same pond views as those from the restaurant. **1571 Poipu Road, at the Hyatt Regency Kauai; (808) 742-1234; www.hyatt.com; expensive; dinner daily.**

Outdoor Kissing

❤❤◖ **MAHA'ULEPU BEACH, Poipu** Adventure usually ignites the flames of passion, so trying to find this beach ought to start that spark. It's not an overly challenging quest to locate Maha'ulepu, but you do drive down unmarked, bumpy sugarcane plantation roads to a run-down shack, surrounded by chickens, where you sign in and continue to the beach. Sound interesting? Well, it is. The only problem is that you may feel like you're trespassing. (Fortunately, Hawaii's beaches are not private property, so you aren't anywhere that you aren't supposed to be; you just have to pass through private sugarcane fields to get to this particular beach.)

Because getting here takes some effort, Maha'ulepu Beach offers more solitude than Poipu's beach area. You still won't be totally alone, but this soft, two-mile stretch of sun-kissed beach does offer a peaceful place to wade through the waves, explore tide pools, or just sit in the shade of the trees. Luckily, it's private enough in places that you'll be quite comfortable sneaking a kiss when the passion strikes. *From the Lihue Airport, travel southwest on Highway 50 and turn left at the junction of Highways 50 and 520. Follow Highway 520 south to Poipu, where it turns into Poipu Road; follow this road beyond the Hyatt's golf courses and continue toward the ocean.*

Romantic Alternative: At the edge of the Hyatt's property, you'll find somewhat more accessible **SHIPWRECK POINT**, a dramatic lookout where the ocean meets a steep, rocky ledge. Cliff diving is said to be popular here, but we didn't see any brave souls trying it. A more romantic pastime is witnessing a glorious sunset from this lookout.

West Shore

Kauai's dry West Shore harbors several nondescript towns tracing the coast and offers few dining and lodging options for tourists. Nevertheless, you'll want to make a day trip here (if not several) to view the West Shore's natural wonders, including the beautiful sandy beaches and breathtaking **WAIMEA CANYON**.

Waimea

Hotel/Bed and Breakfast Kissing

❤❤ **WAIMEA PLANTATION COTTAGES, Waimea** Built in the early 1900s, these picturesque cottages—once the homes of sugar plantation workers—are now yours to rent. Forty-eight homes, in varying degrees of size and desirability, outline a property where very little has changed since the days when farming was Kauai's primary enterprise. Some cottages feature an alluring black-sand beach just yards from your lanai, while others, set on tall stilts, are packed tightly together along a dirt road with little or no view of the water. All homes have been restored, but some still manage to retain an undesirable old-fashioned look, with exposed plumbing and outdated furnishings. The best choices are the cottages set right on the beach, with shady ocean-view verandas complete with cozy wicker furniture. All of the cottages boast a full kitchen, hardwood floors, Hawaiian furnishings made of koa and mahogany, cable TV, a stereo, and a private bathroom. A swimming pool is also available for guests. When we visited, the **WAIMEA BREWING COMPANY** (808-338-9733; inexpensive to moderate) was being constructed adjacent to the lobby in the main building. Only lunch and dinner are served here, so you'll have to look elsewhere for breakfast. **9400 Kaumualii Highway; (808) 338-1625, (800) 992-4632; www.waimea-plantation.com; moderate to unbelievably expensive.**

Romantic Warning: Many cottages are clustered on this property, and the fact that Waimea Plantation Cottages caters to groups and families (children stay free) could pose major privacy and noise problems. This is, however, the only romantic overnight option in Waimea, and it does offer a wide range of prices to fit most budgets.

Romantic Warning: KOKEE LODGE (Waimea Canyon Drive; 808-335-6061; very inexpensive) is the only other lodging option near Waimea. The lodge rents cabins at the top of Waimea Canyon Drive, but think twice before you book a stay in one of these musty, run-down units. Service is gruff, wild roosters roam and crow freely, and large rats are a problem. The only reason to stay overnight up here is if you want do a lot of hiking and would prefer not to drive up and down the hill each day, although the drive really isn't that bad. You'd be better off in a tent than in one of Kokee Lodge's cabins; information on campsites in **KOKEE STATE PARK** (see Outdoor Kissing) can be obtained by contacting the **DEPARTMENT OF STATE PARKS** (3060 Eiwa Street, Room 306, Lihue, HI 96766; 808-274-3444).

Outdoor Kissing

❤❤❤❤ **WAIMEA CANYON/KOKEE STATE PARK, Waimea** "The Grand Canyon of the Pacific," as Waimea was famously dubbed by Mark Twain, lives up to its noble nickname. A long, twisting road journeys up 4,000 feet to stunning vistas that will surprise anyone who thinks all Kauai's beauty lies in its lush gardens. Make your first stop at the **WAIMEA CANYON LOOKOUT** to breathe in the fresh, cool air and admire how the steep, verdant valleys contrast with the bare volcanic rock and rich red soil. A spectacular kaleidoscope of colors surrounds you, ranging from lush green forest to glowing crimson earth laced with chaparral. As you continue up the hill, be sure to pause at the **PUU KA PELE** and **PUU HINAHINA LOOKOUTS**; each stop offers another magnificent perspective on the canyon.

Proceed to **KOKEE STATE PARK**, where you can visit a small natural-history museum and lodge, but stop here only if you're ravenous or need a hiking trail map; otherwise you'll be frustrated by the shabby facilities. Continue on to the **KALALAU** and **PUU O KILA LOOKOUTS**, which are perched above Na Pali Coast. The scenery—a vast green landscape fronting the shimmering blue ocean—is so breathtaking, you may need mouth-to-mouth resuscitation. Hopefully you're with someone who can help. **Department of State Parks: (808) 274-3444.** *Heading westbound on Highway 50, turn right onto Waimea Canyon Drive (Highway 550). The uphill drive takes 20–40 minutes, depending on traffic.*

Romantic Note: Bring along comfortable shoes and a light jacket; the temperature at this altitude is cool but still pleasant, and perfect for hiking. The many trails range from easy walks to rugged hikes, all with incredible scenery.

Mana

Outdoor Kissing

❤❤❤❤ **POLIHALE STATE PARK, Mana** Our curiosity was instantly piqued when we surveyed our Kauai map and discovered that the highway along the West Shore eventually turns into a dirt road, then ends altogether at Polihale State Park. Before we knew it, we found ourselves in search of this intriguing beach, notably one of the longest in the state. Although the dirt road is well marked on the map, we couldn't help but wonder if we had taken the wrong turnoff as we wound our way several miles along the bumpy, potholed road with nothing but dry brush in sight. To our sheer delight, after 15 minutes of dusty trying-to-be-patient driving, we finally came upon a velvety, sandy beach set beside the sheer cliffs of Na Pali Coast. As the sun sank below the horizon, weaving a tapestry of colors across the sky, we were held captive by the beauty of the moment. **Department of State Parks: (808) 274-3444.** *From Lihue Airport, follow Highway 50 south and then west, past the towns of Kekaha and Mana, until the highway ends. Turn left onto the dirt road and follow signs to Polihale.*

Romantic Warning: Polihale Beach has long been celebrated as one of Kauai's most beautiful beaches, which (much to our chagrin) means it isn't really as much of a secret as the lengthy dirt road might lead you to believe. The potholes discourage many tourists, but those with four-wheel-drive vehicles aren't deterred at all—they actually drive right onto the beach. It isn't exactly picturesque to have the shore dotted with trucks, but once the sun starts to set, the dune buggy crowd thins out, and you can focus on the horizon instead.

East Shore

Believe it or not, even Kauai has traffic, and you're most likely to get caught in it on the East Shore. The highway here runs along an overdeveloped coast that, in parts, has more condos, hotels, gas stations, restaurants, and houses than palm trees. The advantage of this area is its extremely affordable accommodations and restaurants, but, unfortunately, only a few of these are worth recommending for an intimate rendezvous. But don't give up the East Shore altogether. We discovered some wonderful places for kissing purposes, despite the traffic.

Lihue

Hotel/Bed and Breakfast Kissing

❧❧ **ASTON KAUAI BEACH VILLAS, Lihue** Affordable luxury is hard to come by on the East Shore, where low-priced, cockroach-ridden, outdated hotels and condos are in abundance. At the Aston's beachfront condominiums, however, affordability and comfort go hand in hand. The ocean is just steps away from your spacious lanai, the bedrooms are air-conditioned, and the prices are fairly reasonable. The Aston isn't what you would call a luxury resort, but when it comes to basic, clean accommodations, the Aston has it all: simple rattan furnishings, pastel blue decor, spacious one- and two-bedroom suites, tennis courts, outdoor swimming pool and Jacuzzi tub, and a luscious white-sand beach out front. **4330 Kauai Beach Drive; (808) 245-7711, (800) 922-7866 mainland, (800) 321-2558 interisland; www.aston-hotels.com; moderate to very expensive.**

Romantic Warning: We didn't see any dust flying, but on the back of the Aston's map it warns that on Saturday and Sunday there is "county-sanctioned motorcycle track usage [from] 9 A.M. to 5 P.M. Please pardon the dust." Their quote, not ours.

Romantic Note: The OUTRIGGER KAUAI BEACH HOTEL (4331 Kauai Beach Drive; 808-245-1955, 800-OUTRIGGER; www.outrigger.com; moderate to unbelievably expensive) next door could be an option . . . if you don't mind casts of thousands. Manicured lawns, waterfalls, three super-sized swimming pools, and a plethora of palm trees are impressive, but

---

Never leave valuables in your rental car (even in the trunk). Just because you're in paradise doesn't mean you don't have to be city smart.

the very standard 341 hotel rooms and, once again, plenty of people don't make this a choice overflowing with romantic possibilities.

Restaurant Kissing

☘☘❀ **GAYLORD'S AT KILOHANA, Lihue** A noble Clydesdale harnessed to a white carriage stands patiently in the circular brick driveway of the beautifully restored Tudor-style mansion that houses Gaylord's. Inside there's a country store and several galleries and, in the backyard, Gaylord's U-shaped, covered dining room replete with brick pillars and charming wrought-iron tables covered in starched white linens. An absence of walls allows everyone to have a lovely view of the courtyard, manicured gardens, and mountains beyond.

The former sugar plantation mansion is no doubt a tourist magnet but, thankfully, the grounds and home still retain a sense of genuine style. The food, on the other hand, could use some help here and there. The steak-seafood-pasta-oriented menu offers such entrées as chicken and rosemary fettuccine with sautéed mushrooms, Thai basil, artichoke hearts, and coconut milk; and Seafood Rhapsody with sautéed prawns, broiled lobster tail, and grilled mahi mahi served with herbed drawn butter. Unfortunately, the sauces can be too rich, and the lack of vegetarian choices can be frustrating if one or both of you are so inclined. Still, the efficient service and lovely setting make lunch or dinner here a tranquil treat. **3-2087 Kaumualii Highway; (808) 245-9593; www.gaylordskauai.com; moderate to expensive; lunch Monday–Saturday, dinner daily, brunch Sunday; recommended wedding site.**

Wailua

Outdoor Kissing

☘☘ **FERN GROTTO, Wailua** The quiet Wailua River meanders through a lush tropical jungle, past a popular swimming hole, and into the naturally formed amphitheater called the Fern Grotto. To fully experience the extraordinary beauty and serenity of this place, we suggest that you decline a tour with hundreds of other travelers on the Wailua River Cruise (it won't be hard to resist). Instead, rent kayaks from **KAYAK KAUAI OUTBOUND** (1340 Kuhio Highway, Kapaa; 808-822-9179, 800-437-3507; www.kayak kauai.com; $25–$35 for a single kayak, $48–$60 for a double). For fewer people-sightings, go early in the morning and survey this jungle river at your own romantic paddling pace. *Follow Kuhio Highway north* *into Wailua. Watch for signs to the Fern Grotto on your left, just past the Wailua River.*

Wailua Homesteads

Residential neighborhoods, sprawling horse pastures, and views of the cloud-covered mountains best define Wailua Homesteads. To reach this commercially undeveloped region, you'll have to take the only route that starts near Wailua and winds up a long, scenic road into the green hills. Once you arrive, sample a taste of quiet Hawaiian life that doesn't involve the beach.

Hotel/Bed and Breakfast Kissing

❤️❤️ **INN PARADISE, Wailua Homesteads** You'll best appreciate Kauai's east shore by staying in a bed and breakfast like Inn Paradise. Modern and eclectic, this residential home offers the senses a reprieve from the hotels and condos that populate much of the island. The inn's wraparound lanai affords views of the countryside and, if you're lucky, distant mountain waterfalls that become visible only when the clouds depart.

Although the three available guest suites share the lanai, all have a decent amount of seclusion, along with private entrances, king-size beds, ceiling fans, and wicker and rattan furnishings. The main difference among the rooms is size. The Prince Kuhio Suite, a studio-type unit with a tiny kitchenette area, is the smallest; the Queen Kapule Suite has a separate bedroom, living room, and small kitchen; and the King Kamualii Suite features two bedrooms, a full kitchen, and separate living and dining rooms. Whichever you choose, you'll receive a complimentary welcome basket filled with fruit, juice, coffee, muffins, honey, and fresh jam, perfect for breakfast in bed. Linger as long as you want. And if those toes are just itching to sink into some sand, the beach is only three miles away. **6381 Makana Road; (808) 822-2542; moderate; minimum-stay requirement.**

❤️❤️❤️ **MAKANA INN, Wailua Homesteads** If country living, rather than instant beach access, is what you seek during your Hawaiian stay, then the two accommodations here will do perfectly. Located at the end of a sleepy cul de sac, Makana Inn is surrounded by mountains and rolling green pastures. You'll find plenty of wide-open space to savor, clean air to breathe, and friendly country critters to keep you company—namely, three horses, three cats, and one dog. And if a day at the beach is on your agenda, it's only a 15-minute drive away.

Our favorite option is the private and spacious guest cottage adjacent to the host's contemporary home. Its hardwood floors covered by vibrant throw rugs, cozy sitting area with concealed TV/VCR, private phone, and kitchenette arranged ideally for light cooking are all you need to feel at home. You can hide away in the bedroom, complete with a huge California king-size bed bedecked with bright Hawaiian-print linens, a standard bathroom, and a lanai opening to views of cloud-cloaked Mount Wai'ale'ale—one of the wettest spots on earth.

The second option, the Garden Apartment, is located in the ground level of the host's home. It features a private entrance and lanai. Guest can enjoy a small kitchenette, a giant-screen TV/VCR, a king-size bed adorned with bright linens, a private bathroom (shower only), and lots of sunny windows. No one will see you down here . . . except maybe the horses. Whether you choose the apartment or the cottage, you will be greeted with an "Aloha breakfast basket" containing fresh fruit, juices, coffee, tea, milk, and muffins. **Reservations through Hawaii's Best Bed and Breakfasts, (808) 885-4550, (800) 262-9912 mainland; inexpensive; minimum-stay requirement.**

❤❤ **OPAEKAA FALLS HALE, Wailua Homesteads** Set on a bluff overlooking the verdant valley and Wailua River, this custom-made, contemporary home not only has excellent views, but a comfortable, detached apartment-like unit that's all yours to kiss in. An aqua-colored spiral staircase leads up to the unit, where you'll find blond rattan furnishings, a full kitchen, a king-size bed, a standard tiled bath, and a washer/dryer. Special touches throughout, such as beautiful blue-tinted windows and concrete construction (for soundproofing purposes), show that some thought was put into making this home as comfortable as possible. Through glass doors, step outside your living room onto a wide lanai that overlooks a pretty cliffside pool. There's also a Jacuzzi tub, but it's gas-powered and the owners charge a fee for your bubbling pleasure. A welcome basket awaits in your refrigerator, as well as a variety of Hawaiian-made treats to enjoy whenever your sweet tooth strikes. **Reservations through Hawaii's Best Bed and Breakfasts, (808) 885-4550, (800) 262-9912 mainland; inexpensive; minimum-stay requirement.**

❤❤❤ **ROSEWOOD BED AND BREAKFAST, Wailua Homesteads** You'll breathe sighs of relief (and contentment) as you leave the busy town of Kapaa and wind your way up into Wailua Homesteads' lush countryside. Within such a pastoral setting, you'll find this picturesque farmhouse looking as traditional as can be, with blooming flower gardens and a white picket fence. You might yearn for the ocean (it's nowhere in sight), but only for a moment—the solitude and peacefulness here more than compensate for the lack of nearby water. Besides, the beach is a mere 15-minute drive away.

Although the main house holds one guest suite, you'll want to stay in one of the two self-contained cottages in the backyard. Directly behind the main house lies the Thatched Cottage, appropriately named for its roof. The inside is simple: no TV or phone, one bedroom and one bath, a kitchenette, and eclectic antique furnishings. Outside there's a private shower hidden among the greenery. We prefer the light, updated, and very sweet Victorian Cottage, with its hardwood floors, full white-tiled kitchen and eating area, sunroom with white wicker couches, bright bedroom with Laura Ashley linens, white-tiled bathroom, and upstairs loft with twin beds. The guest suite in the main house is homey and spacious, but much less private and appropriately less expensive.

Discerning touches such as chocolates on your pillows and champagne for special occasions make any stay here a pleasure. A welcome basket, consisting of fresh papaya and other tropical fruits, organic granola with macadamia nuts, and Kona coffee, is stocked in your refrigerator if you stay in a cottage or presented in the main house if you're staying there. After just one peaceful night, you'll be refreshed and ready for another blissful day in the sun. **872 Kamalu Road; (808) 822-5216; www.rose woodkauai.com; inexpensive to moderate; no credit cards; minimum-stay requirement; recommended wedding site.**

Romantic Note: Rosewood, as a company, manages several vacation rentals throughout Kauai (see **HALE PILIALOHA** in Poipu). Another rental worth noting is the three-bedroom **HALE MAKANI** in Kapaa (moderate; minimum-stay requirement). The advantages of Hale Makani are its hillside location, private Jacuzzi tub, modern and pleasant appointments, full-size kitchen, and large deck from which you can see the ocean, mountains, and surrounding neighborhood. That last point leads us to the only problem we saw. Simply put, many of the residences surrounding Hale Makani need a good cleaning up.

Kapaa

Hotel/Bed and Breakfast Kissing

Stayed here for Honeymoon--very nice! As good as the guide makes it out to be.

❤️❤️❤️❤️ **HALE O' WAILELE, Kapaa** What do you get when you combine eight sprawling acres with more than 100 species of fragrant tropical flowers and palm trees, views of mountain waterfalls, a lava-rock swimming pool, and two homes with ultra comfortable and elegant accommodations? Well, in this amorous travel guide, you get a four-lip rating.

The name of this bed and breakfast, *Hale O' Wailele*, means "House of Leaping Waterfalls," reflecting its prime position at the base of the

Makaleha Mountains. (Depending on the season, you can see anywhere from two to 12 waterfalls flowing down the rocky cliffside.) To us, *Hale O' Wailele* also means true hospitality in one of the most opulent outdoor settings on the island.

As you enter the first home, you pass through an inviting common room filled with leather couches, an attractive entertainment center with stereo and TV/VCR, and windows that showcase the Eden-like surroundings. Hawaiian family heirlooms and stylish contemporary furnishings prove to be pleasing complements.

The three bedrooms in this home surround the common area. The Canoe Suite, the most romantic room on the entire property, is simply exquisite, with Persian rugs set atop hardwood floors, a comfy king-size bed, a TV/VCR, a marble bathroom, and a private Jacuzzi tub on an adjacent outdoor deck. The two other rooms share a spacious and lovely bathroom but, typically, if one room is occupied, the owners won't rent out the other. Ku Lumi Manu, "The Ancient Room," holds a king-size bed and the other, Ka Lumi Manu, "The Bird Room," has two double beds. Both rooms are equipped with handsome linens, cable TV and VCR, and a small refrigerator, and share an outdoor hot tub. In the backyard, where tropical flowers bloom, you'll discover a koi pond next to a lovely swimming pool complete with (what else?) a waterfall.

A short but steep driveway leads you up to the expansive second house, named Waonahele, which means "House at the Edge of the Forest." Like its counterpart below, it features the same meticulous attention to detail. The three bedrooms here are furnished with cream and beige linens, gray slate floors, king-size beds, private marble bathrooms with whirlpool baths, and TV/VCRs. All rooms are adorned with fresh tropical flowers gathered from the surrounding gardens. A common area with comfortable furnishings is lined with gigantic picture windows that take advantage of the stunning landscape.

Regardless of which house or room you choose, enjoy a full Hawaiian-style breakfast buffet each morning at one of two large tables in Waonahele's common area. Breakfast may consist of piping-hot omelets, French toast, fresh island fruit, and sweet breads. If you can muster the will to leave the breakfast table, you will be pleased with all the recreational options available, including a full weight room, golf carts (so you can explore the property), and flower gardens where you can gather blossoms to make a personalized lei. Complimentary snorkeling equipment, beach gear, coolers, and mountain bikes are available for your daily expeditions. **7084 Kahuna Road; (808) 822-7911, (800) 775-2824; www. planet-hawaii.com/kahuna; inexpensive to moderate.**

❤❁ **KAPAA SANDS, Kapaa** Located on the grounds of a former Buddhist temple, this 20-unit condominium complex presents a peaceful, clean, and inexpensive place to relax and savor the refreshing Hawaiian breezes. Despite a slightly unappealing location—sandwiched between sea and street—this place should not be overlooked. All the units are decorated differently, which means some of the units are very nice but some are outdated. Be persistent in giving exact details of the kind of decor you want when making reservations. The units are either studios or two-bedroom condos, and are classified as oceanview (which is somewhat misleading, because all you can really see is the unit in front of yours and a partial view of the ocean) and oceanfront (which, true to definition, does mean you look right out to the churning sea). If you're lucky, you may see sea turtles or monk seals on the beach or in the surf.

All units have a full kitchen, lanai, snug sitting area, and private bathroom. However, the best choices are the two-bedroom units. While the studio units are the least expensive, several are furnished with Murphy beds, which may or may not be your style. There's a sparkling-clean pool but, unfortunately, it borders the parking lot (not uncommon with condos in this area). On the plus side, when we visited the pool it was people-free. Due to heavy undertow, the ocean here is not safe for swimming, but a soft, grassy lawn and sandy beach area await just steps from your unit, and they are great spots for taking it easy on warm Hawaiian afternoons. **380 Papaloa Road; (808) 822-4901, (800) 222-4901; www.kapaasands. com; inexpensive; minimum-stay requirement.**

❤ **LANIKAI, Kapaa** As far as Kapaa condo complexes go, these suites come with ample elbow room. Choose from either one- or two-bedroom units, but select carefully: The master bedrooms are on the ocean side in the odd-numbered rooms and they're on the parking-lot side in the even-numbered rooms. All 18 units offer full kitchens, large soaking tubs and separate standing showers, king- or queen-size beds, and private laundry facilities. Between the beach and lush landscaped grounds is a pleasant seaside pool, a perfect place to soak in the rays and breathe the salty air. So with all this, why the one-lip rating? We were nearly blown over when it came to the price, considering the outdated decor in many units, the lack of air-conditioning, and the busy arterial close by. If Kapaa is where you want to be, and the price doesn't blow your wad, you'll definitely have lots of kissing space here. **390 Papaloa Road; (808) 822-7700, (800) 755-2824; www. castle-group.com; very expensive.**

Restaurant Kissing

☙☙❧ **A PACIFIC CAFE, Kapaa** Although A Pacific Cafe is one of the best culinary experiences in all of Hawaii, we were somewhat reluctant to try it when we discovered this "café" nestled in the middle of a shopping mall. Not surprisingly, we didn't find intimate candlelight dining. Instead, we discovered a well-lit, stylish room, filled with black-lacquered rattan chairs and reddish wood tables, that was much too lively for quiet conversation. Despite the somewhat bustling atmosphere, the waitstaff managed to maintain attentive service, and the entire dining experience never felt rushed or unrefined.

Actually, the hustle and bustle disappear after your first divine bite of scallop ravioli covered in a light lime cream sauce, sprinkled with roe, and garnished with a beautiful array of native vegetables. As the extravaganza of Hawaiian regional cuisine continues, you will marvel over angel-hair pasta with Chinese pesto and grilled Hawaiian fish skewers; lobster and asparagus risotto with shrimp-tomato broth; blackened *ono* with papaya-basil sauce and papaya-ginger salsa; and a white chocolate terrine with strawberry sauce. Forget the candles! With food like this, who needs dim lighting? A spotlight (and a standing ovation) would not be out of place. **4831 Kuhio Highway (Highway 50), Suite 220; (808) 822-0013; moderate to expensive; dinner daily.**

Anahola

Hotel/Bed and Breakfast Kissing

☙☙☙☙ **THE PLANTATION HOUSE, Anahola** Have you ever dreamed of paradise? Your dream can come true if you rent this plantation-style Hawaiian home embracing a stunning expanse of Anahola Bay. Every nuance of this 5,167-square-foot residence brings pleasure to the beholder. Long, winding corridors lead to four well-spaced bedrooms, each with its own sheltered-from-view outdoor shower and patio. The bedrooms and bathrooms are ample throughout, with floor-to-ceiling windows and incredible detailing, but the two master suites located at opposite ends of the home are especially enormous and comfortable.

Enter this island mansion through large koa-wood double doors. Big windows and abundant skylights fill the house with radiant sunshine and provide partial views of the heavenly blue waters of the Pacific. The stunningly large and airy living room and dining area are flanked by 40 feet of sliding glass doors that open to a large, lushly green backyard encircled by towering palm trees. The interior holds a comfortable display of rattan and white furnishings (surprisingly sparse, given the home's grandiose architectural design), plus hardwood floors, a marble fireplace, and an enviable designer kitchen. All the amenities are here, including a TV/VCR and stereo system.

Just a few feet beyond the backyard is the crashing surf of Anahola Bay. Upon waking, brew a fresh pot of Kona coffee, then take cup in hand and stroll out to the beach to breathe in the fresh sea air. Later in the day, be sure to take a walk around this huge stretch of astonishingly empty beach. One side is laden with tide pools, another boasts prime snorkeling conditions, and still another has rocky, lava-encrusted terrain that makes hiking a challenge. **Reservations through Anini Beach Vacation Rentals, (808) 826-4000, (800) 448-6333; www.anini.com; unbelievably expensive; minimum-stay requirement.**

North Shore

The increased rainfall on this side of the island may be a deterrent to some, but the resulting landscape makes it a blessing in disguise. We found the short-lived showers invigorating, and they make everything here extra green and fresh. The North Shore is also home to some incredible beaches (made famous in movies such as *South Pacific*) and the **HANALEI NATIONAL WILDLIFE REFUGE**, a fertile valley set aside for a variety of rare birds.

Kilauea

Hotel/Bed and Breakfast Kissing

❤❤❤ **KAI MANA, Kilauea** Although Kai Mana's plantation-style main house offers four guest rooms, the private dome-shaped cottage (nicknamed "the mushroom") is the most inviting choice for romance. Set on a grassy knoll, the cottage is quaint, cozy, and minimalist in decor, with a full, tiled kitchen at its center. It also boasts a spacious living room with a TV/VCR and comfortable furnishings, a queen-size bed, and a tiny bathroom with shower. Wraparound reflective-glass windows offer all-around views of the water and the stunning sunsets. Use of the Jacuzzi tub on the deck of the main house is included with your stay, and the beach is accessible via a wooded trail. With respect to your privacy, the managers stay well away, even for breakfast, so you'll have to bring along your own provisions for morning meals or that midnight snack.

Two of the four bedrooms in the main house feature a king-size bed, one has a queen-size bed, and the remaining room holds two double beds; all are beautifully adorned with Hawaiian-print bedspreads. We particularly liked the bamboo canopied bed in the Bamboo Room. Each room has uneventful decor, a private bathroom, a private entrance from the lanai, and use of the deck Jacuzzi tub, which is not private, but does have admirable views of the Pacific coastline and famous Kilauea Lighthouse. Each morning, an island-style breakfast is served on the lanai for those staying in the main house.

Kai Mana offers some additional services that may intrigue you, including massage and body work (arranged by appointment), and counseling sessions with Shakti Gawain, the owner of the home and best-selling author of many spiritual books. All are designed to give you a healing and relaxing experience. **Reservations through Hawaii's Best Bed and Breakfasts, (808) 885-4550, (800) 262-9912 mainland; www.kai-mana.com; inexpensive to moderate; minimum-stay requirement.**

❤❤❤❤ **KILAUEA LAKESIDE ESTATE, Kilauea** Sometimes we find a place that is so spectacular, we wonder if we're dreaming. After we pinched ourselves and rubbed our eyes, we realized that Kilauea Lakeside Estate is truly a romantic reality.

On the lush foothills of Kauai, this designer home/vacation rental has its own lake and waterfall, a par-three golf hole, and acre upon acre of privacy. The contemporary Hawaiian home is bordered by grassy lawns, more than 40 varieties of fruit trees, and, best of all, a 20-acre freshwater lake stocked with fish and overflowing with recreational water toys. With its bathtub-warm waters and no neighbors in sight, it's the ideal skinny-dipping spot. (Don't tell us you wouldn't do it if you had a chance!) If that's not enough, explore the nearby hiking trail that leads you to a waterfall and some fascinating rock formations built by the ancient Hawaiians.

In the middle of all this is a dream house with everything a home should have, including three bedrooms and three baths, a fully equipped kitchen, and a large living room with a TV/VCR. Kissing comes easily in the upstairs master bedroom, thanks to its king-size bed, vaulted ceilings, and windows looking out over the grounds. A walk-in shower and Jacuzzi tub with views of the lake complete the wonderful picture. If (and we say this with great hesitation) you need to leave the estate, visit the nearby bird refuge or head down to one of the secluded beaches just a five-minute drive away. But who needs secluded beaches with a place like this? Kilauea Lakeside Estate is truly like having a mini-resort all to yourselves. **(310) 379-7842; www.mmv.com/lakeside; unbelievably expensive; recommended wedding site.**

Romantic Note: Reality bites when it comes to the steep price. However, the home is large enough for two or three couples to easily share, and that brings costs down to the moderate-to-expensive range. If the two of you do splurge, it's about the same price as an oceanfront room in one of Poipu's luxurious hotels.

❤❤❤❤ **SECRET BEACH HIDEAWAY, Kilauea** Private and exquisite, Secret Beach Hideaway is perfect for couples who want the sophistication and luxury of a hotel, but prefer the privacy and comfort of a home. A gate at the entryway ensures that you will have this little oasis all to yourselves—11 acres of lovely, landscaped tropical gardens and a small cottage that really is a romantic's dream come true.

Sumptuous, plush furnishings fill the one-bedroom bungalow, complete with high ceilings, an indoor/outdoor shower, and a separate kitchen and living room area. Everything is top of the line, from the marble countertops to the double-headed shower to the fine linens and soft towels. The cottage is on the small side, but the owner has managed to fit in everything beautifully (including a stereo system, cable TV/VCR, and washer/dryer, all tastefully tucked away in cabinets). Outside you'll find a large lanai facing the ocean, where a private Jacuzzi tub awaits.

If you can bring yourselves to leave this incredible interior, go for a short (albeit steep) walk down to **KAUAPEA (SECRET) BEACH** (see Outdoor Kissing). Banana and papaya trees, haleconias, ginger, and more tropical beauties line the terraced garden path to the beach. After your trip to the grocery store for provisions, you won't want to leave your hideaway again. **Reservations through Hawaii's Best Bed and Breakfasts, (808) 885-4550, (800) 262-9912 mainland; very expensive; minimum-stay requirement.**

Romantic Note: Sharing the same views as the Hideaway is a second oceanfront property, known as the **SECRET BEACH OWNER'S COTTAGE** (very expensive; minimum-stay requirement). This one-bedroom cottage is decorated in Hawaiian rattan and pine furnishings, and features a marble bath, TV/VCR, CD player, and lanai with an outdoor barbecue.

Restaurant Kissing

❦❦❦❧ **CASA DI AMICI, Kilauea** Tucked away in a delightful North Shore "mini-mall" of sorts, Casa di Amici overflows with charm. A white, lattice-framed entrance invites you into the small open-air dining room filled with hanging plants, white holiday lights, rattan chairs, and footed pedestal tables covered with crisp white linens. There's no eye-popping views here, but the soft melodies from the piano more than compensate. As the night rain pounds on the roof and the ocean breezes cool the evening, snuggle closely together and prepare for some culinary delights.

Delicious Italian food is the name of the game here. Start your meal with a fresh salad or an interesting appetizer, such as Japanese blackened shrimp in ginger-beet sauce. For the main course, seafood dishes are especially good; try flavorful Scampi Di Amici: jumbo prawns, garlic, capers, fresh tomatoes, basil, and olive oil served on a generous bed of linguine. More robust appetites can indulge in chicken with sun-dried cherry and port wine sauce, which is superb. Top off your meal with a foamy cappuccino and some local sweetness: a slice of Kilauea sugar loaf pineapple upside-down pound cake with passion-fruit cream and vanilla ice cream. Now that's a mouthful. **2484 Keneke Street; (808) 828-1555; moderate to expensive; reservations recommended; call for seasonal hours.**

Outdoor Kissing

❦❦❦❧ **KAUAPEA (SECRET) BEACH, Kilauea** Even though Kauapea Beach isn't really a secret anymore, most people still call it Secret Beach. That could be because it is not all that easy to find, not particularly easy to get to, and certainly not easy to hike back from. A long, steep descent on a rather precarious path takes you to a mile of sandy shore set at the edge of the Kilauea cliffs. Although swimming isn't recommended because of the strong undertow, you can usually sight playful dolphins in the surf. Beachcombing and wading are also enjoyable options. *Between Kilauea Point and Kalihiwai Bay.*

Romantic Note: Secret Beach is also a well-known nude beach. Some may consider this worthy of a romantic warning instead of just a note, but if you were hoping to do something daring on your vacation that you could never get away with in your hometown, this might be the place to do it. Just don't forget your sunscreen.

Princeville

Hotel/Bed and Breakfast Kissing

❤️❤️❤️ **HALE'AHA, Princeville** You'll find this affectionate bed and breakfast nestled within the master-planned community of Princeville. While the mix of vacation rentals and private estates in this sprawling development can make a tourist feel a bit like an intruder, Hale'Aha is an intimate alternative.

Spanning the entire upper level is the Penthouse Suite, with a king-size bed, a large sitting area with couches, an open-beamed ceiling, a small kitchenette, a washer/dryer, and a private lanai facing the ocean. A Jacuzzi tub big enough for two awaits in the bathroom. On the main level, just off the kitchen, is the Honeymoon Suite, which also has a two-person Jacuzzi tub, plus a king-size bed, a kitchenette, a small sitting area with golf-course views, and a glimpse of the ocean. Both the Bali Hai Mountain Room and On the Golf Course Room are much smaller and their views aren't spectacular, but their lower prices may tempt you. The contemporary decor throughout Hale'Aha relies a bit too much on ultracheery pastels, from the white-washed beams and floral curtains to the peach carpeting, but everything is sparkling clean and guests have ample privacy.

In the morning, breakfast awaits at a large table in the living room. Look forward to fruit smoothies, steamed brown rice with raisins and coconut, hot homemade bread with guava butter, and Kona coffee. **3875 Kamehameha Road; (808) 826-6733, (800) 826-6733; www.pixi.com/~kauai; inexpensive to expensive; minimum-stay requirement.**

❤️❤️❤️ **HANALEI BAY RESORT AND SUITES, Princeville** Much more modest than the neighboring **PRINCEVILLE HOTEL** (see review below), the Hanalei Bay Resort just might fit your style. Most assuredly it will fit your budget. Spread out on 22 acres, this 234-room complex consists of a series of wood-paneled, contemporary buildings. Walking from one end to the other could be a nightmare in the heat of the afternoon, but a 24-hour shuttle service is available to take you to and fro.

Choices for accommodations are limitless, with the least expensive being the "hotel room with refrigerator" (their classification, not ours). The next level in price is the "studio with kitchenette," then a "one-, two-,

---

All beaches in Hawaii are public. As long as you can find public access, you are welcome to enjoy the beaches everywhere.

or three- bedroom suite with full kitchen," and, finally, a "two- or three-bedroom prestige suite with kitchen," at the top of the price range. No matter which unit you choose, you can look forward to soft carpeting, rattan furnishings, a king- or queen-size bed, air-conditioning, telephone, color TV, lanai, and private bathroom. Many rooms and suites have views of the absolutely awe-inspiring mountains and cliffs of Bali Hai, which jut straight up from the Pacific. A full breakfast and two afternoon cocktails are included if you book a suite; otherwise you'll have to make good use of that "hotel room with refrigerator."

Of the two pools at Hanalei Bay Resort, dip your tootsies into the smaller, circular pool behind the Ginger Buildings. It's not as fancy as the curvaceous rock pool below the lobby, but it's also not full of water babies. Be sure to rent some snorkeling equipment and journey down to the beautiful white-sand beach. You'll share the sand 'n' surf with Princeville Hotel guests, and beach space can be tight, but the beauty is worth the price. **5380 Honoiki Road; (808) 826-6522, (800) 367-5004 mainland; www.castle-group.com; moderate to unbelievably expensive; recommended wedding site.**

Romantic Suggestion: Hanalei Bay Resort's **BALI HAI** restaurant (moderate to expensive; breakfast, lunch, and dinner daily) features an open-air setting and is an amazing spot from which to watch the sunset while sharing a cocktail or fruit smoothie. The Pacific Rim cuisine rates just a hair above average, and service is friendly but inexperienced. (Note: When we visited, a new chef was slated to take over, so things may change. It's worth a try.)

❧❧ **HANALEI NORTH SHORE PROPERTIES, Princeville** Although the office is in Princeville, the incredible homes, cottages, and "celebrity hideaways" managed by this company are scattered along the North Shore, from Haena to Moloaa Bay. These vacation rentals range from one to four bedrooms, and most have views; some are even beachfront. Without a doubt, a private home can be a nice alternative to a busy resort or standard condo. Special indulgences may include cook or maid service, or even personal massages. Just be specific and define your romantic needs (as far as lodging goes, that is), and the friendly office staff will gladly accommodate your wishes. **(808) 826-9622, (800) 488-3336; www.kauai-vacation-rentals.com; moderate to unbelievably expensive; minimum-stay requirement.**

❧❧❧❧ **PRINCEVILLE HOTEL, Princeville** Even the most worldly travelers will be wowed upon entering the ornate lobby of this polished, simply gorgeous hotel. Deep green, rust, black, and white marble tiles grace the floor and partially cover the walls. Resplendent, lofty, red and gold tapestries serve as the primary artwork, plush sofas and chairs invite quiet moments, and immense crystal and wrought-iron chandeliers hang from above. Grandiose windows embrace two sides of the lobby, so views of the endless ocean and glorious Na Pali Coast are always within sight. The effect is stunningly aristocratic and illustrious.

An adjacent living room with the same decor provides space for high tea and evening entertainment, while the windswept wraparound terrace holds the **CAFE HANALEI** (moderate to expensive; breakfast, lunch, and dinner daily). From this vantage point, you can revel in the rapturous, unimaginably beautiful paradise surrounding you. Informal dining here, whether for breakfast, lunch, or dinner, is truly a feast for all your senses, as well as your souls and hearts. Throughout the evening, local entertainers light up the night with engaging music.

Fortunately, unlike many other prominent local hotels with impressive lobbies and disappointingly mediocre rooms, the accommodations here equal and sometimes surpass the beauty of the entry. The soft cream carpeting, classic wood furnishings, separate sitting areas with oversize sofas, and king-size beds layered with generous pillows create a wonderful environment. Each unit has a large picture window (but, unfortunately, no lanai) looking out to the mesmerizing Pacific, Hanalei Bay, and the pool area, or to the surrounding mountains, depending on what you're willing to pay. Spacious, utterly sensual bathrooms, done in the hotel's signature dark green marble, seem to have enough room to host a small cocktail party (they are undoubtedly attractive enough). A final distinctive feature is the soaking tub with its huge privacy window; with a flip of a switch, the window becomes opaque for privacy or clear so you can look out to the dazzling view.

The hotel's **LA CASCATA RESTAURANT** (see Restaurant Kissing) serves delicious Mediterranean Italian cuisine in a lavish dining room. An added benefit is that the cheerful ambience here creates a nice change of pace from the hotel's primarily elegant, refined environs. **5520 Ka Haku Road; (808) 826-9644, (800) 826-4400; www.princeville.com; very expensive to unbelievably expensive; minimum-stay requirement seasonally; recommended wedding site.**

Restaurant Kissing

❀❀❀ **LA CASCATA RESTAURANT, Princeville** Bring your sunglasses along with your sweetheart to La Cascata. When the golden orb starts making its final show, the windows take in all the beauty and brightness. While you're at it, you might also need your normal glasses too. For as you dine in this seductive restaurant, replete with soft candlelight and old-world adornments, you might have to look twice to remind yourselves that you're on a tropical island, not the Italian Riviera. The terra-cotta-tiled floors, high-backed upholstered chairs, wrought-iron wall sconces, and bouquets on every table combine Mediterranean warmth with continental elegance. But you only need to glance through the tall windows at the azure Pacific and the misty Hanalei hillside to know exactly where you are.

Delicate spices enhance the flavor of every dish on the ever-changing menu, and interesting pastas with rich, creamy sauces leave your palate begging for more. We highly recommend the splendidly prepared prawn and asparagus risotto, with all flavors present and accounted for, or the more traditional rack of lamb.

Like all aspects of the Princeville, the atmosphere and service is wonderful, and the food is superior. Unfortunately, the restaurant fills up fast around sunset and the noise level increases, plus the tables are too large to foster much intimate conversation. However, as the night continues and the crowds thin out, listen to the soft and melodious acoustic guitar, and share some between-course kisses. **5520 Ka Haku Road, at the Princeville Hotel; (808) 826-9644; www.princeville.com; moderate to expensive; reservations recommended; dinner daily; recommended wedding site.**

Outdoor Kissing

❤❤❤ **KAWEONUI BEACH (SEALODGE BEACH), Princeville** Bring your sense of adventure—finding this romantic spot is half the thrill. A bumpy, overgrown dirt trail wanders down to a little stream you can easily hop over on rocks. Farther along your trek is an imposing mass of black-lava rock jutting over the water's edge. Many travelers stop here, thinking they've reached the end of the journey, but those poor souls don't have our book. The secret to finding Kaweonui Beach is not being deceived by the water on both sides of you. Continue to the left on what's left of the crumbly dirt path, and be careful as you edge around the corner. When you finally (and joyfully) behold the strip of sandy beach tucked into this hidden cove, walk just a little farther and give each other a pat (or more, if you like) on the back—you worked hard to find this special spot.

As hard as it is to find, this beach is not as private as you may hope. It certainly wasn't crowded the day we discovered it, but we would have preferred to have it all to ourselves. Who wouldn't? *Take Highway 56 northbound and turn right onto Ka Haku Road. Turn right on Kamehameha*

Road and follow it to its end at the parking lot for the Sealodge Condos. The trail to the beach begins at the oceanfront corner of the Sealodge, between two units.

Romantic Warning: The hike isn't lengthy, but the trail is a bit steep, narrow, and difficult at times. A healthy heart and shoes with good traction are necessary.

Hanalei

Hotel/Bed and Breakfast Kissing

❤❤❦ **HALE MAKAI BEACH COTTAGES, Hanalei** Besides vacation rental homes, there aren't many romantic lodging options in Hanalei, so Hale Makai is a real find. The four one- and two-bedroom cottages here, nicely spaced from each other, share a beachfront acre. Two units sit right at the edge of the sandy beach, facing the crystal blue water and sometimes turbulent surf. The other two are located behind the oceanfront units, but they still offer peeks of the stunning scenery.

Hawaiian-style rattan and bamboo furniture with pastel cushions adorns each cottage's living room, and the bedrooms have queen-size beds with tropical-print linens. Staying in for meals is a money-saving option, since the fully equipped kitchens come with everything except food. These reasonably priced cottages are popular, but if they aren't available, don't worry. The proprietors, a father-and-daughter team, can help you stretch your vacation dollar in other moderately priced, romantically viable properties they manage. **Reservations through Hanalei Vacations, (808) 826-7288, (800) 487-9833 mainland; www.800hawaii.com; inexpensive to moderate.**

Romantic Alternative: TUTU'S COUNTRY COTTAGE (reservations through Bed, Breakfast, and Beach, 808-826-6111; www.bestofhawaii.com/hanalei; inexpensive; minimum-stay requirement) isn't beachfront—it's located in a residential area close to other homes—but the country-style furnishings are quite comfortable, and you have ample space to yourselves. Also, the beach is only a short walk away.

Restaurant Kissing

❤❤❦ **CAFÉ LUNA, Hanalei** Hanalei is about as authentic an island town as you will experience in Hawaii. Given the quintessential Hawaiian character found here, it is hard to imagine how a thoroughly classic northern Italian restaurant could fit in so beautifully, but it does. Café Luna is a spectacular spot for the heart as well as the palate. The converted home offers soft lighting, well-spaced tables, wood floors, and a congenial owner, which combine to create a captivating dining experience. Whether it is veal shank in a savory brandy sauce, roasted rack of lamb, or seafood cannelloni, everything is perfectly prepared and nicely presented. The waitstaff is helpful and attentive, and the atmosphere warm and cozy. That's a great combination for any couple looking for a memorable island repast. **5-5161 Kuhio Highway; (808) 826-1177; moderate; lunch and dinner daily.**

❦❦❦ **POSTCARDS CAFÉ, Hanalei** The unassuming, bucolic town of Hanalei is the last stop for satisfying your stomach before venturing further to the rugged, almost impenetrable Na Pali coastline. Hanalei's easygoing personality is accentuated by shops and restaurants catering to both locals and tourists. Postcards Café perfectly captures this laid-back attitude with its casual atmosphere and relaxed waitstaff. The picturesque wood-framed exterior is embraced by a wraparound veranda dotted with a handful of wood tables for your dining pleasure. Lush foliage surrounds the property and provides the right amount of tropical fauna to create a cozy island ambience. Inside, the rustic wood interior has only a handful of tables for a more casual, decidedly less tropical experience.

An all-vegetarian menu is served at Postcards Café; the portions are generous and hearty, and the preparations imaginative and creative. Breakfast is a leisurely affair of outstanding pancakes; oversize omelets filled with fresh, island-grown organic produce; or delicious burritos stuffed with black beans, rice, fresh salsa, and melted cheese. In the evening, discover the wonderful melange of flavors in the coconut curried vegetables with tempeh accented by a spicy peanut sauce. Taro fritters with papaya salsa, and grilled jumbo shrimp with teriyaki plum sauce and braised cabbage are also must-try entrées. Perhaps the only drawback is that the laid-back waitstaff tends to be on island time, so adjust your watches and let this be a leisurely meal to remember. **5-5075 A Kuhio Highway; (808) 826-1191; inexpensive; breakfast and dinner daily.**

Outdoor Kissing

❦❦❦ **KAYAK KAUAI OUTBOUND, Hanalei** Unlike other modes of transportation, kayaks can carry couples to an isolated section of paradise. At Kayak Kauai Outbound, the carefree staff will strap a couple of kayaks on your car and send you on your merry way. We felt a bit unprepared at this apparent independence, but it truly was as easy as we had been told, and the tranquillity we found on the Hanalei River was sublime. If we hadn't seen them for ourselves, we wouldn't have believed the many fish jumping out of the water among the brilliant orange *hau* tree flowers floating on the surface.

Kissing might be difficult while sitting in separate kayaks, but be daring—the water is warm and shallow in most places. If you can both swim, the worst that can happen is that you'll be in the water together. Doesn't sound so bad, does it? Chances are, especially if you're beginners like us, you'll get pretty wet anyhow, so dress accordingly.

A word to the wise: Unless you've done this together before, we highly recommend that you rent one kayak each rather than sharing a double. Two beginners could spend all day zigzagging up the river, each person blaming the other for the lack of coordination. It might be funny at first, but trust us—once your arms are sore, it could get ugly. **5-5088 Kuhio Highway; (808) 826-9844, (800) 437-3507; www.kayakkauai.com; $25–$35 for a single kayak, $48–$60 for a double.** *As you enter the village of Hanalei, the rental office is the third building on the right, just off the Kuhio Highway.*

Romantic Note: On this particular river, the first half of the journey is close to the road and breezy, but hang in there—once you travel beneath the bridge, the waters are calmer and the scenery only gets better.

Romantic Suggestion: All this paddling will get your heart thumping and your stomach grumbling, so bring a picnic lunch with you. Before venturing forth, stop by **THE HANALEI GOURMET** (5-5161 Kuhio Highway; 808-826-2524; inexpensive to moderate; breakfast, lunch, and dinner daily), which offers the best lunches in town, with a nice variety of made-to-order sandwiches, pastries, and wines. Insulated backpacks and coolers are available, too. On the sandwich-fixings front: French rolls seem to keep the best, and ask them to go light on the mayo and hold those juicy tomatoes (you'll be carrying your picnic around for a while, so you don't want a soggy sandwich). A perfect stopping point on this adventure is the grassy pasture you'll find at the end of the Hanalei River.

Romantic Option: Kayak Kauai Outbound has another office in Kapaa, and both branches offer guided kayak excursions that include hiking, camping, mountain biking, and snorkeling ($55–$250 per person). Tri-athlete types might be interested in the journeys described in the brochure as "rigorous" or "workouts," but there are also "relaxing and safe" outings from which to choose.

Don't bake your brains . . . wear a wide-brimmed hat. The tropical sun is more intense than you might realize.

Haena

Outdoor Kissing

❤️❤️❤️ **KUHIO HIGHWAY (HIGHWAY 56), Haena** Venture past the surprisingly busy town of Kapaa, and the Kuhio Highway will take you through phenomenal landscapes and quintessential island scenery. Much of the drive is waterside, but even when the ocean isn't in sight, lush foliage and dramatic rocky peaks usher you toward the North Shore. The descent into the verdant **HANALEI NATIONAL WILDLIFE REFUGE** and the roadside lookouts thereafter are the crowning glories of the drive. A narrow road with many one-lane bridges crosses calm rivers; passes popular snorkeling spots like **TUNNELS BEACH,** as well as the impressive **WAIKAPALA'E** and **WAIKANALOA WET CAVES;** and ends at **KE'E BEACH,** where various trails to Na Pali Coast and lush rain forests begin.

At first glance, the end of the Kuhio Highway looks like nothing more than a busy parking lot and a small, crowded beach area. Although Ke'e Beach is usually packed, snorkeling among its coral reefs is a wonderful option. We also recommend heading away from the beach (and most of the beachgoers) on the pathway that follows the far side of the shore. This easy trail leads to a hillside terraced with volcanic rocks, where you can sit and behold the exhilarating arrival of dusk. It's a different painting every night, as the setting sun brushes glorious colors onto the canvas where the ocean meets the sky. Watch the sunset long enough and you might even catch a glimpse of the infamous "green flash": a phenomenon that occurs when the last rays of sunlight hit a particular species of phosphorescent plankton near the water's surface, causing a brief flash of green light. Don't count on a "green flash" every night—conditions have to be just right— and it is best seen from a boat.

Continue a little farther along this trail to another very special place. Turn your gaze toward the Bali Hai mountainside and look for a grove of palm trees; then search out the path that leads there. This grove is a sacred *heiau* (Hawaiian temple), the birthplace of the hula and one of the last sites where human sacrifices were made. Don't worry; these days, small lava rocks wrapped in ti leaves are the only offerings made to the Hawaiian gods.

❤️❤️❤️❤️ **NA PALI COAST STATE PARK, Haena** One of the largest state parks in the United States, Na Pali Coast State Park covers 6,175 spectacular acres. Heaven and earth merge at the exquisitely beautiful Na Pali coastline, a 14-mile-long rocky shoreline that is inaccessible by car. At the base of these formidable cliffs are some of the most remote, unspoiled beaches in the world. Verdant tropical rain forest and deep valleys cover the uninhabited land; slippery red-clay foot trails and stream crossings that increase in difficulty during rainstorms make access tricky for even the most accomplished hikers and backpackers. The combination of such beauty with such difficult access is, perhaps, what keeps this domain more like heaven than earth.

Most of the area is more easily (although not intimately) seen via boat; contact **LIKO KAUAI CRUISES** (808-338-0333; tickets start at $95 per person). The sea caves; lush, rolling hills; mammoth cliffs; and staggering waterfalls are all breathtakingly beautiful. During many boat excursions (particularly early in the day), spinner dolphins, whales, and sea turtles cavort in the waves, providing lively aquatic entertainment. One word of warning: The waters here can be rough and rollicking, making even the most stalwart seasick. Estimate your tolerance level before you head out on a cruise, or what you thought was going to be a romantic excursion could turn into a very unpleasant experience.

Helicopter tours are also available, and give you an overview of this landscape that is unparalleled in enchantment and beauty; we recommend **OHANA HELICOPTER TOURS** (808-245-3996, 800-222-6989; www. ohana-helicopters.com; prices start at $144 per person) or **ISLAND HELI-COPTERS** (808-245-8588; $172 per person). Helicopter tours often include a souvenir video, and they usually take a more in-depth look at the island as a whole.

With the right shoes (it can get wet), athletic prowess (some of the ascents are fairly steep), and provisions (such as drinking water and snacks), you can also hike into the region. For an arduous single-day trek, follow the four-mile round-trip trail starting at **HAENA BEACH PARK** and ending at **HANAKAPIAI BEACH**. Branching off from this path is a four-mile round-trip approach to stunning **HANAKAPIAI FALLS**. Although it takes a relatively healthy body to make this journey, the glimpse of Eden is phenomenal. For those who can kiss and backpack at the same time, the 11-mile (each way) **KALALAU TRAIL** overflows with scenic wonder. Depending on your level of expertise, the hike can take two to three days. **Department of State Parks: (808) 274-3444; free overnight permit required for backpackers.** *At the end of Highway 56 in Haena, look for signs for Na Pali Coast State Park.*

Hawaii—
The Big Island

Waipio

Kawaihae * * Waimea

Hilo

*Kailua-Kona
*Holualoa
*Kealakekua
*Honaunau

*Volcano

Waiohinu

Hawaii—
The Big Island

Almost the size of the state of Connecticut, the Big Island is, without exaggeration, a place with plenty of elbow room. Known as either the Big Island or the island of Hawaii, it's the largest land mass in the Hawaiian archipelago, encompassing over 4,000 square miles of astounding and unique scenery. And thanks to continuing eruptions from Kilauea, the magma-spewing volcano, the island is still growing. Topographically speaking, the Big Island has a stunning assortment of features: snowcapped mountains in winter, endless acres of black lava beds as barren and haunting as the moon, verdant tropical rain forests, and some of the tallest peaks in the United States. In fact, 12 of the earth's 14 climatic regions can be experienced in a single day's journey on the Big Island.

From a tourist's perspective, Hawaii is unlike any of the other Hawaiian Islands. Beaches here are few and far between, and most feature lava rock or black sand. Although you can swim to your hearts' content in these waters (the snorkeling here is extraordinary), most of the shoreline is more conducive to scenic viewing than swimming or sunbathing. But this apparent shortcoming has been an asset for the Big Island. The lack of sandy swimming beaches and the vast beds of encrusted lava have prevented developers from taking hold as they have on the other islands. Also, there are plenty of wide-open spaces—enough so that you never really feel the impact of civilization. The whole island has a population of 135,000, which is sparse in proportion to its size. (Oahu, at one-third the size, has just under 1 million people, and Maui, only slightly larger than Oahu, has approximately 100,000.)

To fully appreciate all the Big Island has to offer, a rental car is essential. Driving around this island makes for a wondrous, but extremely long, excursion (driving the perimeter takes at least eight hours), so set aside a couple of days to see it all. Every mile reveals a new panorama of the island's dramatically disparate landscapes. On the dry northwest side, at the base of Mauna Kea, which rises an imperious 13,796 feet, the rolling acres of chaparral abruptly turn into a desolate expanse of lava field. Just beyond this fascinatingly bleak landscape is the breathtaking

All beaches in Hawaii are public. As long as you can find public access, you are welcome to enjoy the beaches everywhere.

KOHALA COAST, with its magnificent but hard-to-reach shoreline. Although many of the beaches along this stretch of coast are too dangerous for swimming, they offer gorgeous vantage points where you can share a scintillating sunset.

Farther south lies the **KONA DISTRICT. NORTH KONA** consists primarily of the venerable Hawaiian fishing village of Kailua-Kona, which has become increasingly commercialized and, except for the beach area and surrounding hillside, holds little romantic charm. Fortunately, this is really the only place you'll find crowds. **SOUTH KONA**, with its many undersea parks, offers some of the most exquisite snorkeling in all Hawaii. As you continue east you find the tiny, no-stoplight town of Volcano, as well as **HAWAII VOLCANOES NATIONAL PARK**, where you can study and witness firsthand the awesome power of Mother Nature. If you continue northward, you'll come to **HILO**, one of the rainiest cities in the United States and home to the annual Merrie Monarch Festival, a cultural arts extravaganza held in March or April that attracts hundreds to this town.

This is truly an island of natural wonders and romantic seclusion. Thankfully, most of the island's accommodations (with the exception of those in Kailua-Kona and Hilo) are separated from each other by many miles. As a result, relatively undisturbed retreats into the surrounding natural beauty provide couples with sanctuary from life in the fast lane.

Romantic Note: Pure Kona coffee is considered the most flavorful in the world. Coffee lovers should try this magic brew to see why, according to legend, the gods still choose the Big Island as a place to indulge their eccentricities. But be cautious; not everyone serves pure Kona coffee. Some places use a blend of beans containing as little as 10 to 20 percent Kona, with nowhere near the same taste as true Kona.

Kohala Coast

Barren yet breathtaking, the seemingly eternal stretches of black lava end abruptly at the thundering Pacific surf in a strangely surrealistic landscape. The unrelenting beds of lava and the absence of sandy swimming beaches have deterred mass hotel development along the Kohala Coast (and elsewhere on the island), thus relatively little of the land is marred by cement and steel. Consequently, the existing resorts here are few and far between—and exceedingly secluded. Plan to make yourselves at home in the resort of your choice, because there is little in terms of restaurants and shopping anywhere nearby. But who needs shopping? You will have everything you need, and more, in the confines of your hotel and in the surrounding splendor of nearby mountains and water. If you crave privacy more than you crave swimming and sand, the Kohala Coast may be your slice of paradise.

Hotel/Bed and Breakfast Kissing

❧❧❧❧ **FOUR SEASONS RESORT HUALALAI, Kohala Coast** It's obvious the designers of Kohala Coast's newest resort have done their homework. Drawing upon the successes (and avoiding the failures) of other hotels in the area, they have created a resort that is beyond comparison in terms of elegance, comfort, and style. From the minute you arrive at the low-key, Balinese-inspired resort, everything (and everyone) is aimed at making you comfortable, starting with the fruit nectar and cold towel you're offered at check-in. Afterward you are escorted, via golf cart, around the beachfront resort to your room. Thirty-six low-rise bungalows house 243 guest rooms, offering mostly ocean views and some terrific golf-course vistas from their large lanais.

The guest rooms at the Four Seasons are a study in simplicity with slate floors covered by woven mats, warm butterscotch-colored walls enriched by koa wood accents and doors, Balinese-style furnishings, white linen bedspreads, and elegantly framed Hawaiian art. Bathrooms feature deep soaking tubs, glass-enclosed showers, and a variety of little luxuries, such as after-sun cooling gel. No romantic detail has been overlooked. Wake up together and grind your own coffee beans, or take an aromatherapy bath in the deep tub (oils included). For those of you who like to read while your sweetheart sleeps, a clip-on mini-light is provided by the bed. As we said, nothing has been overlooked.

For every day you spend here, you could visit a different swimming pool. Three oceanfront pools and a 25-meter lap pool will have you splashing for joy. One such pool, the natural, seawater-fed King's Pond, is stocked with hundreds of tropical fish and a few manta rays. Snorkeling in the King's Pond can be a bit nippy, but the colorful, living world that waits beneath the surface is well worth some teeth chattering. Besides the pools, you'll be pleased to discover a rough but lovely half-mile stretch of beach, an outstanding Hawaiian cultural center, an 18-hole private golf course (with some of the most romantic, seaside tee boxes we've seen), tennis courts, and an "open-air" sports club and spa that is breathtaking, literally and figuratively.

Romantic dining at the Four Seasons is found beachside at **PAHU I'A** (see Restaurant Kissing). Overlooking the 18th green is the **HUALALAI CLUB GRILL** (moderate to expensive; lunch and dinner daily), a great spot for watching sunsets; for poolside culinary pleasures, there's the **BEACH TREE BAR & GRILL** (moderate to expensive; lunch and dinner daily). **100 Ka'upulehu Drive; (808) 325-8000, (888) 340-5662 mainland; www.fourseasons.com; very expensive to unbelievably expensive and beyond; recommended wedding site.**

❦❦ **HAPUNA BEACH PRINCE HOTEL, Kohala Coast** In Hawaiian, *hapuna* means "spring of life." While officially named after the series of underground springs in this area, the Hapuna Beach Prince Hotel captures this definition in another way as well. Just stay at this elegant beachfront hotel and watch your romance spring to life. It's easy to find love in this luxurious setting. A stunning open-air lobby embellished by towering stone pillars and Asian art pieces greets you as you enter, while 32 acres of terraced lawns and lush gardens await below. Merely looking around will put you in a state of relaxation.

The 350 rooms and suites have that standard hotel look, although each is pleasantly appointed with all the traditional amenities you could want. In addition, each unit has either a view of the ocean (over the grounds) or a direct oceanfront vista. Your proximity to the soft white sands of Hapuna Beach is a definite plus here (and might also explain the exorbitant prices). The beach, often called one of the island's most beautiful, is one of the few spots along the coast where you can swim and play in the tide pools. Overall, the Hapuna Beach Prince Hotel is a place to treat yourselves like royalty while enjoying friendly service, a world-class beach, and all the offerings of a full-scale resort. **62-100 Kaunaoa Drive; (808) 880-1111, (800) 882-6060 mainland; www.hapunabeachprincehotel.com; unbelievably expensive and beyond; recommended wedding site.**

Romantic Note: Restaurant options here include the spacious, circular COAST GRILLE (expensive; dinner daily) for Euro-Hawaiian cuisine accompanied by ocean views in an open-air setting. One of the island's few oyster bars is found here too, featuring specially selected oysters from around the globe.

❦❦❦ **HILTON WAIKOLOA VILLAGE, Kohala Coast** Sixty-two oceanfront acres (but, alas, no natural beach) envelop this palatial wonderland, which includes six restaurants, eight lounges, 1,240 guest rooms, meeting facilities, three swimming pools, two golf courses, several twisting water slides, shopping, a beautiful health spa, a lagoon with trained dolphins, and more. So how do you make your way across this gargantuan property? Just like you do in Disneyland! Hop on the small ferryboat that winds through the connecting waterways or try the electric tram that parallels the water. Either option can be delightful once or twice, but both grow tiresome quickly, especially when there are crowds. Instead, set out on foot (don't forget your map), and wander along flagstone walkways that meander past the stunning Asian and Pacific art pieces that grace this Polynesian palace. Although there are acres upon acres of property to explore, most of it is man-made (waterfalls and lagoon included), and you may find yourselves longing for open stretches of untouched beach and sky. (Isn't that why you came to Hawaii?) To satisfy your cravings, take a shuttle bus from the hotel to the public beach next door.

Once you've finally found your suite, located in either the Ocean, Lagoon, or Palace Tower, you can bask in stately (although pricey) comfort and ocean views. The Club Bay Suites are especially luxurious, with Asian motifs, unusual pottery, magnificent view lanais, queen-size koa-wood beds, marble baths, and Jacuzzi tubs. The Regency Club Suites include exemplary concierge service, breakfast and the morning paper, and evening cocktails with hors d'oeuvres. If your budget can handle it and you're in the mood for miles of hotel and lots of outdoor recreation, you've found heaven. Otherwise, you'll be looking frantically for the exit. **425 Waikoloa Beach Drive; (808) 885-1234, (800) 221-2424; www.hilton.com/hawaii/waikoloa; expensive to unbelievably expensive and beyond; recommended wedding site.**

Romantic Note: The Hilton has six different restaurants to choose from, all just a ferryboat or tram ride away. **IMARI** (808-885-2893; moderate; dinner daily), set in a lovely tea garden highlighted by waterfalls, offers innovative Japanese cuisine and a sushi bar with some of the best bite-size creations around. Another option is the **PALM TERRACE** (808-885-2893; moderate to expensive; breakfast and dinner daily), an open-air dining room set beside a plunging waterfall. Delectable baked goods, fruits, and traditional American and Japanese dishes are served at deluxe breakfast and dinner buffets. **DONATONI'S** and the **KAMUELA PROVISION COMPANY** (see Restaurant Kissing for reviews of both) are also quite good.

❀❀❀ THE ISLANDS AT MAUNA LANI, Kohala Coast

Five acres of man-made saltwater lagoons nearly surround The Islands at Mauna Lani, a property made up of Mediterranean-inspired luxury townhomes. The artificial ponds and waterfalls do not even begin to compare to an actual oceanside setting, but if the idea of having a place all to yourselves sounds appealing, consider staying here. The 46 two- and three-bedroom, split-level homes are all attractively decorated in varying styles. What they have in common are white oak floors and ceilings, expansive windows, a huge full kitchen with pale wood cabinets, a laundry room, central air-conditioning, and a wet bar and gas barbecue outside. The kitchen is stocked in advance with a complete assortment of groceries, and a full-size rental car is yours for the duration of your stay.

You may be saying to yourselves, "All this and only a two-and-a-half-lips rating?" Well, despite beautiful furnishings in many of the homes, the units feel somewhat sterile and they are extremely close to one another, leaving little breathing room. Also, the ocean is nowhere in sight. Thankfully, there is a swimming pool at the center of the property, and beach access is just a short drive away. **68-1050 Mauna Lani Point Drive; (808) 885-5022, (800) 642-6284; www.islands-at-maunalani.com; very expensive to unbelievably expensive.**

Romantic Alternative: MAUNA LANI POINT (68-1050 Mauna Lani Point Drive; 808-885-5022, 800-642-6284; www.maunalani-point.com; expensive to unbelievably expensive) is yet another condominium resort right next door. Roomy one-, two-, and three-bedroom suites feature ocean views beyond a golf course. Unfortunately, the decor is different in each suite, and it ranges from casual contemporary to downright tacky. These units hardly compare to the elegance found at The Islands at Mauna Lani, but if oceanfront is a requirement for your romantic state of mind, this is an option.

❀❀❀❀ **KONA VILLAGE RESORT, Kohala Coast** Picture a romantic island getaway with plenty of privacy and an abundance of sand, water, fragrant flowers, and palm trees around every corner, and you've pictured Kona Village. This is truly an escapist's dream, but those who can't live without modern conveniences (i.e., TVs, telephones, alarm clocks, radios, etc.) will be better off elsewhere. What will you find here? Blissful peace and isolation. Staying at Kona Village is like being transported to an ancient seaside Hawaiian fishing settlement: You sleep beneath a thatched roof in a private, self-contained *hale* (bungalow) designed exclusively for romantic exile. A total of 125 *hales* in a full range of sizes (and prices) dot the resort's 82 creatively landscaped acres, and are decorated in a variety of authentic and colorful Polynesian themes ranging from Samoan to Fijian to Tahitian.

Although furnishings in the *hales* are simple, they include all the required comforts: king-size beds, colorful linens, private baths, and refrigerators stocked with cool drinks. Dusty walking paths meander past cottages tucked beneath palm trees, nestled near a large lagoon teeming with birds, set atop jet black lava rock and black sand, or scattered along a stretch of soft white beach. It feels magical after dark as you walk beneath an arena of twinkling stars. Sit at the water's edge and try to catch a glimpse of the mysterious manta ray, or listen to the gentle rush of the man-made waterfall from the spacious outdoor hot tub or the two small swimming pools.

Civilization feels light-years away, and this illusion is enhanced by the fact that you don't have to worry about money (until you pay the tab, of course). Experience a cashless society where three daily meals are provided (they are included in the room price). Alas, although Kona Village's weekly luau is truly one of the best on the Big Island (see Miscellaneous Kissing), the food at both of the restaurants here is best described as mediocre. **Queen Kaahumanu Highway (Highway 19); (808) 325-5555, (800) 367-5290 mainland; www.konavillage.com; expensive to unbelievably expensive and beyond; recommended wedding site.**

Romantic Note: At Kona Village, children are welcomed with open arms, but with so many activities set up for them to do during the day, they are rarely in sight.

❀❀❀ MAUNA KEA BEACH HOTEL, Kohala Coast

Like so many of the Kohala Coast resorts, the Mauna Kea Beach Hotel resounds with splendor and grace. Yet, compared with many others, this hotel maintains a low profile—a major selling point for couples seeking solitude along with sensuous days and nights. A beautiful koi pond weaves through the hotel's inner atrium, while walkways surrounded by lush gardens lead to bluffs overlooking the sea. Throughout the hotel, from the lobby to the hallways, art pieces accentuate the natural beauty surrounding you.

The romantic potential of the 310 rooms ranks only about average, but truly the most alluring aspects here are the crescent-shaped stretch of soft, sandy beach and the serene turquoise bay fronting the property. Of the handful of restaurants, **THE BATIK** (expensive to very expensive; dinner Sunday–Monday and Wednesday–Friday) rates as the most kiss-worthy. Euro-Asian cuisine, combined with tableside preparation of dishes, classical guitar music, and views of Kauna'oa Bay, make this the resort's premier dining spot. **62-100 Mauna Kea Beach Drive; (808) 882-7222, (800) 882-6060 mainland; www.maunakeabeachhotel.com; very expensive to unbelievably expensive; recommended wedding site.**

❀❀❀❀ MAUNA LANI BAY HOTEL AND BUNGALOWS, Kohala Coast

When *Lifestyles of the Rich and Famous* rated the Mauna Lani Bay the number-one resort in the United States, it probably referred to the five unique, ultraluxurious bungalows (ten lips at least!) that only the rich and famous could possibly afford. Located right on the water's edge, with panoramic ocean views, each one has more space than most homes, along with a sumptuous marble bath, Jacuzzi tub, private pool, personal butler, and plush oversize furnishings, all for $3,625 (and up) a night. If you can swallow that price, you already know about overindulging the senses.

The rest of us (the underpaid and the obscure) are consigned to a large, white plaster hotel shaped like an arrow. Set on the rugged and secluded Kohala Coast, the hotel is surrounded by lush foliage, manicured grounds, waterfalls and protected fishponds, and a premier waterfront golf course etched in black lava rock. A five-story open-air lobby hints of older construction, but you probably won't care once you see the brilliant glass waterfall and the ponds filled with tropical fish and turtles. Guest rooms are attractive and exceedingly comfortable, though somewhat on the snug side. Most have lanais looking out to the spectacular ocean, which creates a more spacious feeling inside. (The Garden Rooms, however, look out over the parking area.)

Resort amenities abound. In addition to the aforementioned championship golf course (you've probably seen it on TV, with its unparalleled over-the-water par-three hole), the Mauna Lani offers tennis courts, a lovely swimming pool, three miles of white-sand beach, a health club, and six restaurants, including **THE CANOE HOUSE** (see Restaurant Kissing). **68-1400 Mauna Lani Drive; (808) 885-6622, (800) 367-2323; www. maunalani.com; expensive to unbelievably expensive and beyond; recommended wedding site.**

❀❀❀❀ **THE ORCHID AT MAUNA LANI, Kohala Coast** Like its namesake flower, The Orchid at Mauna Lani is simply beautiful. Thirty-two acres of lush, tropical gardens and golf course encompass the 539-room hotel. In the sprawling interior courtyard, rocky waterfalls, fishponds filled with koi, quaint footbridges, and lush vegetation surround you as you follow rambling paths past a large, curvaceous swimming pool. It continues to get better from here as you walk along the pathways to a private lagoon, a perfect place for snorkeling in the day and stargazing at night.

The guest suites, while nowhere as magnificent as the grounds, still outshine many on the Kohala Coast in terms of style and comfort. Rich color schemes, plush linens, and an attractive marble bath with separate tub and shower are standard in all rooms. Private lanais, most with rousing views of the surrounding grounds and ocean, make for the ideal in-room breakfast spot.

Complete relaxation comes easy at The Orchid, thanks to its outstanding Centre for Well Being, a comprehensive activity and wellness program. Enjoy tai chi classes under the palm trees, interpretive walks to nearby petroglyphs, or a healing massage by the seaside. When the day winds down, dine at **THE GRILL** (see Restaurant Kissing), The Orchid's formal and elegant dining establishment. Or head down by the water to **BROWN'S BEACH HOUSE** (moderate to expensive; lunch and dinner daily) for Hawaiian regional cuisine. Afterward, stroll through the torch-lit grounds, find an oceanside hammock, and swing together to the sounds of the sea. **One North Kaniku Drive; (808) 885-2000, (800) 845-9905 mainland; www.orchid-maunalani.com; very expensive to unbelievably expensive and beyond; recommended wedding site.**

Unrated THE ROYAL WAIKOLOAN, Kohala Coast Staying on the Kohala Coast can take your breath away, both by the beauty and by the exorbitant prices so many hotels and resorts charge. (Most start at $325 a night.) If you want beauty on a budget, the 545-room Royal Waikoloan may be your answer. When we visited, the hotel was in need of major renovation and that's exactly what was about to happen. While we can't foretell what the $20 million remodeling job will look like, we can say that this hotel fronts one of the nicest beaches on the coast. It's perfect for swimming and snorkeling, and secluded enough for some kissing opportunities. The open-air lobby is quite pleasant, as is the bar area and small pool. Hopefully, the hotel won't raise its moderate rates too high after renovation. The Kohala Coast needs a good hotel that falls into the "reasonably priced" category. **69-275 Waikoloa Beach Drive; (808) 886-6789, (800) 688-7444; www.outrigger.com; moderate to very expensive.**

Restaurant Kissing

❤❤❤ THE CANOE HOUSE, Kohala Coast Considered one of the best restaurants on the coast, The Canoe House comes very close to living up to its challenging reputation. The open-air dining room allows distant views of the gentle water and breathtaking sunsets through swaying palms and tiki torches, making the outside an integral part of your dining experience. Under a thatched roof with wood detailing, soft candlelight and comfortable seating fill the interior with a subtle elegance that blends perfectly with the energy of the waves and the warmth of the air.

Like many of Hawaii's restaurants, The Canoe House serves Pacific Rim cuisine, with a few continental favorites thrown in to round out the menu. Nori-wrapped tempura *ahi* with wasabi soy sauce, and marinated *ono* with wasabi "smashed" potatoes are two delicious entrées. If wasabi doesn't wow you, there's grilled New York steak, hibachi-style chicken with roasted potatoes, and the house specialty: honey-glazed lamb chops served with a *poha* (cape gooseberry) sauce. Presentation and fresh ingredients are emphasized here along with wine recommendations for each dish. But ultimately the taste is the first consideration, and everything is more than delectable. **68-1400 Mauna Lani Drive, at the Mauna Lani Bay Hotel and Bungalows; (808) 885-6622, (800) 367-2323; very expensive; dinner daily.**

❧❧ **DONATONI'S, Kohala Coast** Complete with elegant Tuscan-style architecture and old-world charm, this cozy restaurant is like stepping straight into Italy (although the nearby palm trees remind you that you're in Hawaii). Complementing such surroundings is a menu composed of entirely northern Italian cuisine ranging from gourmet pizzas and pastas to savory meat dishes. Large overstuffed brocade chairs, romantic lighting, and views of the hotel's waterways and surrounding garden create an intimate atmosphere in which to dine in bliss. The waterside patio is a wonderful place to dine, but when we visited the management was extremely inflexible in accommodating our request to sit there. Good luck. **69-425 Waikoloa Beach Drive, at the Hilton Waikoloa Village; (808) 885-2893; www.hilton.com/hawaii/waikoloa; expensive; reservations required; lunch and dinner daily.**

❧❧❧ **THE GRILL, Kohala Coast** Combine rich, dark koa wood, sparkling crystal chandeliers, crisp linens, and plush upholstered chairs, and what do you get? The Grill, an elegant and formal restaurant that showcases seasonal and Hawaiian cuisine with style. Add to this regal atmosphere excellent service and an incredible chef who seeks to reward all the senses within one meal, and what else do you get? A dining destination that meets *our* ever-so-high, romantic-minded standards.

Traditional grilled fare with innovative Mediterranean flair graces the menu. Try such culinary delights as rack of lamb, grilled *kiawe*-smoked breast of free-range chicken, pan-seared herb-crusted sea scallops, and thyme-crusted swordfish steak. Desserts are equally enticing, so save some room. For the best views of The Orchid's torch-lit grounds, request a patio table or an interior table next to the open windows. Feeling that

---

Disposable underwater cameras take surprisingly good photographs. We recommend purchasing one to take along on snorkeling adventures and boat rides so you won't have to worry about getting your nondisposable camera wet.

ocean breeze and looking up at the stars make dining here a celestial experience. **One North Kaniku Drive, at The Orchid at Mauna Lani; (808) 885-2000; very expensive; dinner Tuesday–Saturday; recommended wedding site.**

☙☙❧ **KAMUELA PROVISION COMPANY, Kohala Coast** After you've worked up an appetite exploring the amusement park–like grounds of the HILTON WAIKOLOA VILLAGE (see Hotel/Bed and Breakfast Kissing), hop on the electric tram and go to the Kamuela Provision Company for steak and seafood. (Be sure to ask if you're headed in the right direction; asking for directions is a must at this 64-acre resort.)

At the end of the line, the Kamuela Provision Company borders the oceanfront and is so peaceful and quiet, you might even forget the rest of this massive property. Outdoor seating is especially nice because of the surrounding tropical ambience, and from 6 P.M. to 10 P.M. a guitarist sends soft melodies into the open night air. Inside, tall French doors separate several quaint dining rooms, each holding tables with floral linens and glowing candles, black-and-cream-checked chairs, and hardwood floors. Service is prompt and friendly, and the menu offers hearty choices like Madras curried lamb chops, roasted ancho–marinated chicken, and fresh fish prepared three ways. For dessert, consider sharing a piece of chocolate-macadamia nut pie or a generously sized slice of mud pie served with hot fudge sauce and whipped cream. These desserts are both heavy and heavenly! **425 Waikoloa Beach Drive, at the Hilton Waikoloa Village; (808) 885-2893; moderate to expensive; lunch and dinner daily.**

☙☙☙☙ **PAHU I'A, Kohala Coast** At Pahu i'a, stunning sunsets come complimentary with your dinner, along with unobstructed views of the crashing white surf. The Four Seasons' elegant open-air restaurant has all the details down, from the outstanding setting to the unsurpassed service and flavorful dishes.

Pahu i'a means "aquarium" in Hawaiian and, in keeping with its namesake, an enormous tank teeming with colorful fish greets you upon arrival. Slow-moving ceiling fans, teak and mahogany woods, and Asian artwork seduce you to sit back, relax, and savor the atmosphere. Just as you become comfortable, your palate will be awakened by some decidedly delicious and interesting dishes. Start with the English pea coconut soup, which sounds complex, but is subtle and smooth in taste and texture. For some colorful local flavors, try the Big Island oyster mushroom and purple spinach salad. Entrée specials, drawing upon local and international ingredients, are irresistible. Just one bite into the succulent grilled butterfish with a ginger-herb vinaigrette and you'll taste what we mean. As the stars blanket the sky, finish your meal with the bittersweet chocolate soufflé, filled with crème anglaise at your table. This dessert is so heavenly you might just levitate. **100 Ka'upulehu Drive, at the Four Seasons Resort Hualalai; (808) 325-8000, (888) 340-5662 mainland; www.fourseasons.com; expensive to very expensive; breakfast and dinner daily.**

Miscellaneous Kissing

❤❤❤ **KONA VILLAGE LUAU, Kohala Coast** Kona Village has the best luau in Hawaii, and we don't mean just on the Big Island; we mean it is the best luau in the *entire state*. Judging from the number of locals who frequent this weekly event for special occasions or just to reunite themselves with the Hawaii of old, this luau is the real deal. Polynesian dancers and entertainers perform on a stage beyond a pond area, so the experience isn't "in your face" like at most other luaus (see "To Luau or Not to Luau" on page 15). The high-energy entertainment is excellent, and the food was one of the most memorable parts of our trip.

Our senses were first dazzled by the smoky aroma of the *kalua* pig as it was lifted from the *imu* (an underground oven six feet wide and four feet deep, lined with burning wood and hot lava rocks). This delicious, traditionally prepared meat is the main dish of the feast and, unlike at other luaus, where you might get only a taste, there is plenty of it to go around. Other authentic Polynesian favorites from the intriguing menu include poi, which is mashed taro root and crucial to any Hawaiian meal; *laulau*, seasoned pork with salted butterfish wrapped in taro leaves; *poisson cru*, fresh chunks of raw fish and thin slices of vegetables marinated in lime juice and coconut milk; and banana and papaya *po'e*, mashed bananas and papayas baked with pineapple juice and coconut milk. This luau is an event not to be missed. **Queen Kaahumanu Highway (Highway 19); (808) 325-5555, (800) 367-5290 mainland; www.konavillage.com; free admission for resort guests, $69 per nonguest; reservations required.**

Kawaihae

Hotel/Bed and Breakfast Kissing

❤❤ **MAKAI HALE, Kawaihae** As you wind up the hillside toward Makai Hale, the stunning splendor of the Kohala Coast becomes more apparent. Across the expanse of horizon, the crystal blue Pacific dazzles your eyes while the mountain peak of Mauna Kea rises majestically to meet the sky. Vast black lava beds below drop suddenly to the raging sea. Makai Hale takes full advantage of this view, and guests can take in the heavenly surroundings in a detached two-bedroom suite. Floor-to-ceiling windows, a comfy white wicker bed with floral linens, a standard, rather small bathroom, and unobstructed views from the front bedroom are yours alone. To fully embrace views of the Kohala Coast, slip out the sliding glass door of your suite onto a sweeping cement deck with a large swimming pool, a Jacuzzi tub, and picnic tables where you can relax for hours and contemplate the breathtaking panorama. You'll find breakfast provisions in the small kitchenette; the hosts, who live in the adjacent house, leave your privacy undisturbed. **Reservations through Hawaii's Best Bed and Breakfasts, (808) 885-4550, (800) 262-9912 mainland; inexpensive.**

Restaurant Kissing

❧ **CAFE PESTO, Kawaihae** Tucked—or, rather, trapped—in the middle of a small shopping center, this café is the perfect place for a quick lunch or dinner, despite its very unromantic location. Inside, the casual dining room is distinguished by a black-and-white-checked floor and bright contemporary art. The menu lists a wide variety of salads, calzones, hand-tossed pizzas, hot sandwiches, pastas, and risottos, and fresh seafood prepared in three tantalizing styles. Cafe Pesto's service rates among the friendliest and most efficient on the island, and we know your lips won't be disappointed with the food. **In the Kawaihae Shopping Center; (808) 882-1071; www.cafepesto.com; inexpensive to expensive; lunch and dinner daily.**

Waimea

Up here, at 2,200 feet above sea level, the days can be hot, with warm afternoon rains and cool breezes that blow through gently swaying trees and over idyllic green pasture land. The ocean is only eight miles away, but another world exists at this elevation, and it is worth discovering for yourselves. Waimea is a thriving, quiet country town and home to several thousand islanders. You'll find a variety of restaurants and shops, as well as acres and acres of visual enchantment.

For well over 100 years, the pivotal business of the region has been the **PARKER RANCH**, the largest family-owned ranch in the United States. Currently, more than 225,000 acres are in a charitable trust serving the town of Waimea, but it all began as a two-acre land grant back in 1837 from King Kamehameha I to John P. Parker. For a more detailed historical retrospective, tour the two museums, one of which is in the owners' ranch house.

Instead of spending only a day in this peaceful countryside, consider a longer romantic sojourn. Waimea isn't the tropical Hawaii you usually imagine, but it also isn't as crowded or as expensive as the coastal areas.

Hotel/Bed and Breakfast Kissing

❦❦ **TINA'S COUNTRY COTTAGE, Waimea** At the end of a secluded neighborhood sits a quaint green cottage that's as fresh as the breeze that sweeps down from Waimea's foothills. Immaculate best describes the two-bedroom hideaway featuring a full kitchen, high ceilings, a woodstove for those nippy evenings, and all the electronic amenities needed for entertainment. The spacious master bedroom (the only romantic choice of the two bedrooms) won't wow you with heartstopping amenities, but will satisfy with its queen-size bed, lace curtains, standard but bright bath, and plenty of space, including a large walk-in closet. Throughout, the home is modestly decorated with floral accents, a sprinkling of antiques, and Hawaiian artwork. Protected from the wind, you and your honey can snuggle on the cushioned wicker furniture that adorns the covered front porch. On occasional weekends, the rodeo arena across the yard hosts cowboy roping competitions. Depending on your perspective, this show could be worth watching. The proprietor stocks the kitchen with enough breakfast fixings for your entire stay, so you won't have to rush out for anything. **Reservations through Hawaii's Best Bed and Breakfasts, (808) 885-4550, (800) 262-9912 mainland; moderate.**

❦❦❦❦ **WAIMEA GARDENS COTTAGE, Waimea** As you've thumbed through the Hotel/Bed and Breakfast Kissing selections in this guide, you've probably noticed references to Hawaii's Best Bed and Breakfasts reservation service. Well, the owners of this business have created a "best" bed and breakfast of their own.

An impeccably renovated duplex cottage adjacent to the main house holds two lovingly decorated units (the Waimea Wing and Kohala Wing) bordered by a rushing creek, sweeping lawn, forest, and well-maintained English garden. Forest-green trim on the windows and a picket fence complement the shingled exterior of the duplex. Inside, the country-inspired interiors are flawless, with wood-burning fireplaces, hardwood floors, alcove bedrooms, down comforters, charming kitchens, stereos, and TVs. While both cottages are equally enchanting, the Kohala Wing has the advantage of a full kitchen (the Waimea Wing has a kitchenette), not to mention the bathroom of your dreams. Relax in the deep Jacuzzi tub or bask underneath the open, two-head shower while you enjoy views of a lovely Balinese-style garden. Open the adjoining door and dry off in this secluded spot surrounded by a high wooden fence and lit by the glow of a Japanese lantern.

In the morning, a breakfast consisting of farm-fresh eggs (you cook them to your liking), granola, milk, tropical fruits, and yogurt awaits in your fridge. Every amorous detail has been attended to at Waimea Gardens Cottage, so all you have to do is snuggle together and enjoy. **Reservations through Hawaii's Best Bed and Breakfasts, (808) 885-4550, (800) 262-9912 mainland; www.bestbnb.com; inexpensive.**

Restaurant Kissing

❤❤❤ **MERRIMAN'S RESTAURANT, Waimea** Ask anyone on the Big Island, and they'll tell you this spot serves up some of Hawaii's best regional cuisine. While the Waimea location may be a bit out of the way for those staying in Kailua or along the Kohala Coast, the drive up to these pastoral parts is beautiful and well worth the 30- to 60-minute trip. Besides, the food that awaits at Merriman's is worth driving a million miles to taste.

When we visited, our wok-charred ahi was perfectly done, and the fresh catch of the day *(ono)*, sautéed in a sesame crust and topped with a mango-lime sauce, proved that the locals know what they are talking about. Fresh local meats, including Kahua Ranch lamb, are equally savory and masterfully prepared. The chef takes full advantage of local, organically grown produce in such dishes as the garden-fresh Lokelani tomato salad. As for ambience, tables are situated a little too close to one another for any privacy, and at times the room can be noisy; but the food is so grand, you'll hardly notice these shortcomings. You can save the kissing until you get home, full and satisfied from a delightful meal. **Highway 19 and Opelo Road; (808) 885-6822; moderate to expensive; lunch Monday–Friday, dinner daily.**

Waipio

Outdoor Kissing

❤❤❤❤ **WAIPIO VALLEY, Waipio** Looking down into the breathtaking Waipio Valley from the roadside lookout is an awesome experience. However, an excursion through the valley itself, in a mule-driven wagon, provides passage to gorgeous tropical vegetation, cascading waterfalls, saturated taro fields, and a striking black-sand beach. It is also a journey through history. King Kamehameha I established his long reign over the islands from this location. Formidable battles, human sacrifices, and peaceful agriculture have all been part of life in this mesmerizing valley. The softly wafting breezes here seem to whisper of Hawaii's past, so take a moment to contemplate the ancient stories this area can share. **Waipio Valley Shuttle: (808) 775-7121. Waipio Valley Wagon Tours: (808) 775-9518; $40 per person for a one-and-a-half-hour tour; reservations recommended.** *Call for directions to pick-up locations.*

Romantic Note: If you are interested in a more intimate trek and are also capable of handling a fairly steep ascent out of the valley, hiking is definitely an option. Watertight shoes are a necessity, along with a backpack and light rain gear. Remember, this is the rainy side of the island.

Kona District

Kailua-Kona

Just south of the Keahole-Kona International Airport is the Big Island's major metropolis and largest tourist stopover: the town of Kailua-Kona. Its shores, nearby streets, and highways are bursting at the seams with hotels, restaurants, cafés, gift stores, national retail stores, gas stations, and local residences. This scene is a bit startling once you have explored the rest of the island, because you can go for miles and never see development like this again. Although the crowds in Kailua-Kona hardly compare to those in Waikiki on the island of Oahu, be forewarned that this is not the place to come for quiet refuge on great beaches. Kailua-Kona welcomes you in warm Hawaiian style, offering many options for tourists who seek easily accessible lodging, dining, and entertainment. But this is not the area where you will find anything resembling paradise.

Hotel/Bed and Breakfast Kissing

❤️❤️ **ASTON ROYAL SEA CLIFF RESORT, Kailua-Kona** Although the white stucco exterior may be a bit stark for some tastes, the Aston's elongated design, garden courtyards, and Mediterranean feel are a welcome change from the repetitious, nondescript, and very run-down hotels found throughout Kailua-Kona. Stroll through spacious open-air hallways to your one- or two-bedroom suite. The 154 rental units here are condominiums, but the property is operated (and looks) more like a hotel. Each room has the same plain decor, soothing pastel colors, a large-view lanai, cushioned wicker furnishings, a full kitchen, a large tiled bathroom, and a tropical floral bedspread. The units aren't fancy, but they aren't exorbitantly priced either. In fact, this is one of the few places where we do not recommend the most expensive rooms, even if you are willing to splurge, because the very expensive oceanfront villas are sadly in need of refurbishment. During value season (April through mid-December), you can get a one- or two-bedroom unit with spectacular ocean views for less than $200. Not bad in this neighborhood.

Last but not least, the two outdoor pools (one freshwater, the other salt water) have unobstructed ocean views and are surrounded by a well-groomed landscape with colorful flower beds, a small waterfall, palm trees, and an expansive, lush lawn. When dusk's cool breezes arrive, warm yourselves in the poolside Jacuzzi tubs. Comfort should always be this affordable on Hawaii. **75-6040 Alii Drive; (808) 329-8021, (800) 922-7866; www. aston-hotels.com; moderate to unbelievably expensive.**

❀❀❀❁ KAILUA PLANTATION HOUSE, Kailua-Kona Ah, sweet sanctuary at last. Many of the Big Island's bed and breakfasts are private homes that have been converted to accommodate guests; more often than not, they are too casual for comfort and too home-like for romance. The Kailua Plantation House is a welcome exception. Built and designed to serve exclusively as a bed and breakfast, this inn offers its guests the intimacy and seclusion of a small property with the luxury of a superior hotel. This is a rare combination, especially on the Hawaiian Islands.

Set on the edge of a black lava beach, this impressive two-story plantation-style mansion offers exquisite views of the turbulent Pacific surf from every angle. Busy Alii Drive, right behind the house, is the only potential drawback, but as long as you don't stay in either of the two rooms facing the noisy street, the inn's design is such that you won't even know the traffic is there. You can relish the ocean breezes undisturbed from the spacious common room, wraparound lanai, outdoor Jacuzzi tub, or small triangular dipping pool. And you've only just begun.

Each of the three non-street-side guest rooms has a spectacular ocean view, private bath, private lanai, and enticing details. The deluxe first-floor Pilialoha Suite offers a platform Jacuzzi tub for two, accentuated by an overhead skylight. This is considered the honeymoon suite, but it's too close to the common room and dipping pool for true privacy. The upstairs Kai o Lani ("Heavenly Waters") Room is more secluded, and appointed with a bamboo-and-rattan queen-size half-canopy bed. Its spacious bathroom features a deep soaking tub and a glass-enclosed shower complete with a window looking out to the ocean. Even the smaller, African-inspired Hale Apelika Room next door is beguiling, with its rattan-and-bamboo furnishings and its elegant animal-print bedspread atop the canopied bamboo queen-size bed. You will feel pampered from the moment you arrive, and the morning's full buffet breakfast of fresh-baked muffins, breads, baked dishes, local and exotic fruits, and Kona coffee will make your departure that much more difficult. You just might want to book another night or two. **75-5948 Alii Drive; (808) 329-3727, (888) 357-4262; www.tales. com/kph; moderate to very expensive; recommended wedding site.**

❦❦❦ **PUANANI, Kailua-Kona** Peace and quiet, plus privacy and affordability, are never easy to find under one roof, especially in Hawaii, but they are just what you will find at this bed and breakfast. *Puanani* means "beautiful flower," and this property in a quiet residential area is embellished with a multitude of them. Colorful ti plants and other tropical foliage surround the striking two-story glass-and-cedar home capped with a blue tile roof. Sounds of a flowing fountain and rustling Christmas palms set a peaceful mood. A waterfall trickles into a 40-foot lap pool in the manicured backyard, while the nearby hot tub and tennis court round out the recreational options. All of this tropical splendor was created by the gracious hosts themselves, and they have done an incredible job.

Guests can rent one of three units. In the main house, choose from the one-bedroom Plumeria or the Palm Suite, a one-bedroom unit with separate sitting area. Located on opposite ends of the home, both units are wonderfully secluded and spacious; both have a private bath, kitchenette, queen-size bed covered by a handmade Hawaiian quilt, attractive antique furnishings, and a private entrance. A distant ocean view can be had from both rooms, but the lush grounds will more than satisfy your senses. For water vistas, book the second-story Gardenia. Offering the utmost in privacy, this detached cottage offers a full kitchen, living room, one bedroom, and a private deck. In all units, a simple but filling continental breakfast is left in the refrigerator for you to enjoy at your leisure. **Reservations through Hawaii's Best Bed and Breakfasts, (808) 885-4550, (800) 262-9912 mainland; www.planet-hawaii.com/puanani; inexpensive.**

❦❦ **SEA VILLAGE RESORT, Kailua-Kona** Condominium rental can be an affordable alternative for budget-minded lovers who seek romantic asylum on the Big Island. Of course, with condominiums you run the risk of ending up with interiors that don't suit your style. Such is the case at Sea Village, where most units have somewhat dated tropical decor. On the other hand, Sea Village does provide large one- or two-bedroom, fully equipped apartments with generous privacy at extremely reasonable rates. Rates decrease the longer you stay, so it is to your advantage to extend your Hawaiian vacation.

You can select from garden, ocean-view, or oceanfront suites (the better the view, the higher the price). Each suite comes with a large kitchen, washer/dryer, view lanai, and weekly maid service. Lounge near the small oceanside pool and sip a drink from the convenient wet bar, or hold hands and venture down to the lava-rock beach to watch the turbulent Pacific surf. And for those who like to be near the center of the action, Kailua-Kona's restaurants, shopping, snorkeling, and tourist activities are only a five-minute drive away. **75-6002 Alii Drive; reservations through Paradise Management Corporation, (808) 538-7145, (800) 367-5205 mainland; inexpensive to moderate.**

❤❤❤ **WESTWINDS KONA AKUA HOUSE, Kailua-Kona** What could be more romantic than cuddling together on a cool night, listening to a seasonal tropical downpour tapping on the tin roof? At Westwinds Kona Akua House, high on the hills above Kailua-Kona, such nighttime nature dramas provide the quintessential romantic ambience. This spectacular plantation-style vacation home resides on an acre of lush tropical land with no other houses in sight . . . perfect for savoring the magnificent water views and fiery-orange sunsets. Stroll past nearby macadamia nut orchards or enjoy the innkeeper's beautifully tended gardens that complement the natural surroundings.

The two-story house can sleep up to six, but it's perfect for one couple. Sit on the screened sunporch and watch the day go by, or prepare a meal in the gorgeous tile and koa-wood kitchen. A two-headed shower larger than most bathrooms, a loft bedroom with ocean views, and an elegant living room with green leather couches make Kona Akua a truly romantic place to stay, rain or shine. **(808) 322-5103, (888) 548-5662; www.karuna. com/westwinds; expensive.**

Romantic Note: Unlike at other vacation rentals, here you have two options come breakfast time. The proprietor is happy to prepare a meal for you, or if you'd like you can make breakfast yourselves. Just give the proprietor advanced notice if you select the first option.

Restaurant Kissing

❤❤❤ **EDWARD'S AT KANALOA, Kailua-Kona** Edward's is Kailua-Kona's only oceanfront Mediterranean restaurant and, if we may add to this claim, it's one of the only surf-side restaurants in town where the food complements the location. Situated at the very edge of the Kanaloa Condominium complex, this 60-seat al fresco spot is flanked by a pool and the pounding waves below . . . a two-for-one waterfront dining experience. Although it's open for all meals, the romance hour is after 5 P.M., when the pool crowd has disappeared and the orange orb puts on its final performance of the day. Fewer than two dozen tables, adorned with colorful tablecloths and palm leaf–shaped chairs, are spaced far apart, allowing you to enjoy the evening without hearing your neighbor's opinion on everything.

Mediterranean influences are evident throughout the menu, starting with such treats as a mushroom ragout in a pomegranate seed sauce, peppered *ahi* topped with olives and a garlic beurre blanc, or medallions of pork with prunes and white wine. All delight the taste buds with well-balanced flavors. Moroccan-spiced chicken, roasted rack of lamb, and stuffed squid continue to impress. Desserts tend toward more traditional lines, including a rich flourless chocolate torte that will leave you wanting more. **78-261 Manukai Street; (808) 322-1434; moderate to expensive; breakfast, lunch, and dinner daily.**

❧❧ **KONA INN RESTAURANT, Kailua-Kona** Take refuge from the commotion of Kailua-Kona at the Kona Inn, where you can sink into a high-backed wicker chair, a cool drink in hand, and gaze out over the Pacific Ocean. Nestled in the midst of a somewhat charming stretch of shops, this open oceanfront restaurant provides the perfect retreat for hungry tourists—and plenty of them come here. Walk through a dreary lobby adorned with stuffed game fish, past a potentially noisy open bar, and into a dining room overlaid with Oriental rugs and lined by antique-looking wood tables and chairs. The seating is fairly tight, so request a table nearest the open side of the restaurant. No matter where you sit, you will have a view of the ocean.

Don't expect too much from the mostly seafood menu, which offers a standard selection ranging from sautéed shrimp scampi to steak and lobster combos. Still, the prices are reasonable, and the hypnotic sounds of the surf serve as a lovely serenade. **75-5744 Alii Drive, at the Kona Inn Shopping Village; (808) 329-4455; moderate to expensive; lunch and dinner daily.**

Never leave valuables in your rental car (even in the trunk). Just because you're in paradise doesn't mean you don't have to be city smart.

❦❦ **MICHAELANGELO'S, Kailua-Kona** Romantic inclinations will be well tended to in this Italian restaurant, set on the second floor of a waterfront shopping center. Exposed beams and high ceilings with skylights soar above booths highlighted with swirls of rolled fabric, candles, green paisley linens, and faux marble–painted walls. The eclectic decor is more contemporary and intense than you would expect in Hawaii; but if you sit in the more casual deck area, the ocean views and palm trees remind you that you're still in the tropics, at least until your meal arrives. The ambrosial aromas will take you halfway around the world. A small menu offers mainly traditional Italian dishes with an emphasis on pasta and chicken. Overall, the food is quite standard here, but the service is warm and entirely professional. **75-5770 Alii Drive No. 2; (808) 329-4436; moderate to expensive; dinner daily.**

❦❦❦ **RESTAURANT LA BOURGOGNE, Kailua-Kona** What this place lacks in a view (or windows, for that matter), it makes up for in intimacy and tranquillity. Just a few miles outside Kailua-Kona, in what resembles an industrial strip mall, you'll find this tiny, 12-table restaurant. Decorated in a modest French country decor, La Bourgogne makes no attempts at being too fancy and tends toward the traditional with white linens and a red rose on each table. The lights could be dimmed down some, but perhaps more light is essential in the windowless dining room.

The handful of tables fill quickly, especially during the busy season, so reservations are a must. Request a booth if possible and then prepare your palate for uncompromising French fare, drawing primarily from the Burgundy region. While the main dishes are all excellent, don't pass up the local mango and Maine lobster salad in a passion-fruit vinaigrette, a light and cool combination that is worthy of being an entrée in and of itself. On the dessert front, the chocolate Grand Marnier soufflé will have you saving your diet for another day. **Highway 11, three miles south of Kailua-Kona; (808) 329-6711; expensive; reservations required; dinner Monday–Saturday.**

Holualoa

Hotel/Bed and Breakfast Kissing

❦❦❦❦ **HOLUALOA INN, Holualoa** The colorful melding of Eastern, Western, and Polynesian cultures, traditions, people, and cuisine is a hallmark of the Hawaiian Islands. The Holualoa Inn thoroughly honors this ideal, deriving its bucolic elegance from sources around the world. Reminiscent of the Pacific Northwest, the three-story cedar structure rests upon 40 acres of forested lands, lush fields, and coffee orchards. A testimony to the elegant beauty of wood, cedar walls and cathedral ceilings blend harmoniously with polished eucalyptus floors that extend throughout the rambling house. You'll find ample space for two in the expansive upstairs and downstairs common areas, which are tastefully appointed with unusual, contemporary art pieces and a mixture of modern and antique furnishings. A grand piano and a billiard table provide options for entertainment, and a small kitchenette stocked with complimentary snacks is available for guests at all hours. Borrow a book from the lending library and curl up in one of the many cozy corners. Better yet, simmer in the garden hot tub or catch some rays by the outdoor pool as you soak in the enchanting views of the surrounding countryside, Kailua Bay, and the Pacific beyond.

Choose from six alluring guest rooms with authentic Polynesian themes. All are extremely private because they are scattered throughout the house. Unusual wooden beds, fascinating art, sizable baths, ocean views, and beautiful floral linens will tempt you to forget the beach and stay inside. The Balinese Suite, one of the more romantic options, has treetop views, a private balcony, and a lovely bamboo bed.

Around dusk, visit the rooftop gazebo for the best ocean views and an evening kiss. In the morning, awaken to streaming sunlight and the aromas of a home-cooked breakfast. Sample local fruits (many picked right on the property) and relish the host's coconut coffee cake and eggs Benedict. We're not exaggerating—this place is as romantic as it gets. **Reservations through Hawaii's Best Bed and Breakfasts, (808) 885-4550, (800) 262-9912 mainland; www.konaweb.com/hinn; moderate.**

Romantic Suggestion: Just a short walk up the driveway and along the main road is a charming local espresso bar, HOLUAKOA CAFE (808-322-2233; inexpensive; breakfast and lunch daily). Hide away in the adjoining outdoor garden with your java drink, slice of macadamia nut pie, and, of course, your own sweetie pie.

❤❤❤ **ROSY'S REST, Holualoa** Come to Rosy's Rest for a healthy dose of country charm, warm hospitality, wonderfully sequestered accommodations, and very reasonable rates. All of this awaits in Rosy's rustic two-story cottage, which is trimmed with handcrafted ohia-wood railings. Impressive craftsmanship continues throughout the two units, one on the lower level with a full kitchen and separate bedroom, and the other a second-floor studio with a small kitchenette. Both have stained glass windows, private tiled bathrooms, country-inspired details, and queen-size beds with handmade quilts and rustic wood frames. Although the studio is smaller, a vaulted ceiling gives it an open, spacious feeling. Distant views of Kailua-Kona and the ocean can be seen from both units, but the second-floor studio has the better vantage point from its private tiled patio.

Each room also enjoys a pastoral view of the resident mango-eating pony, Christina, in her corral out front. The only distraction from this otherwise peaceful scene is the road below. Traffic quiets down after dark, but this road is the main highway into the small village of Holualoa.

A Hawaiian/European-style continental breakfast of pastries, fruits, and coffee is left in your fridge every night so you can have an entirely intimate breakfast when the two of you wake. **Reservations through Hawaii's Best Bed and Breakfasts, (808) 885-4550, (800) 262-9912 mainland; inexpensive.**

Kealakekua

Hotel/Bed and Breakfast Kissing

❦❦❦ KEALAKEKUA BAY BED AND BREAKFAST, Kealakekua Nature in all its splendor surrounds you at this bed and breakfast and private cottage rental. On one side resides a state historical park, while the other side consists of forested conservation land. Just beyond the property's edge, past the lush jungle, is what you came to Hawaii to see: the Pacific Ocean. Of course, while all this nature is nice, you do need a place for romance and rest. Venture down a long gravel driveway to the Mediterranean-style home that serves as the main bed and breakfast. Hidden farther below is the Ohana Kai Guest House, which can be yours alone.

The large, stucco home holds three bright and cheery suites. By far the most romantic is the upstairs Ali'i Suite, a spacious room with a king-size bed, stereo with CD player, screened-in windows, and a six-by-six-foot Jacuzzi tub that could almost be classified as a small dipping pool. Surrounded on two sides by windows, you'll be treated to ocean and mountain views as you soak to your hearts' content. Two modest bedrooms await on the ground level, each with Hawaiian print linens, a private bathroom, and a private entrance via a tiled lanai. None of the rooms in the main house has a TV, but if the need arises, the tube can be turned on in the common area. A continental breakfast is served buffet-style on the upstairs lanai, which overlooks a fairway-sized lawn.

If you don't splurge for the Ali'i Suite, we highly recommend the spacious and secluded Ohana Kai House. Accented by dark koa-wood floors and an open-beamed ceiling, this cottage offers two and a half bathrooms, a full kitchen, a spacious eating area, and a living room. Comfy couches set in front of colossal screened windows take full advantage of the natural surroundings. The two bedrooms, each with a queen-size bed, are small but cool and comfortable. This roomy home can sleep eight, but the affordable price makes it just right for two. For the out-and-about crowd, some of Hawaii's best snorkeling is just three minutes away at a nearby marine preserve. **82-6002 Napoopoo Road; (808) 328-8150, (800) 328-8150 mainland; www.keala.com; inexpensive to expensive.**

❀❀❊ **MERRYMAN'S BED AND BREAKFAST, Kealakekua** Witness the spectacular scenery of the Big Island at this inviting two-story farmhouse, set on a breezy hillside in coffee country. Distant, panoramic views of the Kona Coast and close-up looks of the home's expansive lawns and flower gardens are the only things that may distract you from looking at each other. Knotty pine walls, exposed beams, cathedral ceilings, and hardwood floors in the sizable upstairs living room contribute to the distinctive country atmosphere. Unwind in the cozy comfort of cushioned wicker furniture as you gaze through sweeping bay windows to the sparkling ocean beyond. And that's just the common area.

All four guest rooms are beautifully maintained. The Deluxe Master Suite has beautiful linens, a private all-wood bathroom, and a peekaboo ocean view. Downstairs, the Rose Room is augmented with floral linens, sparkling tiled bath, and a private entrance; it's perfect for couples who desire more secluded accommodations. The remaining two upstairs guest rooms share a bath (which is large, but obviously not private), but they still offer sufficient space.

The engaging hosts offer you all the comforts of their sunny home, including a Jacuzzi tub set beneath palm trees in the front yard, a plentiful full breakfast, and complimentary beach and snorkeling gear. If you want to lounge around the countryside or explore the Kona Gold Coast, this is an ideal retreat. And besides, the beach is only a ten-minute drive away. **(808) 323-2276, (800) 545-4390 mainland; www.lavazone2.com/merrymans; inexpensive.**

Romantic Suggestion: KEALAKEKUA BAY is ten minutes from Merryman's, and the drive is well worth every splendid moment. Wind down a tropical residential hillside past coconut and papaya trees, exotic flowers, and noisy, colorful birds. The mesmerizing blue Pacific seems to expand as you descend, beckoning you closer at every turn. Unfortunately, when you finally reach the water's edge, you're apt to find crowds of anxious snorkelers preparing to enter the underwater park. Snorkeling is wonderful here, but you'll probably want to find a spot where the sardine factor isn't so high. One option is to rent a kayak (prices start at $20 per person) and paddle over to **CAPTAIN COOK'S MONUMENT**, where the water is crystal clear and calm, and the sea life is extraordinary.

Honaunau

Hotel/Bed and Breakfast Kissing

❤️❤️ **KALAHIKI COTTAGE, Honaunau** Set high in the hills of McCandless Ranch (with only a peekaboo view of the ocean), this rambler-style cottage is all yours to enjoy. Add onto that a nearby 70-foot swimming pool, inviting blue-tiled Jacuzzi tub, and surrounding indigenous tropical fruit trees, large spice plants, and shrubs, and you'll have it made in the shade up here. (Note: While the pool fronts your cottage, it's not exactly yours alone. The owners sometimes use it too.)

The cottage—formerly a pool house—lacks the typical layout of a home and has only one hallway connecting the bedroom with two bathrooms. Beautifully preserved antique furnishings in the bedroom (they have been in the owner's family for years) liven up the slightly outdated decor. The master bathroom, with its extra-large shower for two, antique Chinese towel rack, and European fixtures, has a private patio with a picturesque view of the bromeliad garden and a stately mango tree. If outdoor living combined with creature comforts is your cup of tea, you'll love the al fresco kitchen, dining room, and living room underneath the spacious covered lanai. Each morning, the innkeeper (who lives in a house beyond the cottage) tiptoes over to brew coffee and put a bountiful continental breakfast in your kitchen's refrigerator. When you wake, enjoy your morning meal on the spacious covered porch. **Reservations through Hawaii's Best Bed and Breakfasts, (808) 885-4550, (800) 262-9912 mainland; moderate.**

Romantic Note: The innkeepers also operate a tour company called **McCANDLESS RANCH** (808-328-9313; $400 per couple). They take you, via four-wheel drive, into the heart of the jungle and then up above the treeline of Mauna Loa. The all-day tour includes breakfast and lunch.

Before flying, be sure both of you are signed up as frequent flyers. Mileage to Hawaii adds up quickly.

Waiohinu

Hotel/Bed and Breakfast Kissing

❦❦ **HOBBIT HOUSE, Waiohinu** Nestled high in the Hawaiian hills, with nothing else in sight but trees, grass, and the distant Pacific Ocean, the Hobbit House is a truly magical place to call home. This spacious and self-sufficient accommodation comprises the ground floor of the multi-level main house. Inside, a fantasy-like atmosphere is created by the intricate, curvaceous, stained glass windows and unique woodwork that fill the two rooms. Everything you need is here for your convenience, including a large kitchen with eating area; a living area with a comfy couch set in front of a picture window with stunning views of the rolling hills; and a quaint bedroom with antique furnishings, a dark wood queen-size bed, and a unique ohia-branch chandelier. What really wowed us was the large tiled bathroom complete with a two-person soaking tub surrounded by tall stained glass windows that open to the lush world below. Those looking for some good, clean fun will find the large tiled shower big enough for two.

In the morning, a variety of cereals, French toast, muffins, fruit, juice, coffee, and macadamia nuts are brought to your hideaway. Either eat inside or sit outside at a picnic table that overlooks the Big Island's untouched beauty. If the two of you love being alone together and want a little fairy-tale home all to yourselves, Hobbit House is the destination you've both been seeking. **Reservations through Hawaii's Best Bed and Breakfast, (808) 885-4550, (800) 262-9912; www.hi-hobbit.com/island/index. html; inexpensive.**

Romantic Note: The Hobbit House is only accessible with a four-wheel-drive vehicle. If you don't have one, the owners will pick you up at a prearranged time and place.

Volcano

There aren't many places in the great state of Hawaii where snuggling up beside a warm fireplace sounds like a good idea. Taking a refreshing swim or cranking up the air-conditioning is more likely to appeal to mainlanders unaccustomed to heat and humidity. But in the tiny, no-stoplight town of Volcano, cool weather, cloudy skies, and misty rain prevail most of the year. This could be seen as a drawback (it is for visitors looking forward to waving palm trees, warm ocean waves, sunny skies, and hot days), but such conditions can also inspire cozy, romantic inclinations.

Volcano can be a moving experience—literally. Don't be surprised if you awaken to a small earthquake in the middle of the night. Rumbling earth is just an accepted part of life in Volcano, along with events such as lava flows closing down sections of roadway. Everything in Volcano, including a bevy of bed and breakfasts, is just minutes away from **HAWAII VOLCANOES NATIONAL PARK** (see Outdoor Kissing), the area's main attraction. Kilauea, the unpredictable volcano, continues its eruptive activity with majestic and destructive glory. Past lava flows have covered a newly built visitor center, annihilated main roads, and demolished the popular local black-sand beach. Nevertheless, if you can calm your apprehensions (locals don't seem worried and say that living in any mainland city is far more dangerous), witnessing the tremendous power of the earth's miraculous birth process is a must. Walk through extinct lava tubes, drive around the volcano's steaming crater, or, if your timing is lucky, survey momentous views of flowing red-hot lava.

Hotel/Bed and Breakfast Kissing

❀❀❀ **CARSON'S VOLCANO COTTAGES, Volcano** Sheltered by a lush tropical forest of camellias, cedars, and Japanese maples, Carson's offers three secluded rooms on its main property. Also worth your consideration are three separate cottages located around the town of Volcano.

The theme-style rooms on the main property are not outstanding, but they are intriguing and have inviting personalities of their own. Plus, they all have private baths and queen-size beds, and are close to the community outdoor hot tub tucked into a wooden gazebo. Nick's Cabin No. 19, also located on the grounds, lacks a discernible theme, and is packed to the rafters with antique knickknacks. While livable, the exposed framing reminded us more of a summer camp cabin than a romantic retreat.

We're happy to report that the three other cottages, found throughout Volcano, are better suited for those with kissing on their minds. Mahina, Koa, and Kilauea Plantation cottages are each tucked into the jungle, so all you'll see is each other . . . and plenty of lush foliage. While all three are decorated in a charming country style, complete with fireplaces, colorful plates accenting full kitchens, and hot tubs on back patios, we liked the new Mahina cottage the best. This small yellow and green modified A-frame has a queen-size bed as well as a sleeping loft that's just right for two. Near Volcano Village, the chocolate and cream–colored Kilauea Plantation with its claw-foot tub and two resident (outdoor) cats is our second favorite. Koa's room configuration didn't appeal to our sense of coziness, but it's still secluded and pleasant.

No matter where you stay, you're welcome to join everyone in the dining room of the main house for a buffet breakfast, consisting of macadamia nut pancakes, breakfast meats, fruits, and perhaps a pineapple upside-down cake. Couples staying in the off-property cottages may find the five-minute drive an inconvenience and might opt for preparing their own breakfast. **505 Sixth Street; (808) 967-7683, (800) 845-LAVA; www. carsonscottage.com; inexpensive to expensive.**

❤❤❤ CHALET KILAUEA—THE INN AT VOLCANO, Volcano Chalet Kilauea, as a company, is covering Volcano like a lava flow. At our visit, it owned and operated six vacation homes, four bed and breakfasts, and two restaurants. Of its collection, The Inn at Volcano (often called Chalet Kilauea as well) is the crown jewel. This shingle-style, two-story home is set in a lush, landscaped lawn accented by Southeast Asian statues. Inside, the inviting, plush common area is filled with exceedingly comfortable, contemporary furnishings and affectionate detailing, which will pique your curiosity about your own accommodations. The delightful Oriental Jade Room is done up in deep green hues, with a green marble Jacuzzi tub in the private bathroom and a queen-size bed in the bedroom. The Out of Africa Room features warm earth tones, while the lovely Continental Lace Room (which the owners also refer to as the bridal suite) is romantically decorated in white and pink and offers a large soaking tub surrounded by white tile. Adjacent to the main house is the more private, two-level Treehouse Suite, with a king-size bed, double Jacuzzi tub, and fireplace. But the ultimate romantic retreat awaits down a forested pathway. Here, you'll find the Hapu'u Forest Suite, a separate cabin with a king-size bed overlooking the ohia and fern forests and a bathroom that dazzles. You'll know why couples in this room are always late for breakfast . . . they want to stay in the bathroom all day, thanks to its marble double Jacuzzi tub and lava-rock waterfall cascading into the shower. Topping it all off are floor-to-ceiling windows that give the feeling of bathing in the jungle.

As the sun starts peeking through the morning mist, venture to the formal dining room for a breakfast fit for a king or queen. Seated at one of the private two-person tables, under a twinkling chandelier, you'll savor a full breakfast served on antique Victorian china. Start with the luscious triple cream and fruit bowl, followed by either the smoked salmon and bagel plate or ham and cheese omelets, plus fresh muffins, fruit, and coffee and juice. In late afternoon, after a day exploring **HAWAII VOLCANOES**

NATIONAL PARK (see Outdoor Kissing), relish complimentary high tea in the common room, followed by a dip in the outdoor hot tub. **Wright and Laukapu Roads; (808) 967-7786, (800) 937-7786 mainland; www. volcano-hawaii.com; moderate to unbelievably expensive.**

Romantic Alternatives: As mentioned, Chalet Kilauea has a collection of accommodations ranging from economy-minded B&Bs to elegant vacation homes. Romance-seekers may want to opt for the **OHIA HIDEAWAY COTTAGE** (moderate), a deep-forest delight with its queen-size bed, all-marble bathroom, wood-burning stove, and plenty of seclusion. On a larger scale, **THE GINGER HOUSE** (very expensive) is better suited for families, but the privacy and steaming hot tub draw romantics, too. Those seeking a bed and breakfast with spacious, comfortable rooms at moderate prices should stay at **LOKAHI LODGE** (moderate), nestled a lava stone's throw from town center.

❤❤❤ **HALE IKI COTTAGE, Volcano** When it's wet and chilly outside (as it can frequently be at 4,000 feet above sea level), Hale Iki is just the kind of place you'll long for. This cozy little cedar cabin is tucked into lush forest surroundings, and it's all yours for supreme kissing and cuddling.

Knotty pine walls, hardwood floors, and a wood-burning fireplace hint of mountain cabin, but the rattan furniture and tropical prints help remind you this is Hawaii. The bedroom is set in a loft, and the main floor consists of a cozy sitting area next to the fireplace. You'll also find a full kitchen, a dining area, and a bathroom with a huge soaking tub for two set next to windows facing the koa forest. The dense shrubbery surrounding the cabin keeps your bath, and your entire stay here, private. Breakfast, a private affair as well, is left in the kitchen for you to enjoy at your leisure. **Reservations through Hawaii's Best Bed and Breakfasts, (808) 885-4550, (800) 262-9912 mainland; inexpensive.**

❤❤ **KILAUEA LODGE, Volcano** Best known for its restaurant (see Restaurant Kissing), Kilauea Lodge also has some charming rooms to cozy up in. This simple country inn offers 12 units in three adjoining buildings. Of the three, we recommend the suites in the Hale Aloha Building. While all the suites in this building are well suited for romance, the upstairs ones are our favorites, with their cathedral ceilings, exposed wood beams, king-size beds with Ralph Lauren linens, fireplaces, stained glass windows, and private baths. Our only complaint is that the walls are thin and voices can be heard through them.

Accommodations in the two original buildings are less fresh and inviting, although they are graced with fireplaces and a country ambience. Fortunately, all of the rooms have central heat, a must for Volcano in the winter. Be prepared to snuggle, since none of the rooms (except Tutu's Place) has a TV. No matter where you stay, a simple but filling complimentary breakfast is waiting for you every morning in the lodge's handsome restaurant.

Of all Kilauea Lodge's offerings, the off-property Tutu's Place is the spot to hang your safari hat if you enjoy jungle living. This two-bedroom cottage, hidden in the lush foliage along a quiet neighborhood road, is perfect for those seeking solitude. Built in 1929, this little yellow house with a red roof brings a bit of nostalgia into the picture with an old-fashioned kitchen and antique radio. There's an odd-looking wall mural, modern living-room furnishings, a TV/VCR, and a gas stove to round out the scene. The Lodge is a half mile away, so walking to breakfast in the morning mist is a short but refreshing experience. **Old Volcano Road; (808) 967-7366; www.kilauea-lodge.com; inexpensive to moderate; recommended wedding site.**

✿✿❀ MOUNTAIN HOUSE AND HYDRANGEA COTTAGE, Volcano

Informed couples know just where to find romance in Volcano: hidden among the ohia trees, *hapu'u* ferns, orchids, magnolias, and hydrangeas of the Mountain House. This once-private estate and adjacent cottage have been lovingly converted into an elegant bed and breakfast that provides guests with sumptuous surroundings and utter seclusion.

Depending on your means, the Hydrangea Cottage might be the better choice for a romantic retreat. For the same price as a suite in the main home, you get an entire luxury cottage that's tucked into the jungle. The spacious living room has plush modern furnishings, a large kitchen area stocked with breakfast foods, extensive windows that allow an infusion of natural light, a wood-burning fireplace, and a VCR (upon request). The bedroom and private bath are equally special. It's hard to believe they don't charge more, but we won't tell the owners if you won't.

Different, but equally intriguing, is the colossal Mountain House, where the owners once lived. Placed at opposite ends of the home to ensure privacy, the two bedrooms are graced with lovely color schemes, handsome linens, and spacious private baths. There's a hint of 1970s decor here and there, but we didn't mind. (A third room is available, but it's too small to be considered romantic. However, its unbelievably low price might change

---

Don't leave home without insect repellent. Hawaii's trade winds tend to keep bugs on the move, but in the more tropical, jungle-like areas, mosquitoes are a pesky problem.

your mind.) An extravagant gourmet kitchen, so large it almost looks like it's been transplanted from a restaurant, sits in the middle of the home. The kitchen is shared by all house guests, so you may have company if you cook. A complimentary continental breakfast is provided for each couple in an individually marked basket. The house's Asian-influenced decor, koa-wood details, and beautiful views of the surrounding woodland and gardens encourage long hours of rest and relaxation. If there's a golfer in your twosome, no need to wander far for some chipping and putting practice. With the provided clubs, practice your short game on the undulating green lawn. Or, just lie low and cuddle up on the bench under a beautiful old magnolia tree. If you're lucky, you might have the entire house to yourselves. Otherwise, it is large enough for everyone to share. **Reservations through Hawaii's Best Bed and Breakfasts, (808) 885-4550, (800) 262-9912 mainland; moderate; recommended wedding site.**

❀❀❀❀ **VOLCANO RAINFOREST RETREAT, Volcano** During every update of *The Best Places to Kiss*, we discover a new bed and breakfast that leaves us in awe. Volcano Rainforest Retreat is such a place, with three delightful cottages hidden in the jungle. Black lava–stone paths loop throughout the two-and-a-half-acre property, while sun- and moonbeams alike weave their way through the dense canopy of ferns and trees. Hawaiian, Southeast Asian, and Buddhist art from the innkeepers' travels embellishes all the cottages, as well as the pathways leading from cottage to cottage.

The trio of cedar-and-glass accommodations all share the same open and light design, but the Guest Cottage is the most desirable, with its own entrance and carport. The jungle cloaks this cottage in privacy, so you can soak in the tiled tub with the surrounding windows wide open. An upstairs loft holds a queen-size bed, while downstairs you'll find a full kitchen, a living room, a wood-burning stove surrounded by a pebbled hearth, and a fantastic stereo/CD system.

Past the outdoor Japanese soaking tub and shower (available to all guests) awaits the second accommodation, known as The Sanctuary, a small, six-sided, all-window cottage. Relax in the sea-blue surroundings, adorned with Balinese masks, a water fountain, wood-burning stove, and double futon. There's a small kitchenette and bathroom, but you'll have to venture outside to the community shower for some good clean fun. Shades on each side insure your privacy.

Near the owner's home (called the Gathering Hale) is the last of the three units, the octagon-shaped Forest Hale. French doors open to a black iron bed, two comfortable chairs fronting a gas stove, and a kitchenette.

Neither the windows nor the front porch faces the Gathering Hale, so you'll feel quite secluded.

No matter where you stay, enough breakfast fixings for two mornings are left in your refrigerator. The delightful innkeepers often hold retreats at the Gathering Hale, including many on romance in relationships. But we don't think you'll need a workshop . . . just stay here and watch the romance in your relationship bloom. **Reservations through Hawaii's Best Bed and Breakfasts, (808) 885-4550, (800) 262-9912 mainland; www. volcanoretreat.com; inexpensive to moderate.**

Romantic Note: Volcano is limited in dining options, so why not invite a chef over to prepare the cuisine of your choice? The innkeepers can arrange for a professional chef to cook for you in your cottage or, if you wish, deliver dinner right to your door. The very reasonable price of $50 per couple includes a four-course dinner. You won't find this kind of romantic meal deal anywhere else in Hawaii.

❧❧❧ **THE VOLCANO TEAPOT, Volcano** If you wish to steep yourselves in love and romance, The Volcano Teapot is your kind of spot. Hidden in a lush neighborhood near Volcano, this darling two-bedroom 1912 home is bubbling over with charm. While the namesake teapot theme is evident (especially in the kitchen, where you'll find no fewer than two dozen types of teas), the motif is tastefully done. A mix of Hawaiian art as well as English country accessories blend to make this place feel like a home rather than a vacation rental. Lace curtains, white-washed wood floors, a TV, and a wood-burning stove occupy the comfortable living room, while a claw-foot tub awaits in the bathroom. The master bedroom holds a four-poster queen-size bed.

A continental breakfast, served daily, is best enjoyed on The Teapot's most enchanting feature: a large, covered front porch. Sip your tea and while away the day here listening to the native birds and, of course, each other. **Reservations through Hawaii's Best Bed and Breakfasts, (808) 885-4550, (800) 262-9912 mainland; inexpensive.**

Restaurant Kissing

❧❧❧ **KILAUEA LODGE RESTAURANT, Volcano** The earth may be rumbling beneath Volcano, but when it comes to satisfying your churning stomach, choices in this town are few and far between. Luckily, there is the Kilauea Lodge Restaurant, considered by most to be not only the best, but the *only* fine dining option here. Despite its lack of competition, the restaurant maintains its reputation by consistently preparing excellent dishes with a well-balanced mixture of European and Hawaiian influences.

Cuddle up in the provincial dining room next to the Fireplace of Friendship, which pays tribute to Kilauea Lodge's past as a YMCA camp with a collection of artifacts from children's groups around the world. Hardwood floors, koa-wood tables, fresh flowers, and artistic renditions of Pele's fiery temper enhance your dining enjoyment. It isn't exactly fancy, but the atmosphere is warm and the service is friendly. Begin your meal with warm Brie cheese coated in herb batter and coconut flakes, served with fresh hot bread; then sample the fresh local fish (prepared three ways) or one of the nightly specials. The delightful flavors and generous portions (soup or salad is included) may just entice you to return again and again during your stay. Kilauea Lodge Restaurant is open only for dinner unless you are a guest at the lodge (see Hotel/Bed and Breakfast Kissing), in which case breakfast is included with your stay. **Old Volcano Road; (808) 967-7366; moderate to expensive; dinner daily; recommended wedding site.**

Romantic Alternative: Finding lunch in Volcano is a bit of a challenge. Packing a picnic or munching on snacks until dinnertime is an option, but if you would prefer to eat in a restaurant, consider the **VOLCANO GOLF AND COUNTRY CLUB RESTAURANT** (Piimauna Drive, at Hawaii Volcanoes National Park; 808-967-8228; inexpensive to moderate; breakfast and lunch daily). The restaurant's soups, salads, and sandwiches aren't exactly gourmet and the plastic table coverings are less than romantic, but it is pretty much the only game in town when it comes to lunch. Luckily, the food, service, and casual atmosphere aren't all that bad.

Romantic Warning: Your red-hot lava love might turn to stone after seeing **VOLCANO HOUSE** in Hawaii Volcanoes National Park (808-967-7321; moderate to expensive; breakfast, lunch, and dinner daily). Avoid this place at all costs. It is set up to cater to busloads of tourists who visit the park. Although it is one of the only dining options in the park itself, its grim and greasy atmosphere can spoil anyone's appetite for food and romance.

❧❧ **SURT'S AT VOLCANO VILLAGE, Volcano** Here in the heart of Volcano is a corner café with all the culinary sophistication of a big-city restaurant. Thank goodness, too! Despite the thousands of tourists who visit the region and national park, the town only has a handful of restaurants and, of those, only a few could be called upon for a satisfactory and romantic dining experience.

After passing by the glass-enclosed kitchen, you'll enter a dining room adorned with glass-top tables, tall ceilings with ohia-wood pillars, wood floors and walls, and colorful artwork and decorations, including a collection of plates and glass bottles. The seating is tight, but that can't be helped in the small room. Several patio tables provide more space; however, we discourage sitting here. Bugs and a parking lot–view (plus fumes) can ruin your appetite.

Specializing in a mix of Southeast Asian and Italian cuisine, Surt's dishes up some fantastic curry lunches and excellent pasta dinners. No matter what time of day, you can enjoy the tried and true spring rolls, chicken eggplant linguini, and a selection of salads worth savoring. Come dinner, indulge in sautéed chile squid with basil, New York strip steak, or beef Panang. A must-try on the dessert menu is the creamy, light, mango tiramisu. However, if you'd rather have a sweet finale that captures Volcano's best, indulge in the crème brûlée. It's served hot with the custard in molten form. **Corner of Old Volcano Highway and Haunani Road; (808) 967-8511, (800) 937-7786; reservations recommended; lunch and dinner daily.**

Romantic Note: Around the corner is Surt's smaller, less sophisticated sibling, **THE STEAM VENT CAFE** (808-985-8744; inexpensive; breakfast, lunch, and light meals daily). Besides having the only ATM in town, which it proudly advertises, the café serves up espresso drinks, hot teas, pre-made gourmet sandwiches, four types of salads, and enough sweets to keep you satisfied until you kiss. It's the ideal place to stop and pick up picnic supplies (and money) for a day out exploring the steam vents.

Outdoor Kissing

❤❤❤❤ **HAWAII VOLCANOES NATIONAL PARK, Volcano** If capricious Kilauea is in the mood to erupt, don't hesitate to witness it for yourselves. Without question, it is a once-in-a-lifetime event. Unlike any other natural wonder, a volcano (and the power of the fire goddess Pele, according to legend) moves the soul in a way that is hard to describe.

At various times over the past millennium, but more specifically in the past 100 years, Kilauea has displayed its awesome force in a passionate fury that spews up from the earth in rivers and fountains of 2,000-degree molten lava. Thick, flaming red fingers move across the land through an array of lava tubes, then spill into the sea in hissing explosions that turn the liquid fire into black powder and rock.

There are two ways to experience this phenomenon. One is to drive to the end of **CRATER RIM DRIVE** at night to see fountains of molten rock shooting up from the earth. When conditions are safe enough, you can even hike down to the ocean over a well-marked lava field to take a closer look. (Warm clothes, water, snacks, and flashlights are essential for this excursion.) For the less hardy, or for those with more liberal expense accounts, a helicopter tour is a must. Several flight services will take you aloft to survey the devastation from above it all. The pools of bubbling, fiery lava moving through collapsed caverns and open fissures are literally astounding. Sit tight and clasp hands; you're going on the ride of your lives. **(808) 985-6000; www.nps.gov/havo; $10 per car.** *From Hilo, head south on Highway 11 about 28 miles and look for signs to the park's entrance near the town of Volcano.*

Romantic Note: After all this, we must warn you that Kilauea is unpredictable. Depending on all kinds of geological forces, you may not see as much volcanic activity as you had hoped to experience. Fortunately, even if the lava flow has slowed down, you can at least witness the orange glow of the lava's path from the end of **CRATER RIM DRIVE** after dusk. Visibility and safety conditions are posted at the park's visitor center, and the staff there is extremely helpful.

Hilo

Hotel/Bed and Breakfast Kissing

❤❤ **THE BAY HOUSE, Hilo** Feel the power of Hilo Bay's thundering surf as you sit on your private lanai watching the blue water whip into a froth. Built on the water's edge, this contemporary, sparkling white home has two guest rooms, each with a private bath, huge California king-size bed, and an outstanding view of Hilo Bay. Plenty of windows give the rooms a bright touch, while the green leather couches, colorful floral print bedspreads, and white walls lend a clean, contemporary sparkle. A breakfast buffet, served in the common room, brings fresh fruit, pastries, granola, and Kona coffee to the table. Such an upbeat bed and breakfast, complete with friendly hosts, is ideal for Hilo, one of the country's rainiest cities. **Reservations through Hawaii's Best Bed and Breakfasts, (808) 885-4550, (800) 262-9912 mainland; inexpensive.**

❤❤ **SHIPMAN HOUSE, Hilo** If there ever was a house on Hawaii that was built to impress, the Shipman House is it. Situated high on a hill, the century-old, stately Victorian mansion certainly makes a strong impression,

---

Many restaurants offer early-bird dinner specials, which often include soup/ salad, entrée, and dessert. Inquire at the restaurant of your choice and then dine early. You can usually catch the sunset too.

especially to those who find that a historical setting and romance go hand in hand. If you have an hour or so, the home's owner (the Shipmans' great-granddaughter) will give you a tour that churns up plenty of interesting Hawaiian history.

Grandiose rooms, floor-to-ceiling windows, and original fixtures and detailing throughout the home will definitely dazzle. The three guest rooms in the main home radiate with natural light and spaciousness thanks to ten- to 12-foot-high ceilings. Each has a bright, modern bath (one is detached), a refrigerator, antique furnishings, and fresh flowers. Our favorite is Auntie Clara's Shell Room because of the spectacular view of Hilo Bay, windows that open to the jungle below, and its beautiful shell collection. The only drawback to this room is that you'll have to do the down-the-hall dash to reach your private bathroom. (Kimonos are provided.) The nearby guest cottage, built in 1910, has two identical rooms each with a big tiled bathroom, private screened-in porch, Hawaiian artwork, and fresh red flowers.

After a breakfast of cornbread, banana bread, popovers, poi muffins, and assorted fruit, take a stroll around the equally impressive grounds. Or just snooze on the wraparound front porch dreaming of days gone by. **Reservations through Hawaii's Best Bed and Breakfasts, (808) 885-4550, (800) 262-9912 mainland; www.hilo-hawaii.com; moderate.**

Romantic Warning: Like most older homes, the Shipman House is a work in progress. When we visited, all the antique photos were off the walls waiting to be refurbished. Take such renovation work into account if you stay here.

Lanai

* Lanai City

Lanai

All the interisland airlines offer daily flights to and from Lanai. There is also daily passenger-only ferryboat service from Lahaina, Maui, to Manele Bay, Lanai, via Expeditions (808-661-3756, 800-695-2624 interisland; reservations required). If you take the boat between December and March, hang on tight and watch for whales—they often accompany the crossing.

Of the millions of visitors who come to Hawaii each year, most never visit the island of Lanai, and their absence is one of its most alluring features. This tiny island is only 18 miles long and 13 miles wide, and lies just seven miles west of Maui. With a resident population of only 2,800, Lanai has all the tantalizing details of paradise, especially solitude and conspicuous tranquillity. Enjoy "talking story" with the locals who love their land and welcome visitors; hike along trails in the cool, tree-covered hills; or four-wheel drive to hard-to-reach sandy beaches where you and your loved one will be the only strollers for miles around. Lanai offers truly remote resort hotels with all the sumptuous, accommodating services you would expect from the most elegant of destinations, and no tourist attractions. We'll repeat that because we know it's hard to believe—*no tourist attractions*. Romance is the very soul of Lanai.

You won't find the lush vegetation of the other islands here—there's not enough surface water on Lanai to sustain a rain forest—but every other facet of a blissful tropical paradise awaits. Lanai's arid interior is covered with pine-covered highlands, rocky cliffs, rolling red-clay hillsides dabbed with green, and pineapple fields healing from years of operation. Only one road leads from the boat landing up to Lanai City, 2,000 feet above sea level. This same road eventually splits into two branches that are suitable only for four-wheel-drive vehicles. Car rentals are expensive ($100 a day or more), but worth it for a long day of exploration (see Outdoor Kissing).

Lanai has a fascinating recent history. In the 1920s, 98 percent of the island was purchased by Jim Dole, who developed and planted the illustrious pineapple crop canned by his plantation. For years virtually all of Lanai's usable land was covered in cultivated fields. Eventually, U.S. costs grew too high, and South America became the new center for pineapple production. The last pineapple harvest on Lanai occurred in 1993. Employment prospects in this isolated corner of the world would have been devastated had the Dole Food Company (also flirting with financial woes) not built two of the most charming, exclusive hotel properties in all of Hawaii. Now tourism is the major industry on tiny Lanai, but more development is just around the corner, including the construction of luxury, million-dollar homes.

Is paradise lost? Far from it. For now, Dole is the only developer and, thankfully, it is moving slowly. In the meantime, Lanai awaits in all of its splendid glory.

Lanai City

Hotel/Bed and Breakfast Kissing

❤❤❤❤ **THE LODGE AT KOELE, Lanai City** Unlike any other destination in Hawaii, the architecture and the atmosphere at The Lodge at Koele may make you feel like you're in the wrong state. Unmistakable Pacific Northwest decor marks this lodge, which stands proudly on top of an idyllic verdant hillside. The building resembles an incredibly luxurious ski lodge, and a casual alpine spirit envelopes you the moment you cross the threshold. Inside, the enormous great hall, with its high-beamed ceilings and two formidable stone fireplaces, is adorned with plush furnishings and beautiful antiques from all over the world. An opulent Hawaiian plantation feeling is evident in a series of luxurious sitting rooms where guests can enjoy complimentary afternoon tea, watch TV, or while away the hours playing billiards or other games.

Some of the 102 guest rooms are located on the second level above the main lobby; however, most await in the more secluded adjacent building. Each uniquely decorated room is utterly charming and cozy. Four-poster beds, wicker chairs, pine furniture, large soaking tubs, and private lanais are all affection-inspiring. After you've checked into your room, stroll through the immaculate gardens bordered by Norfolk pine forests, or practice your short game on the 18-hole putting course set in a grove of giant banyans. Centered in the midst of all this lushness are two hot tubs and a large pool.

The lodge's restaurants display the same high standards and attention to detail. Of particular interest are the **KOELE TERRACE** (expensive; breakfast, lunch, and dinner daily) and the **FORMAL DINING ROOM** (expensive to very expensive; dinner daily). Both serve sumptuous meals with a mastery almost unparalleled on any of the islands. In particular, the Formal Dining Room is outstanding; its menu offers a creative commingling of Mediterranean and Pacific Rim cuisine, and every bite is a memorable experience. **Reservations through Lanai Resorts, (808) 565-7300, (800) 321-4666; www.lanai-resorts.com; expensive to unbelievably expensive and beyond; recommended wedding site.**

❀❀❀❀ **THE MANELE BAY HOTEL, Lanai City** You may not know how to describe paradise, but you'll definitely know it when you see it. Luckily, you need not look any further than The Manele Bay Hotel, where you'll discover paradise in addition to luxury, grandeur, and gracious, sincere hospitality. Enter the magnificent two-story lobby where towering etched glass doors open to a grand pool area. You'll also find exquisite furnishings, poshly decorated dining rooms, a fire-warmed game room, and a variety of stately terraces. In the distance, a rocky bluff outlines the ocean, nearby beach, and pristine countryside.

In the guest rooms, European comfort and refinement impart serene relaxation. Each large room features expansive sliding glass doors that open to a private lanai overlooking either lush gardens and their reflecting pools or the pounding surf below. Bright yellow English floral fabrics, plantation-style furnishings, and an attractive bath further enhance each guest room.

Both of the dining rooms here are pleasantly sophisticated and surprisingly excellent (a real relief, considering they are pretty much the only game in town besides the two dining rooms at The Lodge at Koele). Share a casually elegant breakfast or dinner at the Mediterranean-inspired **HULOPO'E COURT** dining room (expensive; breakfast and dinner daily), where Hawaiian regional cuisine is the specialty. For a more intimate interlude, schedule an evening at the **IHILANI DINING ROOM** (expensive to very expensive; dinner daily). The menu is eclectic, ranging from Hawaiian regional to Mediterranean cuisine, and the dining room is tastefully adorned in a Hawaiian monarchy theme. Complimentary shuttles transport guests between the hotel and **THE LODGE AT KOELE** (see review above), and to and from the panoramic 18-hole golf courses. For superlative solitude and a pampered interlude together, The Manele Bay Hotel is a true taste of paradise. **Reservations through Lanai Resorts, (808) 565-7700, (800) 321-4666; www.lanai-resorts.com; expensive to unbelievably expensive and beyond; recommended wedding site.**

Romantic Note: HOTEL LANAI (828 Lanai Avenue; 808-565-7211, 800-795-7211; www.onlanai.com; inexpensive to moderate; minimum-stay requirement seasonally) is the only other available place to stay on Lanai. In comparison to the Manele and the Koele, it is too disappointing for words, but even judged on its own merits, it isn't anything to write home about. Built in 1923, it has been modestly refurbished. Rooms are small and sparse, with few windows. Its casual restaurant, **HENRY CLAY'S ROTISSERIE** (dinner daily), serves up American country cuisine at moderate prices. Its price tag is infinitely lower than that of the other two properties, but that's where its attraction ends.

Outdoor Kissing

❤❤❤ **RED ROVER, Lanai City** As the saying goes, there are two types of cars that go anywhere: a four-wheel drive and a rental. On Lanai, the two types are rolled into one vehicle for an off-road, wildly romantic experience you won't soon forget. A fleet of Land Rovers (those *Out of Africa* mobiles) await the adventurous couple thirsty for dust-filled trips down to secluded beaches and up to lush mountaintops. For the truly rugged twosome, opt for a soft-top, but expect to be covered in Lanai's famous red dust by the time you return. (Warning: It doesn't come out of clothing in the wash.) Hard-top vehicles offer that one creature comfort most can't do without: air conditioning. After a briefing on how the emergency radio works, how to read the map, and what the off-limit areas are, you and your honey can explore Lanai to your hearts' content. (Oh, by the way, although it's tempting, don't drive on the beaches unless you want to end your delightful day by having to be pulled out of the soft sand.) Plenty of beautiful beaches await your discovery, as do some hard-core, kidney-killin' mountain roads. Whatever path you travel, you'll find yourselves mostly alone on the back roads. **The Old Labor Yard, Lanai Avenue; (808) 565-7722, 1-87-RED-ROVER; www.onlanai.com/rover.htm; rentals start at $139 per day per couple.**

Romantic Suggestion: Before you begin your land-roving adventure, stop by **PELE'S OTHER GARDEN** (811 Houston Street; 808-565-9628, 888-POG-DELI) and pick up their "Off-Road Picnic Basket" for two (inexpensive). Inside an insulated cooler, you'll find two made-to-order sandwiches, pasta salads, desserts, and drinks.

Molokai

* Maunaloa

* Waialua

Molokai

Formerly known as "The Forgotten Isle" and "The Lonely Isle," Molokai has been trying to change its image over the years to "The Friendly Isle." Molokai will seem most friendly to those searching for little commercialism, relative isolation, and a slow-paced vacation. Since the demise of its extensive pineapple-farming operations in 1988, the island has come to rely on tourism as its major industry. Even so, many islanders are strongly opposed to promoting tourism for fear that Molokai will become another Oahu. Fortunately, at the current rate of development (virtually none), we don't foresee that happening anytime soon, and the feeling of "old" Hawaii is still prevalent on Molokai.

The arid western side of the island consists mostly of dry, dusty roads; rolling cattle pastures; and former pineapple fields dotted with leafless gray trees. However, the east end of the island is a true tropical fantasy. The magnificent, rugged coastline is hemmed with palm trees, which are not found anywhere else on this island, and the surrounding jungle-like countryside is luxuriously thick and green. Alas, the beach area is limited because the water comes right up to the grass or rocky shores, with very little, if any, sand between the ocean and land.

Molokai is only 38 miles long, but it takes nearly an hour to get to the east shore from the west end, which is where you're likely to be staying. Fortunately, the dramatic change of scenery and gorgeous vistas make every minute in the car worthwhile. Take turns driving each way so you can both enjoy the views; the narrow, curving road demands all of the driver's attention.

An unusual point of interest on the island is **PHALLIC ROCK**, located in **PALAAU STATE PARK**. You'll have to use quite a bit of imagination to see the phallic likeness, but according to legend, women who could not get pregnant would spend the night at the base of the stone, then return home pregnant. (We didn't see anyone camping out when we were here, but if you're hoping to conceive on your honeymoon, it might be a worthwhile stop.)

Some of the most dramatic scenery (and intriguing history) is found on the **MAKANALUA PENINSULA**, better known as the site of **KALAUPAPA**. From a distance, this lovely green peninsula, set beneath Molokai's majestic seaside cliffs (some of the highest in the world) and surrounded by turbulent ocean surf on the remaining three sides, bears no traces of its poignant past. Closer up, mile after mile of gravestones reveal the final resting place for patients of the state's Hansen's Disease Leprosy Treatment Center. People suffering from leprosy (properly known as Hansen's disease) were cruelly exiled here by fearful governments in 1866, in an attempt to keep the disease under control. People afflicted with Hansen's disease were essentially left here to die and were not provided with even the most basic necessities. In 1873, Father Damien Joseph de Veuster, a Belgian priest who was deeply concerned about the misery of the people at Kalaupapa, settled his ministry here and brought hope and healing to this lonely peninsula. Father Damien was the first person to recognize the needs of the people at Kalaupapa, and he spent the remainder of his life serving this community. Today, many refer to Father Damien as a saint and a martyr; sadly, he contracted Hansen's disease himself and died of the disease in 1889.

Thanks to sulfone drugs developed in the 1940s, Hansen's disease is now curable (and not contagious). Yet many recovered patients have chosen to remain in Kalaupapa; today, fewer than 100 people live in this small community. They encourage visitors to learn more about their private peninsula and its past. Despite its somber history, Kalaupapa is a powerful place to behold and a true testament to the strength of the human spirit.

Romantic Note: This peninsula is accessible only by foot (it's a steep and strenuous four-hour, round-trip hike) or by plane. You are required to call DAMIEN MOLOKAI TOURS (808-567-6171) for entrance permission. The ground tour alone is $30; airplane/helicopter tours vary in price and you must contact a flight company separately. Mule rides into the valley used to be available but, due to insurance problems, are no longer an option.

Maunaloa

Hotel/Bed and Breakfast Kissing

❤️❤️❤️ PANIOLO HALE, Maunaloa After you've followed a long, winding driveway through somewhat barren scenery, the well-tended grounds and spacious condos of Paniolo Hale are a pleasing sight. All of the studio, one-, and two-bedroom units have one outstanding feature: a large, fully screened-in porch, perfect for letting the trade winds refresh the rooms (while keeping unwanted critters out). Every unit also comes equipped with a full kitchen and a washer and dryer; in some of the two-bedroom units, a Jacuzzi tub is available for an additional daily charge. Although the decor throughout the condos tends to be Hawaiian-inspired, some are decorated more elaborately than others. If you're looking for something extra-special and have flexible travel dates, describe your preferences to the amiable staff and they will gladly accommodate you.

Other noteworthy features of the resort are its swimming pool, golf course, tennis courts, barbecue grills, and picnic tables. In addition, the resort is located right next to Kepuhi and Papohaku Beaches. Although swimming is strongly discouraged due to strong currents, Papohaku is one of the longest sandy beaches in Hawaii, and the scenery is absolutely breathtaking. **190 Lio Place; (808) 552-2731, (800) 367-2984; www.lava.net/paniolo; inexpensive to expensive; minimum-stay requirement.**

Romantic Note: The only other lodging options on the island are various condominium complexes (which tend to be run-down) or the **KALUAKOI HOTEL AND GOLF CLUB** (Kepuhi Beach; 808-552-2555, 888-552-2550 mainland, 800-435-7208 interisland; www.kaluakoi.com; moderate to very expensive). Unfortunately, the rooms are small and plain, and the entire hotel is in desperate need of renovation. Until that happens, we cannot recommend staying there.

Restaurant Kissing

❤ **OHIA LODGE, Maunaloa** If you time your reservations right, you can witness a glorious sunset and look out over the sparkling Pacific from a table at the Ohia Lodge. Unfortunately, nature's scenery is the only romantic reason to come here. Like the resort it resides in, the decor is painfully dated and the standard surf and turf fare is terribly disappointing, as is the service. We only recommend drinks and appetizers at sunset. **Kepuhi Beach, at the Kaluakoi Hotel and Golf Club; (808) 552-2555; moderate to expensive; breakfast and dinner daily.**

Romantic Alternatives: Dining options on Molokai are limited and not what we would typically deem romantic, but we did find several places worth recommending. Excellent local steaks are served at **THE VILLAGE GRILL**, the only restaurant in Maunaloa Village (808-552-0012; moderate; lunch and dinner daily). Decorated in a charming ranch-style, the restaurant recently won some interior design awards. If the night is nice, enjoy dining in the screened-in porch room. For a true taste of island living, visit **KUALAPUU COOKHOUSE** (Farrington Road, Kualapuu; 808-567-6185; inexpensive; breakfast, lunch, and dinner Monday–Saturday), where you must try the chocolate–macadamia nut pie. Just plan on staying awhile, since they operate on island time too. For a slice of another kind of pie, visit **MOLOKAI PIZZA CAFE** (Wharf Road, Kaunakakai; 808-553-3288; inexpensive; breakfast Monday–Saturday, lunch and dinner daily), which also delivers its tasty pizzas.

Waialua

Outdoor Kissing

❀❀❀ **MILEPOST 17 TO MILEPOST 21, Waialua** No, the mileposts aren't the kissing spots, but what lies beyond certainly is. The string of beaches from milepost 17 to 21 on Highway 450 are rimmed with vast reefs full of fish. Unfortunately, seclusion is out—everyone seems to know about these small strips of beach along the main highway. But the water is divine, and by no means will you be bumping fins with fellow snorkelers. *Drive along Highway 450, which borders the ocean, until you reach the above-mentioned mileposts. Parking is limited.*

    Romantic Suggestion: Be sure to bring along snacks, drinks, or a lunch since there are no restaurants along the way.

Midway Atoll

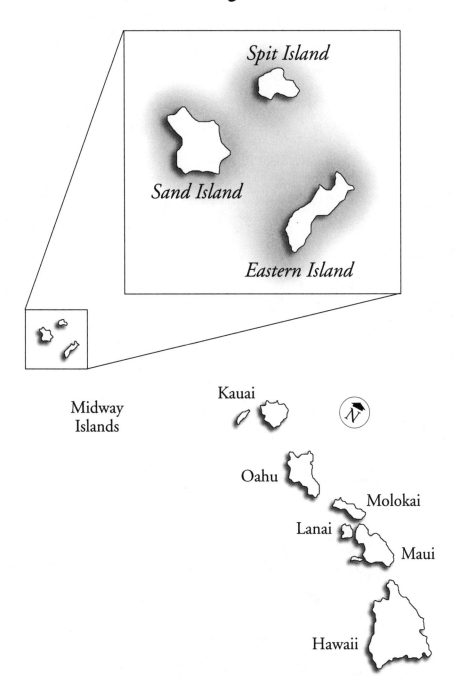

Spit Island

Sand Island

Eastern Island

Kauai

Midway
Islands

N

Oahu

Molokai

Lanai

Maui

Hawaii

Midway Atoll

There are two ways to travel to Midway: on your own or through an activity-related organization. If scuba diving, deep-sea fishing (primarily catch-and-release), or biologist-led research expeditions catch your attention, you're in luck. Midway Sport Fishing and Diving, Inc. (770-254-8326, 888-BIG-ULUA; www.midwaysf.com, www.midwaydive.com) can handle everything from booking your accommodations to organizing daily activities. Those interested in volunteering on research projects should call Oceanic Society Expeditions (415-441-1106, 800-326-7491). Independent travelers should contact the Midway Phoenix Corporation (888-MIDWAY1; www.midwayphoenix.com) to arrange travel plans, including flights, accommodations, and meal plans. All visitors to Midway must pay a user fee of $5 per day. If you stay longer than one week, the maximum fee is $35 per person. All fees go directly to maintaining and improving the Midway Atoll National Wildlife Refuge. If you have questions about the fee program, call the Fish and Wildlife Service Office. Dial (808) 599-5888, wait for the tone, and then dial (808) 421-3363.

Just when you think you've smooched your way through Hawaii, think again. If you stop that lip-motion for a moment and put your nose to the map, you'll discover that the Hawaiian Islands don't end at Kauai. Like a necklace of small emeralds, the archipelago winds northwestward approximately 1,200 miles into the vast Pacific, ending at some tiny jewels called the Midway Islands. While this marks the end of the Hawaiian chain, it is just the beginning of one of the most unique and remote kissing destinations on earth: Midway Atoll.

It's amazing that anyone ever found these small, sandy specks that reside midway between Asia and North America. Three islets compose the Midway Islands (or Atoll). The largest is the inhabited Sand Island, measuring a mere one mile by two miles. The other two, Spit and Eastern Islands, are just big enough for the birds—the only residents allowed. An immense coral reef circling the threesome provides protection from the white-capped waves of the open sea. Within the lagoon, clear, calm waters prevail, harboring Hawaiian spinner dolphins, colorful reef fish, Hawaiian green turtles, and the occasional tiger shark.

The first documented discovery of these islands was in 1859, and by 1867, Midway had become the first offshore island to be annexed by the U.S. government. Almost a century later, Sand Island served as a regular fuel stop for Pan American Airway's China Clipper in the 1930s and then as a U.S. naval air station beginning in 1940. The day that Midway will always be remembered for, however, is June 4, 1942, when Japanese forces launched a major air attack on the tiny atoll. The pivotal World War II Battle of Midway that ensued brought worldwide attention to this sandy spot. Today, Midway is making history again, albeit in a more peaceful manner. After five decades under naval operation, guns have given way to gooney birds (albatross), the island's most famous and long-term residents. In the mid-'90s, Midway Atoll was declared a national wildlife refuge, becoming the first remote island refuge in the Pacific open for public visitation.

A whole world of wildlife awaits visitors, starting in the clear, sandy-bottomed waters surrounding the atoll. A snorkeling platform near the reef allows Midway guests to swim and survey some 200 varieties of fish. Due to the isolated conditions, many fish here are twice the size of their siblings found off the more popular Hawaiian Islands. Looking out across the lagoon, you may spot a large pod of Hawaiian spinner dolphins performing aerial leaps or, closer by, the threatened Hawaiian green turtles swimming in the shallows. If you're lucky, you might see, from afar, the highly endangered Hawaiian monk seal asleep on the cool sand. In order to allow these seals to give birth in peace, much of the beach that surrounds Sand Island is closed to human access. On Midway, animals' livelihood takes precedence over many aspects of human habitation and recreation, a refreshing attitude whose time has come. (By the way, all new visitors attend a mandatory, yet educational and entertaining presentation about protecting animal life on Midway. Roll call is taken.)

One can't write about Midway's wildlife without mentioning the birds, in particular the albatross, which arrive by the thousands each winter. These seabirds—close to goose-size with seven-foot-long wingspans—are an attraction in and of themselves, especially when they engage in elaborate mating dances and nesting rituals. The show continues when thousands of fluffy, hungry chicks arrive on the scene and start waddling around the place. If you miss the albatross season (typically November through July), you still won't be lacking in avian entertainment. Dozens of bird species

Be sure to pack comfortable walking shoes. Sandals may not provide enough traction for the various hikes on each island.

nest here year-round, including the very curious white terns, which check out visitors by hovering above them like little white helicopters.

There's no doubt that Midway remains the choice nesting site for birds, but what about lovebirds of the human variety? Is Midway a romantic resting 'n' nesting site for them? It can be, *for the right people*, and we can't stress this enough. If steamy Jacuzzi tubs, poolside lunches, service with a snap, and lush 'n' plush hotel rooms ignite your passion, Midway won't deliver the kindling. But for the intrepid traveling couple who crave up-close and personal wildlife experiences, a remote location where animals' welfare comes first, pristine surroundings dotted with rusting World War II artifacts, and humble but comfortable accommodations, Midway won't disappoint.

Here's what to expect: First and foremost, dismiss any connections with the Hawaii you are used to. Midway may be the final link of the Hawaiian chain, but it lacks the lushness and size of its popular siblings to the southwest. Needless to say, Midway is free of resorts, swimming pools, golf courses, and swaying palm trees. Forget about year-round 80-degree weather, too. Winter and early spring can bring rainy, windy, and cool conditions. What this atoll offers to those seeking romance is a long section of soft-as-talcum-powder beach with only the birds to keep you company (see Outdoor Kissing); an oceanfront French restaurant (see Restaurant Kissing); and, perhaps best of all, a respite from civilization. Only 100 visitors are permitted at a time, so you won't be bumping elbows anywhere. Overall, life on Midway Atoll is unhurried, unpretentious, and unique.

As the albatross flies, Midway is a five-hour journey from Honolulu International Airport aboard a 25-seat turboprop aircraft. Flights leave twice a week to/from Midway and always arrive/depart well past dusk so as not to disturb, i.e., fly into, the flocks of birds. Due to its remoteness, Midway is not a trip to be taken on a budget. While the accommodations and meal plan run into the moderate-to-expensive range, it's the round-trip airfare that empties the pocketbook. Expect to pay more for a round-trip ticket to Midway than you paid for the flight from the mainland to Honolulu. And one more thing: You're only allowed 40 pounds of checked-in luggage on most flights, so pack accordingly.

For independent travelers who come simply to explore, snorkel, bird-watch, and learn about Midway's history, we recommend staying only four days. This time frame gives you a taste of the atoll, but not a case of island fever. Remember, this is a wildlife refuge first and foremost, and self-guided activities are limited in order to maintain an undisturbed environment for the animals.

Romantic Warning: Birds, birds everywhere and not a spot to sit. Such a saying isn't to be taken lightly when visiting Midway, especially when the albatross arrive to raise their young (November through July). Nothing is sacred. The birds build nests everywhere, those darling fluffy chicks squawk all night, and you may have to equip yourselves with an umbrella . . . if you know what we mean. On the other hand, witnessing such a mass spectacle is truly a once-in-a-lifetime experience. Take both sides into consideration and determine if nesting time is the right time for you to rest on Midway.

Hotel/Bed and Breakfast Kissing

❦❦ **MIDWAY'S ACCOMMODATIONS, Midway Atoll** There's a small sign on the entrance to the guest lodgings that reads, "Officers returning from beach are requested to remove footwear prior to entering." Not quite the sign you'd expect to see at most accommodations. Then again, Midway's lodgings aren't like most places. Two rectangular buildings, formerly naval officers' quarters (hence the sign), have been renovated into rooms and suites for visitors. Let's face it; these concrete structures built in the 1950s resemble a cross between your old college dorm and a nice motel. But, for being a thousand miles from civilization and on a former military base, they aren't that bad.

Each guest room has a queen-size bed or two single beds, air-conditioning, satellite TV, and your choice of a private and/or shared bath; the more spacious suites also feature pleasant sitting areas. Efforts have been made to decorate all 59 rooms and suites with contemporary prints and bright, pleasant colors. If you think of these plain, clean, and comfortable rooms as a place to rest, you'll be more than satisfied. Save kissing for the beach.

When choosing a room, be prepared to also select a meal plan. (This is about as close to Club Med as Midway gets.) We recommend the more expensive deluxe plan ($50 per day per person) over the standard plan ($25 per day per person). With the deluxe plan, you'll be able to savor the phenomenal food accompanied by breathtaking sunsets at the ultraromantic French restaurant **THE CLIPPER HOUSE** (see Restaurant Kissing).

Last, you'll need some transportation to get around on the flat atoll. Walking in the hot sun isn't the most comfortable option, unless, of course you're barefooting it on the beach. Rent a one-speed bicycle (with optional basket) or go big by chartering a golf cart ($5 per day and $25 per day, respectively). Either way, you'll notice that everyone on Midway waves as you whiz by. **Call one of the reservation companies listed on page 201; moderate to expensive.**

Restaurant Kissing

❤❤❤❤ **THE CLIPPER HOUSE, Midway Atoll** One of the most romantic French restaurants we've encountered resides just where you'd least expect it: smack-dab in the middle of the Pacific. Mouths drop open when visitors to Midway learn that savory French food awaits in a lovely restaurant only steps from the beach. (Need we mention that the beach gets our romantic rating as a definite four-lipper?) Light pink sand, peppered by flocks of black noddies, separate this plantation-style restaurant from the atoll's aqua waters. Colors continue to dazzle as the sky turns from fiery orange to light lavender within half an hour of sundown. Be sure to sit at a window table for upfront seats to this sky show, or, if you prefer to color the evening on your own, hide away in a booth near the bar area. While the outside naturally dazzles, the interior imparts an open, modern look with high, beamed ceilings; wood and metal accents; and contemporary light fixtures. A hint of Midway's past is added by the vintage Pan American Airways posters. Crowds aren't common here and the linen-covered tables are spaced well apart, creating a perfect romantic setting.

The French couple who run The Clipper House do an extraordinary job of bringing delicious French dishes to the table with style, especially considering the difficulties they encounter. Due to uncontrollable supply-and-demand circumstances that arise when the nearest market is 1,200 miles away, the menu can and does change, and special requests can't always be accommodated. When we dined, the atoll's supply ship was long overdue, thus limiting the wine selection to only a few bottles. Our advice: Bring your appetite to this restaurant, along with an ounce of flexibility and a pint of patience.

Usually the three-course set menu revolves around whichever type of fish was pulled from the sea that day. The fishing boat returns around 5 P.M., and the versatile and creative chef has the catch on your table by 7 P.M. Talk about fresh! One night we dined on poached *ono* complemented by a light ginger butter, followed by an extraordinary raspberry mousse. The next evening, fish and fowl took the stage together with an *ahi* pâté appetizer and chicken breast in a tarragon sauce entrée. A luscious crème caramel, as sweet and delicate as a kiss, concluded the perfect meal. Midway may be for the birds, but the food at The Clipper House certainly isn't. **Moderate to expensive; breakfast and dinner Monday–Tuesday and Thursday–Saturday.**

Romantic Note: We mentioned that Midway's accommodations may remind you of your college dorm. Well, the only other dining alternative on island, **THE GALLEY CAFETERIA** (inexpensive to moderate; breakfast, lunch, and dinner daily) may bring back memories of chowing down at the college canteen. Most likely you'll eat lunch here (and maybe a dinner or two). It's cafeteria-style dining at its best, right down to the person who punches your meal ticket. No, it's not romantic, but remember, Midway isn't catering to this market. Despite the lack of ambience, eating here affords you the opportunity to chat with other interesting people and taste some of the best curry this side of Asia. Many foreign-nationals working on Midway come from Sri Lanka and Thailand, so prepare your palate for authentic and very spicy curries. Of course, there's more on the menu besides curry, although lacking on the lineup is fresh fruit—a shortage no doubt caused by being in such a remote outpost. Just compensate by loading up on vegetables, including eggplant and lettuce, which come fresh from the atoll's gardens.

Outdoor Kissing

❦❦❦❦ **MIDWAY ATOLL BEACH, Midway Atoll** Monk seal habitat may lay claim to most of Midway's beach area, but there is one gorgeous stretch of sand open to those with two legs (birds included). Take off your shoes in front of **THE CLIPPER HOUSE** (see Restaurant Kissing) and barefoot it westward to a place called **RUSTY BUCKET**. Most likely you won't see another soul while walking hand in hand between these two points. Luckily for the tootsies, the light pink sand doesn't heat up during midday, although the temperature may rise with all the kissing going on. Cool off by swimming in the sandy-bottomed shallows, with water as clear as a pool. The beach's only eyesore are the fuel tanks on the far east side—leftovers from the Navy's occupation. But if you try looking at them as just another part of Midway's history, their presence becomes less intrusive. A raised platform at Rusty Bucket marks the perfect place to hold each other and watch the cumulous clouds reflect the colors of the setting sun.

Romantic Note and Warning: Along with this beautiful beach comes the birds. Expect them, accept them, and admire them from afar. On a more serious note, if you happen to see a monk seal or green turtle, stay at least 100 feet away so as not to disturb them. Last but not least, tiger and Galapagos sharks occasionally patrol the waters. They pose little danger to humans, but to be on the safe side, always swim/snorkel together and limit water frolicking to daylight hours.

Index